Law and Disorder in Tudor Monmouthshire

Ben Howell

MERTON PRIORY PRESS

Published by Merton Priory Press Ltd
7 Nant Fawr Road, Cardiff CF2 6JQ

First published 1995

ISBN 1 898937 03 6

Typeset at Oxford University Computing Service
Printed by Hillman Printers (Frome) Ltd
Handlemaker Road, Marston Trading Estate
Frome BA11 4RW

Contents

A Calendar of the Monmouthshire Quarter Sessions and Gaol Deliveries Roll of 18–19 Elizabeth I (1576–77)

Plates

Map

Table

Acknowledgements

I am greatly indebted to Merton Priory Press for accepting this book for publication, to Mr Philip Riden for his skilled guidance in preparing it for publication, and to Ms Christine Jones for help with typing. I extend my warm thanks to Dr Gwynfor Jones for his kindness in writing a Foreword; my debt to him as a leading authority on Tudor Wales will be evident from the footnotes. The late Revd Norman Miles gave me generous, invaluable and scholarly help with the Roll. The map was expertly prepared by Miss Elizabeth Forrest and I wish to thank her warmly for it. My cordial thanks are also due also to Mr Brian James for helpful suggestions, for assistance in preparing the Bibliography and for reading the proofs. I acknowledge with gratitude the help I have received from the courteous staff of the National Library of Wales, the Library of the University of Wales, Cardiff, and Cardiff Central Library.

I am especially grateful to my wife for her ever-ready assistance in all aspects of the preparation of the text.

September 1995   Ben Howell

Foreword

Surviving Quarter Sessions records for parts of Wales in the sixteenth century provide a basis for the study of law and administration in local community life. The Monmouthshire Quarter Sessions and Gaol Deliveries Roll of 18–19 Elizabeth I (1576–77) preserved among the Morgan of Tredegar family papers enables the historian to examine the manner in which local government was managed in the shire created in 1536 out of marcher territory. It is a key source for the study of the justices of the peace and their sessions in the mid-Elizabethan period.

The Roll transcribed and studied in this volume amply provides information on aspects of the social and economic life of Monmouthshire, particularly in view of the increasing responsibilities entrusted to the landed gentry. The record also discloses the degree of formality imposed by successive Tudor governments on local administration. The activities of the squirearchy, chiefly as justices of the peace in the court of Quarter Sessions, provide valuable data regarding the degree to which law and order were maintained in Monmouthshire and supplement the historian's knowledge of the social structure of a shire community. Despite the problems that beset local officials in conducting their routine business affairs they maintained the administrative framework and made the new office an effective instrument of Tudor government in a traditionally unstable area. Despite the increasing volume of judicial business managed by the courts of Quarter Sessions it is evident that magistrates, as natural leaders of their local communities, strengthened their control of regional affairs in a period of increasing social and economic tension. The Roll of 1576–77 represents a period when the central government, principally through the agency of the Privy Council and the Council in the Marches, taxed further the resources of the landed gentry of Tudor Wales.

It is my privilege to provide a foreword to this handsome volume by Benjamin Howell, whose labours in transcribing, translating and analysing the contents of this Roll have revealed how significant a contribution it is as a study of Tudor administration in Wales. His work is based largely on earlier investigations which he conducted under the supervision of Professor William Rees. The fruits of that research are, in part, published in this volume which offers further dimensions to the historian's knowledge and understanding of the mechanics of Elizabethan local government in Monmouthshire and in Wales.

University of Wales   J. Gwynfor Jones
Cardiff

Preface

This study of local government and law and order in sixteenth-century Monmouthshire is based on a number of sources but especially on the county's Quarter Sessions and Gaol Deliveries (Assizes) Roll of 1576–77, the contents of which have not previously been published. The Roll is a document of considerable significance in that no other Welsh county, apart from Caernarfonshire, has quarter sessions records dating back to the sixteenth century, and it is possible that no other county on the Oxford Circuit, to which Monmouthshire was attached, has surviving assize records from before the 1640s.

The book is divided into two sections. The first is concerned with explaining how medieval Gwent, with its virtually independent and sometimes disorderly marcher lords, was transformed into the shire of Monmouth, thus coming more firmly under the control of the Crown. This was brought about by the Act of Union of 1536 which, together with the Act of 1543, also introduced into the new shire justices of the peace and their quarter sessions, together with assizes and other features of the English system of local justice and administration. For the implementation of these and other changes the government depended to a great extent on the co-operation and diligence of largely amateur (except for the circuit judges) and unpaid local officials, ranging from sheriffs and JPs of the county to the high constables of the hundreds into which the shire was divided, and the petty constables and other officers of the parishes and townships. A major feature of this system was its broad participatory base. Thus, not only the higher echelons of society but also its minor gentry, yeomen, husbandmen and artisans also took part in various capacities.

The incidence of crime and disorder among all sections of society, and the procedure of quarter sessions and gaol delivery, are examined. An attempt is also made to assess the effectiveness of the Tudor settlement in promoting law and order in the county.

The second part of the book contains a calendar of the Roll of 1576–77.

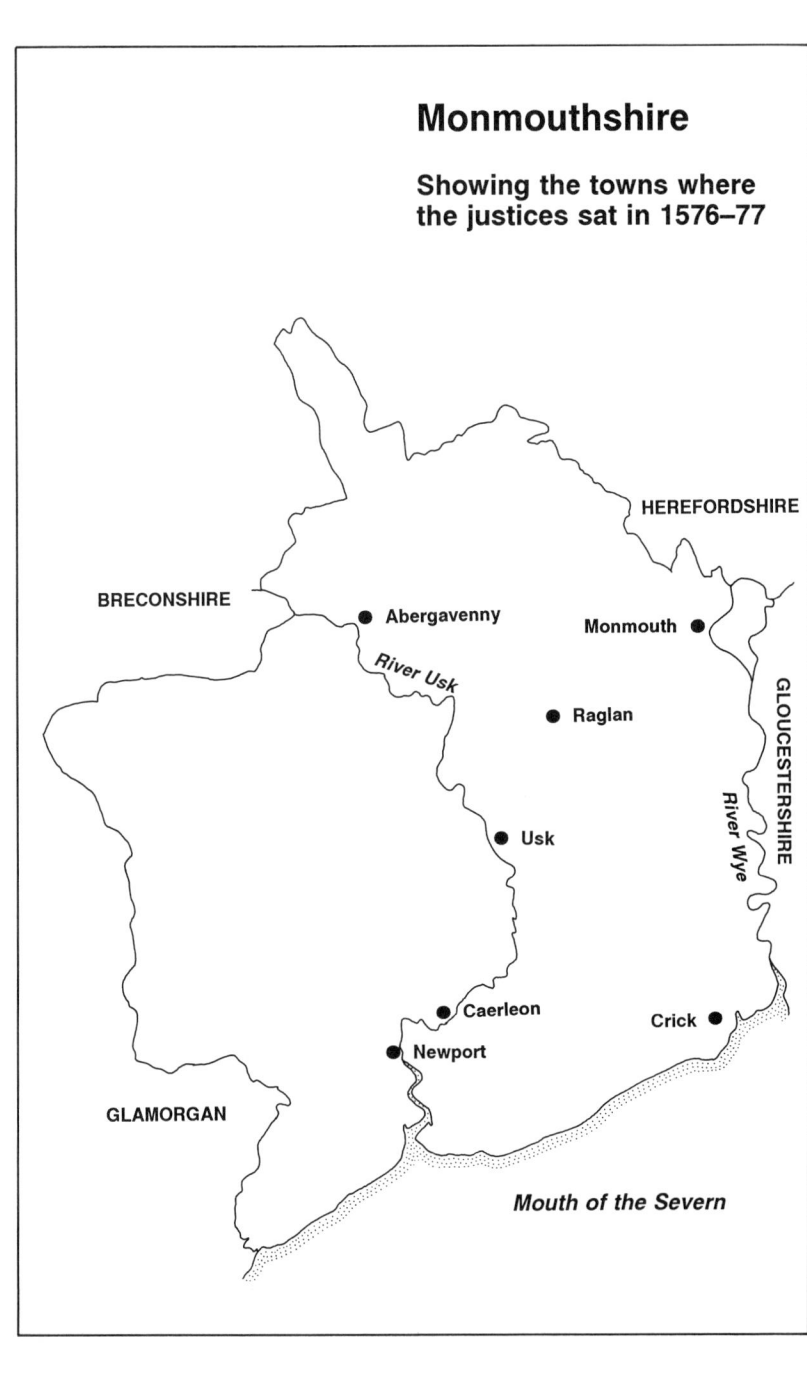

Monmouthshire

Showing the towns where the justices sat in 1576–77

HEREFORDSHIRE

BRECONSHIRE

● Abergavenny

Monmouth ●

River Usk

● Raglan

GLOUCESTERSHIRE

River Wye

● Usk

● Caerleon

Crick ●

● Newport

GLAMORGAN

Mouth of the Severn

1

Medieval Gwent

The shire of Monmouth was a creation of the Act of Union of 1536, which,
together with the second Act of 1543, also introduced into the county justices
of the peace and their quarter sessions, together with assizes and other
features of the English system of local justice and administration.[1] These
changes are reflected in the hitherto unpublished Quarter Sessions and Gaol
Deliveries Roll of 18–19 Elizabeth I (1576–77) — hereafter referred to as
'the Roll' — a calendar of which follows this introductory essay.

The unified system introduced in 1536 and 1543 replaced the various
marcher lordships into which medieval Gwent had been divided, and which
had been formed by Norman invaders in 'private' conquests over the native
Welsh rulers of the Kingdoms of Gwynllwg, Gwent Iscoed and Gwent
Uwchcoed. In this process the old Welsh local divisions of *cantrefi* and
cymydau were 'obliterated and mangled' and replaced by lordships, castleries
and manors.[2] Thus the area we now know as Gwent became a part of 'the
March' or 'the Marches of Wales', which, with its disunity and disorder,
posed a serious problem to the English Crown in the Middle Ages.

After William FitzOsbern's initial cautious incursions (1067) from his
castle at Strigoil (Chepstow), Gwent, like two-thirds of Wales, was
eventually fragmented into a number of lordships, of which the chief were
Newport, Caerleon, Chepstow, Caldicot, Abergavenny, Trelech, Usk (out of
which the lordship of Raglan was later carved) and Monmouth.[3] For
centuries Anglo-Norman hold on Gwent was tentative, especially in the
Welshries of the uplands where Welsh law, customs and language flourished.
Their hold and control of the lowlands and coastal plain were more secure
and their anglicising influences were most marked. The lords, usually absen-

---

[1] P. Riden, *Record sources for local history* (1987), pp. 70, 159–60. Some of these
changes prevailed until the nineteenth century and, in the case of quarter sessions (shorn of its
administrative work in 1888) and assizes, until 1971, when the two were merged to form the
present Crown Court system.

[2] R.R. Davies, *Conquest, co-existence and change. Wales 1063–1415* (1987), p. 21.

[3] P. Courtney, 'The rural landscape of eastern and lower Gwent, 1070–1750' (Unpublished
University of Wales [Cardiff] Ph.D. thesis, 1983), Summary, argues that the Norman invasion
of Gwent 'was a much more prolonged and piecemeal process than has previously been
recognised'.

tee, were often members of powerful aristocratic families who exploited the resources of their lordships in order to finance their English ambitions.

To assist him in administration, the lord had his own council and chief officers, the constable, steward and receiver. From these offices the native Welsh were at first usually barred, but by the later Middle Ages, as we shall see later in the case of Gwent, a number of rising local gentry had become prominent office-holders, at least one had become a marcher lord and his son had achieved eminence in Welsh affairs and in the Wars of the Roses. Generally, however, 'there was so much unchecked self-interest and venality in the March that little honest administration and impartial justice prevailed'.[1]

The marcher lord enjoyed a great measure of independence of the Crown, having his own army, courts and law, together with the right to create boroughs, markets and fairs; he was 'king and justiciar' in his lordship.[2] The most obvious symbol of Anglo-Norman occupation was the castle, the chief one of which was the lord's administrative centre and was usually sited at an important communication point, such as Newport, Chepstow, Abergavenny, Monmouth, Caerleon and Usk. Each of the last four of these castles was also located on the site of a Roman centre and this reflects continuity of these settlements from early times.[3] So too does the Roll, which shows that sixteenth-century quarter sessions were held at all these places, except Chepstow, and at Raglan. By the eighteenth century, quarter sessions had ceased to be held at Raglan but continued at the other centres, and also at Chepstow.

The lord's power did not extend beyond the boundaries of his lordship and criminals fled from one lordship to another to seek protection and to join the new lord's army of retainers. It is not surprising that Gwent and the rest of the March was frequently in turmoil — exaggerated though that might have been by Tudor propagandists.[4]

Another element contributing to disorder was the frequent power struggles and changing alliances between monarch, marcher lords and Welsh leaders, in which Gwent was frequently involved, and at times provided the stage for

[1] Glanmor Williams, *Recovery, reorientation and reformation. Wales 1415–1642* (1985), p. 254.

[2] Davies, *Conquest*, p. 286.

[3] Courtney, Thesis, p. 69.

[4] Davies, *Conquest*, p. 392. Lawlessness in the shires of the Principality (Anglesey, Caernarfon, Merioneth, Flint, Cardigan and Carmarthen), under the direct jurisdiction of the king, also caused concern.

events which affected the course of conflicts in England.[1] The Glyndwr rebellion of the early fifteenth century also spread to Gwent, where his forces gained some successes and suffered severe reverses. The organiser of the anti-Glyndwr forces in the south was the Monmouth-born Prince Henry, later to become Henry V and the victor of Agincourt. The devastation in Gwent resulting from the revolt was even worse than that of the Black Death and subsequent plagues of the previous century. Another consequence of the revolt was the passing of a series of penal laws, as a result of which the Welsh suffered various disabilities. 'Among the most galling prohibitions of the rising Welsh *uchelwyr* (i.e. gentry) was to be excluded from holding office under the Crown and from full participation in the land market.'[2] Individuals, it is true, obtained letters of denizenship exempting them from some of the restrictions, and as time went on the legislation became 'irksome rather than effective.'[3] However, there was no systematic release from the restrictions until Henry VII (1485–1509) issued his charters of enfranchisement.

Meanwhile, a number of economic and social changes, gave an impetus to estate building by the gentry.[4] In that competitive and acquisitive age the *uchelwyr* were keen to obtain 'land, heiresses and office' in order to extend their estates and status. One way of raising money in order to purchase or lease land in those years of a buoyant land market was by holding office in a lordship or religious house, the fees from which helped the gentry to advance their own interests — and made them more creditworthy with usurers. Self-enrichment and advancement could also follow from taking service in wars. In that age of soldiers of fortune one of the best known in Gwent was Sir William ap Thomas, the common ancestor of the Herberts. He married Elizabeth Berkeley, the widow of the marcher lord of Raglan, and, on her death, gained possession of the lordship in his own right.[5]

---

[1] R. Howell, *A history of Gwent* (1988), p. 77.

[2] P.R. Roberts, 'The Welsh language, English law and Tudor legislation', *Trans. Hon. Soc. Cymmrodorion* (1989), 19–75. Details of the penal laws are given in Davies, *Conquest.*

[3] G.E. Jones, *Modern Wales. c. 1485–1979* (1984), p. 69.

[4] Williams, *Recovery,* pp. 83ff; M. Griffiths, 'The emergence of the modern settlement pattern, 1450–1700' in D.H. Owen (ed.), *Settlement and society in Wales* (Cardiff, 1987), pp. 225–48.

[5] The Herberts, through marriage, were adept at establishing themselves in the seats of the older gentry: Glanmor Williams, 'The economic life of Glamorgan, 1536–1642', in *Glamorgan County History,* IV (1974), p. 30.

On William's death his estate passed to his eldest son, Sir William Herbert,[1] who became a leader of the Yorkists in the dynastic struggle and was regarded by some as the 'son of prophecy', the poet Guto'r Glyn hailing him as the potential unifier of Wales against English domination.[2] In 1461, he led a successful attack on Pembroke castle and captured young Henry Tudor, whom he took to Raglan castle, where he was 'honourably educated and in all civility brought up' in the household of one of the foremost Welsh bardic patrons of the age.[3] By 1469, William, now earl of Pembroke, and chief justice of both south and north Wales, was at the height of his power, but in the next year, after a Yorkist defeat, he and his brother were executed. The children of his marriage to Anne Devereux included William, who became second earl of Pembroke, but later resigned that title in favour of Huntingdon, Sir Walter Herbert of Caldicot and Sir George Herbert of St Julians. They also had a number of daughters (six of whom married peers) including Maud, who her father had planned to marry Henry Tudor. Two of his base sons were Sir Richard Herbert of Ewyas and Sir William Herbert of Troy.[4]

William Herbert, the second earl, died in 1491, leaving only a daughter, Elizabeth, who married Sir Charles Somerset; as the illegitimate son of Henry Beaufort, third duke of Somerset, he was a cousin of Henry Tudor, whom he supported in exile and on to Bosworth and afterwards. Sir Charles was given several offices in south Wales and the March, created earl of Worcester in 1514 and acquired through his wife most of the Herbert lands; although the principal seat of the Herbert family throughout the period was Raglan Castle, they were also influential in Glamorgan.

The second son of Richard Herbert of Ewyas, yet another William, who was more at home in Welsh than in English, came to prominence in 1549, when he helped to put down the rising in the West Country and in overthrowing the Protector Somerset in the reign of Edward VI. This brought him a grant of lordships in Monmouthshire (as it was by then) and Glamorgan, the Wiltshire estates of the Protector and the title of the earl of Pembroke (of the second creation); he and his successors were powerful magnates in the Elizabethan period, by which time the family seat was at

---

[1] Howell, *Gwent*, p. 105, n. 5, suggests that he was reluctant to continue with the use of the Welsh *ap* and that this led to his choice of the surname Herbert, which may have been an attempt to claim a connection with the FitzHerberts.

[2] P.R. Roberts, 'The Welshness of the Tudors', *History Today*, 36 (Jan. 1986), p. 8.

[3] Glanmor Williams, *Henry Tudor and Wales* (1985), p. 21.

[4] J. Hunt, 'Monmouthshire wills proved in the Prerogative Court of Canterbury, 1414–1560' (Unpublished Cardiff Local History Diploma Dissertation, 1985), p. 152. See *Dictionary of Welsh Biography*, p. 354 for William Herbert, 1st Earl of Pembroke.

Wilton in Wiltshire. As will be seen, other families such as the Morgans of
Tredegar, Llantarnam and elsewhere had also risen in the locality by the
Tudor period.

In 1471, the Yorkist Edward IV was restored to the throne and Henry Tudor,
now regarded as a strong Lancastrian claimant — and the new 'son of
prophecy' — was taken by his uncle, Jasper, into exile in Brittany; he
remained there until the events which led to Bosworth and his accession as
Henry VII in 1485. (Among the Welshmen who served Henry abroad was
David Seisyllt of Alltyrynys in Ewyas, described by one historian as 'a
yeoman-turned-gentleman and allegedly an innkeeper'.)[1] His grandson,
William Cecil, unquestionably a gentleman, became Elizabeth's chief
minister and was raised to the peerage as Lord Burghley; he was succeeded
as chief minister by his son, Robert, later to become earl of Salisbury.

At the beginning of the Tudor period the basic problems concerning law
and order in Wales, and especially in the March, remained the same. The
Council in the Marches, which Edward IV had set up and which Henry VII
revived, had little effective authority. The most vital element in his policy
was the forging of an alliance with the Welsh gentry, whose most prominent
members wanted equality with the English, opportunities to build up and
consolidate their estates and to hold offfice under the Crown.[2] They were
prepared to support the new regime since it offered them such opportunities.

Although by now most of the marcher lordships had come into the hands
of the Crown — including the lordships in Gwent of the Duchy of Lancaster
(Monmouth, the Three Castles and Caldicot), of the Earldom of the March
(Usk, Caerleon and Trelech) and the Buckingham lordship of Newport — in
práctice authority was vested in the offficers of the lordship, and their
neglect and misconduct encouraged crime. The king's steward in these
lordships was Henry, second earl of Worcester, and he was no more
effective than other officers. The various members of the Herbert family,
who were the earl's kinsmen, were among the greatest dangers to good
order. The royal lordship of Magor became a sanctuary for criminals, all
protected by Walter Herbert of Magor, who was Worcester's deputy steward
there: this small lordship harboured twenty murderers, of whom three were
members of the Herbert family and ten were Walter's servants, besides at

[1] D.M. Palliser, *The age of Elizabeth. England under the later Tudors, 1547–1603* (2nd ed., 1992), p. 100.

[2] Jones, *Modern Wales*, p. 61.

least ten thieves and outlaws. Some of this lawless band were also involved in serious riots in Newport in 1533.[1]

In his handling of Welsh affairs down to 1536 Henry VIII continued his father's policy of attempting to restrain the worst abuses of the lordships by the system of indentures imposed on the lords and their officials. But what was required was to turn the March into shires and introduce there the English judicial and administrative systems. Such a plan was put forward in 1531 and the king is said to have shown some interest in it — 'it weare a gracious deede to reform Wales' — but by then he had other pressing matters to consider arising out of his 'divorce' and the crisis of the Reformation.

Nevertheless, Wales could not be completely ignored by Henry and his minister, Thomas Cromwell. Its disunity and lack of governance were sources of weakness to the English realm, and a potential centre of disaffection and a springboard for attack on England. Cromwell jotted down a frequent 'remembrance' to look 'to the state of Wales'.[2] He also included this ominous item in his agenda of business (1533) for the next session of Parliament, 'A bill of justice in Wales and that no Welshman to be an officer there according to the old lawes of the lande.'[3] But this threat of fully reactivating the penal laws (they had never been repealed) was not to be realised, for within three years a radical change of policy was formulated in the legislation of 1536.

Before that, however, a firmer rule was discernible from 1534, when the ruthless Rowland Lee was appointed President of the Council in the Marches. He was soon active in tracking down and punishing offenders, including a certain Richard ap Howell, 'the murderer of Monmouth'.[4] He was of the opinion that the 'maliciousness' of the March would soon cease if Wales were 'applyed' a little while.[5] Various measures were also passed by Parliament, some infringing marcher rights and all designed to reduce crime, including cattle raiding on both sides of the Severn.[6] But neither this legislation nor Lee's policy of repression was felt to be a solution and the

---

[1] T.B. Pugh, 'The ending of the Middle Ages, 1485–1536', in *Glamorgan County History*, III (1971), pp. 564ff. The author is of the opinion that the Act of Union of 1536 was 'in large measure a consequence of the tyranny and corruption which had flourished in the marcher lordships by Worcester's malpractices'.

[2] *Letters and Papers*, VI, p. 386.

[3] Cited in Roberts, 'Welsh language', p. 24.

[4] *Letters and Papers*, X, p. 130.

[5] Ibid., X, p. 31; VIII, p. 584.

[6] I. Bowen, *The statutes of Wales* (1908), pp. 51ff.

government's new policy toward Wales (it was also a policy adopted for Calais, Ireland, the northern March, the south-west and attempted against Scotland) in pursuit of integrating peripheral areas in the *imperium* and of ensuring that the royal writ ran fully throughout the realm in both secular and religious administration,[1] was embodied in three Acts in 1536.

The first Act established justices of the peace — an office which had existed for some centuries in England — in the six shires of the Principality and in the royal lordships of Glamorgan and Pembroke. The office was extended to the rest of Wales by the Act of Union of 1536. By the second, inter alia, the regal jurisdiction of the Welsh marcher lords was abolished; henceforth all writs were to be issued and all indictments made in the king's name and (apart from the survival of manorial and ecclesiastical courts) the power of doing justice became a royal monopoly. The third Act, known as the Act of Union, was for 'Laws and Justice to be Ministered in like form as in this realm'.[2] This is the Act that brought the shire of Monmouth into being and gave it the shire system that had existed in the Principality and in England for centuries. Lee strongly opposed the new policy, especially the appointment of JPs.

For some years after 1536 the Crown's policy was marked by alteration and indecision, and, in consequence, the implementation of the Act was slow and tentative. But finally in 1543, the second Act, 'An Act for certain ordinances in the King's Dominion and Principality of Wales'[3] completed the process, and in some ways 'legislated after the event' when it purported to introduce the Courts of Great Sessions and Quarter Sessions, when in fact they were already in operation.[4]

The effects of the Union varied from one part of Wales to another. In the new shires of the March, such as Monmouthshire, which had consisted of a number of independent lordships and where there had been no unity, the break with the past was more radical than in the Principality where a shire system had long existed. The Roll of 1576–77 gives some indication of the impact of these changes in Monmouthshire forty years after its creation.

The next chapter will examine the chief clauses of the Acts of Union and especially those which affected Monmouthshire.

---

[1] The religious changes of the 1530s were accepted in Gwent, as elsewhere in Wales, with but few signs of serious opposition.

[2] 27 Hen. VIII, c. 26; see Bowen, *Statutes*, pp. 75ff., and William Rees, 'The union of England and Wales', *Trans. Hon. Soc. Cymmrodorion* (1937) (and published separately).

[3] 34 and 35 Hen. VIII, c. 26; Bowen, *Statutes*, pp. 101ff.

[4] P.R. Roberts, 'The union with England and the identity of "Anglican" Wales', *Trans. Royal Hist. Soc.*, 5th series, 22 (1972), p. 56.

2

The New Shire of Monmouth

Certain provisions of the Acts of Union affecting Monmouthshire will be treated in greater detail in a later section of this chapter. But first a summary of the general changes which these Acts inaugurated is given. By the Act of 1536 Wales was 'incorporated, united and annexed ... to ... the imperialle Crowne of this Realm',[1] and Welshmen were granted equality with Englishmen. The shiring of Wales, begun in the thirteenth century, was completed by the creation of seven new shires, including Monmouthshire (the others being Glamorgan, Pembroke, Brecknock, Radnor, Montgomery and Denbigh), out of the various marcher lordships, the remainder of which were added to some of the existing Welsh or English border shires. The lords lost their regal status, but retained certain feudal rights. Wales was to be represented in Parliament by one knight for each shire, except Monmouthshire, which had two, and one burgess for each shire town, except Harlech; in 1543 Haverfordwest was made into a county borough and given one representative.

The English system of local administration and law enforcement was extended throughout Wales, and sheriffs, justices of the peace, escheators, coroners and chief or high constables of the hundreds into which shires were divided exercised their various duties; some, like the JPs and chief constables, for the first time in the thirteen shires, others, like the sheriff, for the first time in the new shires. (Parochial administration was not provided for in the Acts but developed subsequently.) All courts of law were to be conducted in English and all holders of office under the Crown had to be able to speak that language. The Welsh shires (omitting Monmouthshire) were to have their own system of higher law courts (independent of the courts of Westminster) called the Court of Great Sessions; the shires were divided into four circuits of three shires each, where a judge was to hold assizes twice a year. There was to be similar independence in fiscal matters, each group of three shires having an exchequer to which local officers rendered their accounts. Monmouthshire was excluded from the Great

---

[1] What the Act stated was that Wales had always been annexed and subject to the English Crown, but this was true only of the Principality since 1284.

Sessions and fiscal arrangements, for greater convenience and as the Welsh shire nearest to Westminster. Nevertheless, like all the twelve shires and the English border shires, it came under the general supervision of the Council in the Marches, which, by the Act of 1543, was given statutory recognition. The Act of 1543 also abolished partible inheritance (but this continued to be practised in various places in Monmouthshire and elsewhere).[1] The 1536 Act authorised the setting up of a commission to divide the new shires into hundreds, the work to be done before November the same year.

The provisions of the 1536 Act for Monmouthshire were more detailed and complete than for the other new shires; the 1543 Act provided for the other shires in the main, although the elaboration of the various officials also applied to Monmouthshire. It is improbable, however, that the shire machinery was set in motion earlier there than in the other shires.

The new shire of Monmouth (the name adopted from the lordship of that name) was to comprise the 'lordshippes, Townshippes, parishes, commotes and cantredes'[2] of medieval Gwent, but did not quite conform with it in extent of territory; it did not include the lordships of Ewyas Lacy and Ewyas Harold,[3] a Welsh-speaking area, which was added to Herefordshire, nor that part of the lordship of Strigoil to the east of the river Wye, which was annexed to Gloucestershire. Thus the shire, deprived of these outlying districts, achieved a greater compactness, its boundaries defined by the Wye, the Monnow,[4] the Black Mountains, the Rumney and the sea. (The manor of Bicknor, on the right bank of the Wye, was a detached portion of Monmouthshire until 1844, when it was joined to Herefordshire.)[5]

It was enacted that Monmouth should be the shire town.[6] It seems surprising that this town, in the farthermost limit of the shire, and difficult of access, should have been so appointed. The choice possibly resulted from a combination of factors: it was the most considerable town in the shire, it was the borough of the lordship from which the shire derived its name and

[1] See, e.g., M. Gray, 'The dispersal of Crown property in Monmouthshire, 1500–1603' (Unpublished University of Wales [Cardiff] Ph.D. thesis, 1984), pp. 9, 20; J.G. Jones, *Wales and the Tudor state* (1989), p. 29.

[2] W. Rees, 'The union of England and Wales', *Trans. Hon. Soc. Cymmrodorion* (1937), p. 83.

[3] The monastic lands of Llanthony were separated from the lordship of Ewyas Lacy and were included in Monmouthshire: ibid.

[4] In order that the town and parish of Monmouth 'should be wholly within the newly-formed county, that part of it on the farther side of the rivers Monnow and Wye ... was included in the new county', J.A. Bradney, *History of Monmouthshire*, I, p. 1.

[5] Gray, Thesis, p. 6.

[6] Rees, 'Union', p. 82.

which had long been associated with the Crown, it was better able to provide accommodation for an assize court and county gaol — Lee, however, complained that Monmouth Castle needed repair — and, in view of the fact that the county was to be in the English legal system, it was also the most accessible town for English judges on circuit.[1] Monmouth was also one of the centres at which the sheriff's county court was to be held to hear pleas under 40s., the other being Newport.[2] Interestingly, Leland regarded Abergavenny to be the most flourishing town of the shire.

The Act of 1536 differentiated between Monmouthshire and the twelve shires in three important respects: in the administration of the higher law courts, in revenue and in parliamentary representation. Monmouthshire, not included in a Great Sessions circuit, was added to the jurisdiction, both criminal and civil, of the courts sitting at Westminster, and its officers and inhabitants were subject to the Lord Chancellor and to the royal judges precisely like an English shire. For example, it was enacted that actions of the sum of 40s. or above were to be sued by writ out of the Court of Chancery and tried before the 'Kinges Justices in England or by Assize or Nisi Prius'.[3] It was also provided that the 'Kinges Justices of his Benche ... at Westminster shall have full power ... to directe all maner processe to the sheriff' of the county, as well as writs of *venire facias* for the trial of every issue joined before them.[4] Monmouthshire was later attached to the Oxford circuit.

In fiscal matters, while each group of three shires had its own exchequer to which local officers were to make their account, the Monmouthshire sheriffs, escheators and other officers were to account to 'the Kinges Exchequier in England'[5] as other English shires did. The 1543 Act also directed that all fines, amerciaments and forfeitures of quarter sessions in the twelve shires were yearly to be estreated to their local exchequer; presumab-

---

[1] See also K. Kissack, *Monmouth. The making of a county town* (1975), p. 11. Ecclesiastically, Monmouth town and some neighbouring parishes formed part of the diocese of Hereford until 1845, while the remainder of the shire was in Llandaff, except the parishes of Cwmyoy, Llanthony and Oldcastle, which were in St David's until 1845.

[2] Rees, 'Union', p. 83.

[3] Ibid., p. 84, n. 2. *Nisi prius* is a writ addressed to the sheriff of a county commanding him to bring the men empanelled jurors in a civil court to the court at Westminster on a certain day, 'unless before' that day the judges come to the county to hold the assizes.

[4] Ibid., p. 84. *Venire facias* is a writ directing the sheriff to summon jurors and other persons required to appear in court. For an example issued by quarter sessions, see Roll, Caerleon 2.

[5] Ibid., p. 85.

ly the clerk of the peace of Monmouthshire was to despatch his estreat roll to the Exchequer at Westminster.

In the matter of MPs, the 1536 Act, while not according the same representation as in England, where two knights were chosen for each shire and two burgesses for each borough, gave it a privileged position over the rest of Wales. The two knights were chosen by the 40s. freeholders, while the burgess was elected by the freemen of Monmouth and of the 'contributory' boroughs; they were to receive the same fees as English MPs.[1] William Rees suggested that the smaller representation of the thirteen shires may have been due to the government's fear of their inability or their reluctance to maintain their full quota of MPs in fees and expenses,[2] although by this period the ancient practice of paying members was breaking down. Possibly, too, it was felt that the thirteen shires, lacking in parliamentary tradition, except in the fourteenth century, when the Principality sent representatives to Westminster on two occasions, should serve a probationary period before receiving a greater representation — but no change was made in the number of Welsh MPs until the nineteenth century.[3] Monmouthshire's representation was, perhaps, the result of a compromise between the policy to approximate it to an English shire and the fear expressed above, a fear only too well-founded, if we are to judge from the experience of Kynnyllyn.[4]

The commission to delimit the new shires was not set up immediately, as the 1536 Act required; in fact, some years elapsed before we hear anything of its activities or of the emergence of the new shires. Monmouthshire shared in this delay. The first hint of the changes that were to take place are given in a letter written by Lee to Cromwell dated 21 June (year not given).[5] It is addressed from Monmouth where, doubtless, he was engaged in the task of

---

[1] 35 Hen. VIII c. 11 (Bowen, *Statutes*, p. 133) gives details of the method of payment; it also extended the franchise to the freemen of the contributory boroughs. One of the first burgesses of Monmouth, Thomas Kynnyllyn, sued officers and inhabitants of some of these boroughs (Abergavenny, Caerleon, Newport and Chepstow) for non-payment of the fee due to him 'as burgess of the parlyament of and all the borowes and towns of the Sheir': E.A. Lewis, *An inventory of the early Chancery proceedings concerning Wales* (1938), p. 228.

[2] Rees, 'Union', p. 57.

[3] In 1536 Calais was represented by two burgesses and the county palatine of Chester by two county and two borough members.

[4] See n. 1 above.

[5] The letter is printed in H. Ellis (ed.), *Original letters illustrative of English history* (3rd series, III, 1846), p. ccclxii, and in *Letters and Papers*, X, 1178. In the latter it is included under 1536, but Ellis fixes the year as 1540. If the latter is correct, then news of Cromwell's arrest on 10 June that year had obviously not yet reached Lee.

supervising the 'translation' of the area into shire ground. He complained that Monmouth castle was

> all decayed and in ruyn (the hall and walls only excepte). And forasmoch as it shalbe a Shire town and that also this Counsaile [i.e. the Council in the Marches] shall for sondry causes repayre thither I think it expedient the Priory[1] here, viz. the mansion of the same, as stones, tymbere and other things to be reserved for the re-edifying of the saide Castelle.

It is reasonable to conclude from this letter that preparations were afoot for the formation of the new shire and that Monmouth Castle had been earmarked as a convenient centre where county, and possibly Council, legal and administrative business could be conducted, important officials based and a county gaol established.

On 25 July 1540, the first important appointment for the shire was made, that of the Clerk of the Peace and of the Crown, in the person of Hugh Huntley.[1] It is likely that clerks of the peace were appointed some time before justices of the peace and of the quorum because of the need to set up the organisation of the new quarter sessions, but the length of the intervening period is difficult to estimate and varied from county to county.[2] The first mention of JPs in Monmouthshire is of a list of acting justices in 1542; the first commission of the peace for the county, which appeared in February 1543, contained more than the maximum of eight justices, apart from 'honorary' justices, laid down by the Act of 1543.[3] One of the justices was to hold the office of *Custos Rotulorum*, the Keeper of the Rolls, chiefly responsible for keeping the records and establishing legal precedents;[5] it was usually held by a senior member of the bench. The property qualification for a place on the commission of the peace (£20 p.a. in land) was waived in 1543 as a concession to the relative modesty of Welsh landed income. Later in the century, George Owen of Henllys (Pembs.) commented on this as a concession to enable Welsh gentry to serve as JPs despite their relative

---

[1] See D.H. Williams, 'Monmouth Priory at the Suppression, 1534–37', *Monmouthshire Antiquary*, 3 (1970–78), 186–91.

[2] *Letters and Papers*, XV, 940. Huntley's will is in Hunt, Dissertation, p. 89. A clerk had already been appointed for Glamorgan in July 1539: J.R.S. Phillips, *The justices of the peace in Wales and Monmouthshire, 1541–1689* (1975), p. xi.

[3] Phillips, *Justices*, p. 344.

[4] Ibid.

[5] Jones, *Wales and the Tudor state*, p. 49; idem, *Concepts of order and gentility in Wales, 1540–1640* (1992), p. 173.

poverty and lack of learning. He said that most of them 'could neyther wryte nor read.'[1] What the clause in the 1543 Act actually did was to allow the admission to the bench of those not 'learned in the laws of the lande' so long as they were 'of good name and fame'.[2] They were, however, by the 1536 Act to be able to 'use and exercise English' and quarter sessions and other courts were to be held in that language. There is little doubt that the Welsh squires who held administrative or judicial office in Wales, including Monmouthshire, were bilingual and eligible to serve under the terms of the 'language clause' of 1536. In addition, although court proceedings were to be held in English, interpreters were probably employed.[3] The sixteenth-century quarter sessions records for Caernarfonshire and Monmouthshire — the only Welsh quarter sessions records extant for that period — were kept in Latin.

Meanwhile, the other important appointments had been made. The first sheriff of the county, Charles Herbert, was appointed in November 1541.[4] In November 1541 the first writ of summons for Parliament was addressed to the sheriff. An escheator, two coroners and the keeper of the county gaol had been chosen by 1542.

No precise information is available to determine when the first assizes were held in the county, nor when it was first included in the Oxford circuit. Among the ancient indictments of the King's Bench, J. Conway Davies found a writ of *certiorari* dated 11 August 34 Henry VIII (1542), to the Keepers of the King's Peace and the King's Justices assigned to hear and determine the several wrongdoings in Monmouthshire and to his justices assigned to take assizes in the county.[5] Does this suggest that the assizes had already been held before that date? The first intimation in published State Papers of the county's inclusion in the Oxford circuit is found in the

---

[1] 'Dialogue of the government of Wales', in H. Owen (ed.), *The description of Penbrokshire*, Part III, pp. 555–6, cited in Roberts, 'Language', p. 28, who adds that Owen was given to exaggeration.

[2] Bowen, *Statutes*, p. 113, s. 56.

[3] That this was true for Monmouthshire in the nineteenth century is shown in an entry for 25 March 1803 for payments to be made to court interpreters, in the Treasurer's Account Book (1803–14), among the quarter sessions papers at the Gwent Record Office. See M.Ll. Chapman (ed.), 'A 16th century trial for felony in the Court of Great Sessions for Montgomeryshire', *Mont. Collections*, 78 (1990), 167–70, concerning oral evidence in Welsh being allowed in the trial. See also W.O. Williams, 'The survival of the Welsh language', *Welsh History Review*, 2 (1964), 67–93, and Roberts, 'Language'.

[4] *Letters and Papers*, XVI, 305.

[5] J.C. Davies, 'Report on the records of the county of Monmouth' (Typescript, Gwent Record Office), p. 176. This writ, issued directly out of King's Bench, enabled records of proceedings made by a lower court to be removed and certified before the Westminster court.

grant in June 1542 of a commission of gaol delivery to Sir Edward Mervyn and William Portman, justices of assize of that circuit; their commission included the delivery of the gaol at Monmouth Castle.[1] The first Oxford circuit commission of oyer and terminer to include the county by name is dated 12 February 35 Henry VIII.[2]

By 1542, also, the shire must have been divided into seven hundreds, Skenfrith, Raglan, Trelech, Caldicot, Usk, Newport (or Wentloog) and Abergavenny.[3] The activities of the commission set up for this purpose are not known, but it must have completed its work by that date, for the Act 34 & 35 Henry VIII c. 26 refers in s. 3 to the limits of the hundreds 'of late made', while s. 69 of the Act provided for the appointment, by the JPs, of two 'substantial gentlemen or yeomen' to be chief constable in every hundred.

Thus Monmouthshire made its appearance in 1540 and by 1542 all features of shire administration and justice had been established. But was it in Wales or England?[4] The 1536 Act states that the lordships and other divisions constituting the new shire were in the 'countrey of Wales',[5] but it provided different judicial and other arrangements for the county from those of the rest of Wales. The 1543 Act separated it from the statutory twelve shires,[6] but neither Act specifically consigned it to either country. Perhaps the question does not really arise since it was not the intention of Henry VIII to preserve the identity of Wales but to incorporate, unite and annex it and Monmouthshire to the 'imperialle Crowne of this Realm as a verrye membre and ioynte of the same'.[7]

---

[1] *Letters and Papers*, XVII, 443.

[2] Ibid., XX, Part 2, 622. J.S. Cockburn, *A history of English assizes, 1558–1714* (1972), p. 23, n. 1, claims that Monmouthshire was added to the Oxford circuit by 34 and 35 Hen. VIII c. 26, but he is surely mistaken.

[3] Roll, Caerleon 2.

[4] For a discussion of this see Rees, 'Union', pp. 74ff, and B. Howell, 'Local administration in Monmouthshire, 16th–19th centuries' (Unpublished University of Wales [Cardiff] M.A. thesis, 1951), Chapter 3.

[5] Rees, 'Union', p. 83.

[6] 34 and 35 Henry VIII c. 26, s. 2; Bowen, *Statutes*, p. 101.

[7] Rees, 'Union', p. 81.

3

Society

Sixteenth-century society in Monmouthshire, as elsewhere, was imbued with hierarchy and degree and the Roll of 1576–77 reflects the various gradations which existed there, from the aristocracy in the person of William, third Earl of Worcester, and his son, Edward Somerset, Lord Herbert, to the lowliest pauper.[1]

Hierarchy, organic unity and order were the fundamentals upon which contemporaries formulated their theories about the nature of society, government — and the universe.[2] Within the chain of being linking creation from top to bottom, man was ranked in order from kings to the unfree. All had their appointed places in a divinely ordained hierarchy, and to overthrow it was to return the universe to chaos. The sacred right to rule had been conferred by God upon the monarch who, in turn, devolved it upon those through whom the realm was governed. It was laid down in the Homily of Obedience of 1547 that

> every degree of people ... had appointed to them their duty and order; some are in high degree, some in low, some Kings and Princes, some inferiors and subjects, masters and servants, fathers and children ... take away rulers and there must needs follow all mischief and utter destruction.[3]

Sir Thomas Elyot, in his influential book, *The Governour* (1531), a treatise on the education of the 'better sort', stated that where there was no due regard to rank and obedience to superiors 'there lacketh ordre; and where ordre lacketh, there all thynge is odiouse and uncomely', and the 'publike-weale' suffered.[4] The preservation of good order thus depended on the maintenance of grades and the need for the complete subjugation of the individual to superior authority. In this deferential society the key symbols

---

[1] Roll, Newport, 26; Raglan, 1; Abergavenny, 31.

[2] Lawrence Stone, *The crisis of the aristocracy* (1965), p. 21.

[3] B. Howells, 'The lower orders', in T. Herbert and G.E. Jones (ed.) *Tudor Wales* (1988), p. 53.

[4] Quoted in J. Hale, *The civilisation of Europe in the Renaissance* (1993), p. 356.

were the whip and the hat: the use of the former was confined to lesser subjects, such as servant, apprentices and law-breakers, as a means of enforcing obedience, and the doffing of the latter gave visible proof of a person's acceptance of the principle of subordination.[1] An English knight refused to give his daughter in marriage to an earl, saying, 'I do not like to stand with my cap in my hand to my son-in-law.'[2]

The Welsh poets were staunch bulwarks of 'order and degree' with frequent references in their eulogies and elegies to the *gradd* (status) and *stad* (estate) of their patrons.[3] At every level social status was reflected in outward appearance, lifestyle, speech and responsibilities. At every level also there was much mobility into and out of all social grades, downwards as well as upwards. Those who climbed to eminence from comparatively humble origins, such as Lord Burghley, were sometimes derided by members of old-established families. The Cecils were regarded as 'new men', whose status had been earned by 'clerkship'. 'What are the Cessels', complained an opponent in 1601, 'are they better than pen-gent?'[4]

The Aristocracy

At the apex of this hierarchical society in Monmouthshire were the earls of Worcester and Pembroke, with strong family connections.[5] The Somersets, the earls of Worcester, destined to be powerful in the seventeenth century, were for most of Elizabeth's reign withdrawn from national politics and lived in state at Raglan Castle, where old customs lingered; the then earl was said still to have been waited on at table by 'many gentlemen's sons from two to seven hundred a year bred up at the castle,'[6] although by then most gentry were sending their sons to be educated at the universities and elsewhere. The earls of Pembroke, of the second creation, loyal servants of the Crown (with lapses) who spent much time at Court, were, by Elizabeth's reign, absentee landlords of their Monmouthshire estates, now making their home at Wilton. Of the two, the Pembrokes were the more influential, but both were active

---

[1] Stone, *Crisis*, p. 34.

[2] D.M. Palliser, *The age of Elizabeth. England under the later Tudors* (2nd ed. 1992), p. 95.

[3] J.G. Jones, *Wales and the Tudor state* (1989), p. 123.

[4] Stone, *Crisis*, p. 60.

[5] *Dictionary of Welsh Biography*, p. 350 (Herbert, earls of Pembroke, second creation); p. 916 (Somerset, earls of Worcester).

[6] Stone, *Crisis*, p. 209.

and much sought after patrons of a cousinage and clientage network; as
Burghley commented to his son, a gentleman without a patron was 'like a
hop without a pole.'[1] The first earl of Pembroke (1507–70) gained a great
reputation as 'the eye of Wales' during his presidency of the Council of
Wales and the Marches in the 1550s, as did his son later in the same office,
in virtue of which the latter also held the newly created post of lord
lieutenant of the Welsh and border counties. The father attracted to Ludlow
an increasing number of young Welsh, including Monmouthshire, gentry, and
appealed to them to be conscious of their responsibilities 'to the public good
of the whole estate'.[2] It was an age when nobles and gentlemen were almost
all literate; John Aubrey, however, maintained that the first earl, though a
Privy Councillor, 'could neither write nor read', but Pembroke's signatures
survive to cast doubt on the story.[3]

The Gentry

The first earl of Pembroke was described by a contemporary as one who
enhanced the prestige of his family by his leadership, magnanimity, love of
learning, 'wisdom linked with courage, moderation tempered with justice.'[4]
J.G. Jones explains that these qualities reveal some of the basic concepts of
gentility and were those extolled in people of gentle birth. Much was made
of the attributes of the gentry elite who were to help the Tudors to govern.
Military service was still important, as in the case, for example, of the
Morgans of Pencoed and of Pencarn, a number of whom were knighted in
Tudor campaigns abroad and fell into debt in the process;[5] but the Crown
was also anxious to have men 'fytte for the peace'[6] and the ideal 'governor'
was expected to be a rounded person possessing $virtu$[7] and, according to

[1] B. Howells, 'Government and politics, 1536–1642', *Pembrokshire County History*, III
(1987), p. 129.
[2] J.G. Jones, *Llen Cymru*, 15 (1984–86), p. 77.
[3] Palliser, *Age of Elizabeth*, p. 419, citing John Aubrey, *Brief Lives* (ed. A. Clark), I, p.
315.
[4] J.G. Jones 'Concepts of order and gentility', in idem (ed.) *Class, community and culture
in Tudor Wales* (1989), p. 150.
[5] See A.C. Miller, 'William Morgan of Pencoed', *Welsh History Review*, 9 (1978–9),
1–31.
[6] J.G. Jones, *Concepts of order and gentility in Wales, 1540–1640* (1992), citing R. Kelso,
Doctrine of the English gentleman, p. 39.
[7] W.P. Griffith, 'Beth oedd y dyn Tuduraidd' in D.G. Jones and J.G. Jones (ed.), *Bosworth
a'r Tuduriaid* (1985), p. 31.

Elyot, 'should seem to all men worthy to be in authority, honour and noblesse'.[1]

The Tudors had no standing army, nor a professional police force, and only a small body of permanent salaried officials. This was one reason why the Crown had to rely so heavily on the co-operation of nobles, gentry (especially the JPs) and some members of the lower orders, in filling the offices (all unpaid) in local administration and justice. This also made for a situation of 'government by the informal mechanism of consent'.[2]

Greater attention was coming to be paid to education, and the gentry were now sending their sons to the new Welsh grammar schools — such as the one at Abergavenny — or to schools in England and thence to the universities or the Inns of Court, which assumed the role of a third university. Jesus College, Oxford, founded in 1571, the first principal of which was a native of Abergavenny, Dr David Lewis, was popular with Welsh students. By about 1590 a quarter of the active JPs in Wales had attended a university or an Inn and by 1630 the number had increased to half.[3] As already noted, young gentry also went to Ludlow to seek political and legal education at the Council of Wales and the Marches. The conviction that government was the preserve of those born at a certain social level was enshrined in a memorandum of 1559, which specified that no one was to study law 'except he be descended from a nobleman or gentleman'.[4] A number of Welshmen distinguished themselves in the legal profession, including Sir Richard Morgan of Blackbrook and Dr David Lewis, both Monmouthshire men. Knowledge of the law was also useful for the gentry in estate management, in performing the responsibilities of office, such as on the bench, and in litigation, in which many of them engaged. Sir Thomas Smith, in his oft-quoted definition of a gentlemen, held that

> whosoever studies the laws of the realms who studies at the
> universities ... who can live idly without manual labour, and will
> bear the port, charge and countenance of a gentleman, he shall
> be called master, for that is the title given to esquires and other

---

[1] Cited in Jones, *Concepts of order and gentility*, p. 185.

[2] Palliser, *Age of Elizabeth*, p. 351.

[3] W.P. Griffith, 'Y dyn Tuduraidd', pp. 34–6. J. Hunt, 'Monmouthshire wills proved in the Prerogative Court of Canterbury, 1414–1560' (Cardiff Local History Dissertation, 1985) notes occasional bequests by Monmouthshire gentry 'to find a son to school' (e.g. p. 22). Meredydd ap Sir Phillip of Abergavenny left money to his son 'for his exhibition in the Inns of Court, London' (p. 62).

[4] A. Fletcher, *Reform in the provinces* (1986), p. 40.

gentlemen.[1]

The gentry were the most powerful social group in Monmouthshire. They were divided into various loosely tiered status groups, precedence being given to knights (and baronets from 1611), below whom were the esquires, who were relatively wealthy and possessed substantial estates, and finally the gentlemen, including the minor or 'parish gentry' who were often indistinguishable from yeomen. Movement up or down through the grades was not inflexible: for instance, the Aldey family of Chepstow had been classed as yeomen but described themselves as gentry when they bought land in Hardwick. What property qualification determined membership of the gentry class has often been discussed by historians but in the last resort it probably came down to what status a family considered it enjoyed and whether or not its own assessment was accepted by the community. It is difficult to divide society into clear-cut categories; perhaps 'Howell James of Llantellyo Cryssenny ... yeoman, otherwise called Howell Herbert of Llantellyo Cryssenny, gentleman',[2] had some difficulty in getting himself accepted among the gentry, a base-born Herbert though he might have been (illegitimacy was not usually a bar). Some yeomen counted themselves gentry since they were often descended from armigerous stock.

Within the ranks of the gentry there were wide differences in wealth but most were distinguished from the rest of the community through their role as landlords and the offices which they held. Monmouthshire gentry would undoubtedly have echoed the words of a seventeenth-century English knight who wrote to his grandchildren, 'If thou has not some command in the country (i.e. county), thou wilt not be esteemed of the common sort of people who have more fear than love in them.'[3] Some families, especially knights and esquires, came to fill those posts which buttressed the Tudor state, the offices of justices of the peace, custos rotulorum, sheriff and deputy lieutenant; some lesser gentry served as high constables and members of grand juries. The county oligarchy, the Somersets, Herberts and Morgans, naturally monopolised the county representation in Parliament between 1542 and about 1590.

Established families had already obtained experience in administration by holding posts in the marcher lordships and religious houses. In the lordship of Newport, the office of coroner was filled by members of the Morgan or

---

[1] N. Heard, *Tudor economy and society* (1992), p. 97. It is probable that not many Monmouthshire gentry could afford to live 'idly'.

[2] Roll, Monmouth I, 12.

[3] Fletcher, *Reform*, p. 31.

Kemeys families, the office of steward by the Morgans of Machen and that
of receiver by John Huntley and the Morgans.[1] The various offices in the
Duchy of Lancaster were dominated by the Herbert families.[2]

In the administration of his Monmouthshire estates the second earl of
Worcester (1526–49) appointed his Herbert kinsmen to high office: Sir
Walter Herbert of St Julians as steward and receiver of the lordship of
Caldicot, Sir Charles Herbert of Troy, steward of Monmouth, William John
Thomas, steward of Raglan, all gentlemen of considerable local influence,
and Watkyn Herbert, steward of Chepstow, a member of the lesser gentry.
Grants of office were the most important means of rewarding the earl's
principal adherents and they looked to him to support them in disputes and
appointments. For his part, the earl regarded his local officers as his principal
retainers and supporters; Walter Herbert is known to have had many retainers
of his own.[3] Among others who held lordship office were Thomas and his
brother Walter ap Robert of Pant-glas.

The office-holders of the religious houses included Charles Herbert of
Troy (the first sheriff of Monmouthshire), who was steward of four houses,
while his younger brother, Thomas, was his deputy at Grace Dieu. Charles's
successor as sheriff, Thomas Herbert of Moor Grange, was bailiff of Tintern.
Among other office-holders were the Morgans of Tredegar and Machen and
Philip Williams of Mathern.

A number of leading county families in Monmouthshire, when land came
on the market after the dissolution of the religious houses, either did not buy
at all or bought only little, unlike the gentry of Glamorgan. Among those
who bought or were granted ecclesiastical land were the two earls (Worcester
was granted Tintern); Thomas Herbert of Wonastow, deputy steward of
Grace Dieu, bought the abbey's estate; William Morgan bought the property
belonging to Llantarnam abbey, and, with other purchases, built up a
considerable estate; Roger Williams of Llangwm in Usk bought the site and
demesnes of Usk priory, together with other property, including the manor
of Tregrug; James Gunter purchased Abergavenny priory; and Nicholas
Arnold bought Llanthony cell. Arnold's main residence was in Gloucester
but he maintained a house at Llanthony and eventually settled its estate on

[1] A.C. Reeves, *Newport lordship 1317–1536* (1979), pp. 105–111; T.B. Pugh (ed.) *The
marcher lordships of south Wales 1415–1536* (1963), pp. 24, 255, 295.

[2] R. Somerville, *The Duchy of Lancaster*, I (1953), pp. 646ff.

[3] W.R.B. Robinson, 'Patronage and hospitality in early Tudor Wales: the role of Henry,
Earl of Worcester, 1526–49', *Bull. Inst. Historical Research*, 51 (1978–9), 20–36; idem, 'The
officers and household of Henry, earl of Worcester, 1526–49', *Welsh History Review*, 8 (1976),
26–41.

SOCIETY   xxxi

his illegitimate son, John, who established a family of influence.[1]
The purchasers built new houses worthy of their status. William Morgan,
who demolished the abbey to make way for a *plasty* (mansion), Roger
Williams, who built a *plasty* at Llangybi from stones, doors and fireplaces
taken from Usk castle and John Gunter, who adapted the priory for domestic
use, were all from local families, as indeed were most of the county gentry.
The Morgans of Llantarnam and the Williamses of Llangybi came to be
among the county's leaders.[2] Other new owners built mansions for
themselves on their estates; the Williamses of Monmouth and the Joneses of
Usk, like the Gunters, adapted all or part of the conventual buildings as their
new plasty.[3] The *plasty* was the focal point of the entire community and was
usually located in favourable surroundings. It was not only the centre of the
social graces but it was also where the *uchelwr* carried out many of the
duties associated with the public offices which he might hold. The sixteenth
century also witnessed the rebuilding of a number of medieval houses in the
county, resulting from greater prosperity due to the increased profits from
wheat production.[4] The third earl of Worcester preferred to alter his existing
property rather than build a new house; he also made gardens there.[5]

In spite of the apparent reluctance of some to take advantage of a buoyant
market, land was always important to the gentry. It was not only the
soundest long-term investment, but also brought prestige to them in their
locality. They felt that it was their place to rule in their neighbourhood; land
endowed its possessors with the autonomy and leisure which were the
prerequisites for virtuous government. It was felt that men of mean estate
would be bound to put private interests first. The landed gentry were
educated to believe that their responsibility in life was to administer,

[1] See *Dict. Welsh Biog.*, p. 19 for the Arnolds; p. 635 for the Morgans of Llantarnam; and
pp. 635ff. for the Morgans of Tredegar Park and elsewhere; see also J. Gwynfor Jones, *Y
Morganiaid o Dredegyr* (1988).
[2] By the eighteenth century the Morgans of Tredegar had become the dominant county
family. When John Morgan of Tredegar died in 1719 the bells of Bassaleg and Newport were
tolled for fifteen days: G.H. Jenkins, *Hanes Cymru 1530–1760* (1983), p. 27.
[3] For the disposal of Crown lands see M. Gray, 'The dispersal of Crown property in
Monmouthshire, 1500–1700' (Unpublished University of Wales [Cardiff] Ph.D. Thesis, 1984),
pp. 114–16, 237ff.; idem, 'Change and continuity: the gentry and property of the church in
south-east Wales and the Marches', in Jones (ed.) *Class, community and culture*, 1–38.
[4] W.R.B. Robinson, 'The Valor Ecclesiasticus of 1535 as evidence of agrarian output',
Bull. Inst. Historical Research, 56 (1983), 27; C. Fox and Lord Raglan, *Monmouthshire Houses*
(National Museum of Wales, 1951–4), II, 14–15.
[5] E. Wiliam, 'Domestic architecture' in Jones (ed.), *Class, community and culture*,
159–193; E.H. Whittle, 'The sixteenth- and seventeenth-century gardens at Raglan Castle',
Monmouthshire Antiquary, 6 (1990), 69–75.

adjudicate and serve the community.

Emphasis on public service was matched by adulation of ancient lineage. A recurring theme in the history of the *uchelwyr* was the overwhelming importance of the family, which added to the sense of continuity and stability already created by ancient house and estate. Attachment to the sentiment of family pride caused Sir William Herbert of St Julians to stipulate in his will that his daughter should marry a gentleman bearing the name of Herbert or forfeit her right of succession to his property.[1] It was this pride of family that persuaded the squires that the best way to perpetuate their memory was by setting memorial stones, tombs and chapels in their parish churches, as for example George Lewis's memorial stone in St Pierre church; the chapel of the Morgans at Machen church and of the Herberts at St Mary's, Abergavenny; and the tomb of John Philip Morgan in Skenfrith church (at the foot of the tomb are the arms of the Cecils, to which family his wife belonged).[2]

This sense of continuity — and of good 'stock' — was also stressed by ornate and long genealogies.[3] The poet Dafydd Benwyn had a close knowledge of the pedigrees of his patrons; for instance, in his poem to the Morgans of Tredegar he refers to them as the men of the 'West Country', for they claimed descent from Cadifor Fawr of Dyfed:

> Goreu yn f'oes gwyr am win,
> Goreu ymysg y werin,
> Gwelaf yn lanaf o lin — brenhinoedd
> Gwyr lluoedd y Gorllewin.[4]

There was much intermarriage among the gentry families of the county, as pedigrees in Bradney and elsewhere show. This, of course, led to county families being related and in appointments to office cousinage was an important factor. The ties of kinship, however, did not prevent serious rivalries, feuds and factions among them in their struggle for dominance. Illegally armed retainers of the Morgans of Tredegar and the Herberts of St Julians frequently caused disturbances and riots in the markets or the streets

---

[1] G.D. Owen *Elizabethan Wales* (1962), p. 13.

[2] Hunt, Dissertation, passim.

[3] Francis Jones, 'Welsh genealogy', *Trans. Hon. Soc. Cymmrodorion* (1948) p. 307, notes that 'Genealogy is an essential part of Welsh history ... it should not be allowed to remain the harmless plaything of dilettante squires, parish antiquaries and maiden aunts'.

[4] 'The boldest with the winecup / The leaders of the people / The brightest of that race of Kings / The men of the West Country'. J.K. Fletcher, *The Gwentian poems of Dafydd Benwyn* (1909), p. 10.

of Newport; the Court of Star Chamber tried 30 cases of riots and violence
in the town in eighty years.[1] There were a number of other Star Chamber
cases involving Monmouthshire gentry.[2] This feuding, a feature of gentry
life in Elizabethan times, was mainly concentrated in towns and coincided
with markets and sittings of quarter sessions. It was often perpetrated by
justices appointed to maintain law and order in their localities, or in William
Lambarde's words in 1586, 'to put the laws in ure (i.e. into use) with the
edge of the sword and authority thereof to cut in sunder those offences that
work confusion in the country'.[3] A number of Monmouthshire gentry appear
on the Roll published here for various breaches of the law: Thomas Roberts
of Dingestow (with others) accused of affray and assault; Thomas John of
Usk (with others) the same offence; William Saunders, Llangoven, assault;
Thomas Powell, Abergavenny (lately deputy sheriff), with others, extortion
(acquitted); Arnold Welshe, Llanwern, with others, riot; Richard Herbert,
Goytre, assault and affray.[4]

  Let the last word on the gentry — in this chapter at least — be on their
more peaceful pursuits in their patronage of the bardic orders and their
interest in genealogy, heraldry and antiquities. Among the great patrons of
the bards before the sixteenth century had been Ifor Hael of Gwernyclepa,
a member of a branch of the Morgan family who was visited by the famous
poet, Dafydd ap Gwilym; and the first earl of Pembroke (of the first creation)
to whose patronage previous reference has been made. Raglan came to have
a valuable collection of Welsh manuscripts. The first earl of Pembroke (of
the second creation) often spoke Welsh at Court and reminded Elizabeth of
her Welsh ancestry; it was to him that Gruffydd Robert, the Catholic exile
in Milan, dedicated his *Welsh Grammar* (1567), thanked him for being an
unceasing patron of the Welsh language and for using it at every
opportunity, and urged him to continue to give it his support.[5] Others of the
Herbert family were also well disposed toward the bards. Edward Morgan,
Llantarnam, possessed a good library of Welsh books. William Evans, Ll.B.,
a native of Llangattock-vibon-avel and related to the Herberts, was a member
of the commissions of the peace for both Monmouthshire and Glamorgan,
and chancellor and treasurer of Llandaff, where he showed a keen interest

---

[1] B.P. Jones, *From Elizabeth I to Victoria. Newport. 1550–1850* (1957), p. 30.

[2] I. ab O. Edwards, *A catalogue of Star Chamber proceedings relating to Wales* (1929),
pp. 108, 109, 113 and elsewhere.

[3] Cited in J.G. Jones, 'Concepts of continuity and change in Anglesey after the Act of
Union, 1536–1603', *Anglesey Antiquarian Society and Field Club Transactions* (1990), p. 26.

[4] Roll, Caerleon 9, 24; Usk, 5; Newport 31; Abergavenny II, 49; Crick, 4 and 5; Usk, 36.

[5] H. Hayes, *Cymru a'r Dadeni* (1987), p. 12.

in the bardic craft and judged bardic entries in an eisteddfod there.[1] The poet-parson Thomas Jones of Llandeilo Bertholau, motivated, perhaps, by a mixture of a love of the Welsh language and a desire to promote Protestantism in a county where recusancy (especially among the gentry) was strong, at the Christmas service in 1588 urged his hearers, some years before Vicar Pritchard did the same, to sell their shirts in order to buy a copy of William Morgan's Welsh translation of the Bible which had recently appeared.[2]

Gwent, unlike Glamorgan, never played a conspicuous part in the literary life of the region. It contained many famous households which extended generous hospitality to visiting bards, some from North Wales, but it produced few poets of note. Dafydd Benwyn, from Glamorgan, was the best known of the visiting bards and among the gentry for whom he composed poems were William Evans, many members of the Herbert and Morgan families, together with a lady, Blanche, wife of Rowland Morgan of Machen and a descendant of William Herbert, earl of Pembroke (first creation).[3] The poet reminds us that it was only with the indispensable help of the gentlewoman of the household, whose lineage was as good as that of her husband, that generous charity and entertainment were dispensed within the plasty. By the second half of the sixteenth century however, bardism and the scale of gentle patronage were in decline.

The Lower Orders

The major social division in the Tudor period was that between the 'gentle-born', that is the nobility and the gentry on the one hand, and the 'non-gentle' sections in society, the lower orders, on the other.[4] Many of the latter, who comprised most of the population, relied upon farming as their chief means of subsistence. As the Roll testifies, the struggle for land no less than the struggle to make a living out of it, absorbed much of men's time and energies. A number of cases which came before the Monmouthshire JPs concerned forcible entry, ejecting owners or tenants and retaining possession,

---

[1] G.J. Williams, *Traddodiad llenyddol Morgannwg* (1948), pp. 88–9. The Roll shows that he sat at the quarter Sessions at Caerleon, Newport, Crick and Usk, and the quarter Sessions and second gaol delivery at Monmouth.

[2] Glanmor Williams, *Recovery, reorientation and Reformation. Wales, 1415–1642* (1985), p. 322.

[3] Bradney, *Monmouthshire*, II, p. 303.

[4] B. Howells, 'The lower orders', in T. Herbert and G.E. Jones (ed.) *Tudor Wales* (1988), 41–66.

destroying hedges and crops and the like.[1] Their lives were hard and their economic difficulties increased during the Tudor period when there was an increase in population, in which Monmouthshire shared;[2] this, with other factors, led to inflation, increased prices, land hunger, an increase in the number of landless and masterless people, a labour surplus and relatively low wages. At times there were epidemics and harvest failure leading to distress, malnutrition and increased mortality; the years of greatest mortality in Caerwent were 1572, 1587–88, 1590, and 1597; at Grosmont 1592 and 1598; 1593 at Llanbaddock, and at Llantilio Pertholey in 1597–98.[3] Indeed, the 1590s was a very difficult decade throughout the county.

As with the gentle-born, there were social divisions among the lower orders: the more substantial farmers or yeomen, the smaller farmers or husbandmen, craftsmen, the labouring class and the impoverished.

The Tudor gentry regarded themselves as distinct from and socially superior to the yeomen but the differences between them were often blurred. Some yeomen were descended from the cadet branches of gentry families and it was not uncommon for them to be wealthier than the poorer gentry. It was, in any case, a relative question, for

> A Knight of Cales
> And a gentleman of Wales
> And a laird of the North-Countrie
> A yeoman of Kent
> With his yearly rent
> Will buy them out all three.[4]

Yeomen emerged in Wales in the fifteenth century, though in smaller numbers than in England. The Welsh term *iwmon* is first recorded in the words of a poet from the south-eastern border (i.e. Gwent), where yeomen were likely to have appeared earlier and in greater numbers than elsewhere in Wales.[5] They came to be set apart from the rest of the peasantry by virtue of wealth, style of living, sturdy farmhouses and size of farms; they

---

[1] Roll, e.g. Caerleon, 27; Newport, 34; Abergavenny, 29, 30; Usk II, 60; Monmouth II, 9.

[2] D. Williams, 'A note on the population of Wales, 1536–1801', *Bull. Board of Celtic Studies*, 8 (1937), 359–63, suggests that Monmouthshire's population increased from about 20,000 in 1536 to 27,807 by the end of the century.

[3] B. Howells, 'The lower orders of society', in Jones (ed.), *Class, community and culture*, p. 240.

[4] E. Wiliam, 'Domestic architecture', in ibid., p. 171.

[5] Williams, *Recovery*, p. 104.

might also engage in other pursuits, such as keeping an alehouse.[1] Some of them were freeholders, others were copyholders or leaseholders; some copyholders in lowland Monmouthshire (1610) were still scattered over three common fields, others were consolidated as farms of 120–150 acres while others, both customary tenants and freeholders, had between 200 and 250 acres.[2] Leland noted that 'al venteland' (i.e. most of the county) was 'very fertyle of corne' although men there 'study more of pastures'. This mixed arable and pasture farming did not extend to the uplands between the rivers Ebbw and Rhymney in West Monmouthshire, which Leland considered 'better for catelle than corne'.[3] The yeoman was helped in working his farm by his family and farm servants. Thomas Fuller called the yeomanry 'an estate of people ... living in the temperate zone between greatness and want'. The principal characteristics of the yeoman were his frugality of living and his contentment with a simple way of life; even when he could afford more comfort, he was, in Fuller's phrase 'a gentleman in ore' (i.e. esteem) and he could live without the expenses of a gentleman.[4] Hugh ap Howell of Llanvetherine, yeoman, in his will (1543) refers to 'my manor of Gellthewege with all my lands, tenements etc. in the parishes of Llanferyn and Llanvyhangle Kyleconell ... my mansion house ... my lands, tenements etc. in the parish of Llanthewye Skyrd', but seems contented with his status.[5]

Yeomen, some of whom were literate, were invaluable administrators and men of influence in a locality, as members of hundredal, coroner's, petty and sometimes grand juries in quarter sessions and assizes, serving as high constables of hundreds, and in the various parochial offices. A number of them voted in parliamentary elections as 40s. freeholders. The Roll records that some yeomen were not always law-abiding and were involved in such offences as assault and affray, trespass and contempt, riot and unlawful assembly.[6]

Husbandmen were small farmers comprising one of the groups which made up, in the words of Sir Thomas Smith, 'the fourth sort of men who do not rule', though they might be asked to serve occasionally as parochial officers or as trial jurors. For many of them life was a ceaseless round of

---

[1] Roll, Newport, 55, 56, 57.

[2] F. Emery, 'The farming regions of Wales,' in J. Thirsk (ed.), *The Agrarian History of England and Wales*, IV (1967), 113–60.

[3] Robinson, 'Valor Ecclesiasticus', 27.

[4] G. Batho, 'Noblemen, gentlemen and yeomen,' in *Agrarian History*, IV, 276–306.

[5] Hunt, Dissertation, p. 75.

[6] Roll, e.g. Newport, 4, 12, 8, 21.

toil, often on the edge of penury. As land hunger grew they faced greatly increased rent and entry fines, without being able to produce enough to profit from increased prices. Some worked about 20–30 acres of land but the majority had only 15 acres or less and a few livestock. Jayne Tanner of Redwick, husbandman, in his will of 1543, left 14 acres to his wife, but he also left other land (unspecified).[1] Their farms were usually held on short leases and on termination they would have to look for a new landlord who could afford to choose his tenants and demand higher rents. Many husbandmen were vulnerable to economic disaster such as cattle disease or crop failure. Some worked as part-time craftsmen — they and full-time craftsmen were essential members of the rural community — while their wives and daughters were engaged in spinning, weaving and dairying.

The husbandman had to find money to pay rents, fines, local rates, taxes and debts to shopkeepers in the neighbouring town. George Owen explains that he raised money by selling some livestock, wool and produce in the fairs which were held between May and November.[2] But 'from November to May they have nothing wherewith to make money' and until the following summer had to live on credit with the shopkeepers of the towns for the purchase of iron, salt, oil, pitch, tar, spice 'and such things that are to be had out of towns'. He was careful, however, to be in debt for less than 40s. to any shopkeeper; actions for small debts were settled in the county court, whereas cases involving larger sums went to the assizes which meant heavy legal and other expenses. Those who failed to meet their financial obligations, especially in finding a new tenancy, might be reduced in status to that of a cottager, with two or three acres, common rights and a few livestock, or cease to belong to the farming community and have to join the growing numbers of landless labourers.

There was an abundance of cheap labour in Elizabethan times and labourers, male and female, comprised a quarter of the population. In the countryside most of them worked in employment connected with farming. The conditions of employment affecting them were set out in the Statute of Artificers (1563) which laid down that the period of hire of a servant or workmen should not be less than a year; that masters should not dismiss their servants, or servants leave their employment without the permission of a JP; those employed in a craft were to serve a seven year apprenticeship; that unemployed males should be employed in husbandry and unemployed girls in domestic service; that the parish constable could compel any man to help in the harvest; that fixing annual wage rates was to be transferred from

---

[1] Hunt, Disssertation, p. 74; see also Roll, Raglan, 5.

[2] Cited in Howells, 'Lower orders', in Herbert and Jones (ed.), *Tudor Wales*, p. 56.

Parliament to the JPs. Masters who dismissed their servants were to be fined 40*s*., whereas servants who left their employment or refused to work were to be imprisoned or sent to a house of correction, to be disciplined into obedience. In rural areas farmers could compel sons of poor parents, aged between 10 and 18, to serve as apprentices in husbandry until they reached the age of 21. The JPs, as employers, were tempted to fix the wage rate below the rate of inflation.[1] Among the aims of the Act were that as many as possible of the lower orders should be in employment; that everyone should have a master and, if possible, be part of a household (masterless men and women were regarded as a danger to social stability); and that labour mobility should be restricted through, for instance, compulsory seven-year apprenticeship and forbidding workers to change their employers without permission.[2]

The whole system was oppressive, the labourers being entirely at the mercy of their masters and kept in order by the strict master-servant discipline which prevailed. If they were in distress some might resort to theft — a Surrey MP wrote in 1597 that it was 'hard in poverty not to sinne'[3] — the penalty for which could be hanging or whipping; or become vagrants, the punishment being branding, whipping or both. Among a number of cases in the Roll involving labourers were charges of riot and unlawful assembly, forcible entry and repeated failure to answer to various felonies and murders, for which they were outlawed.[4] It was not, however, an utterly wretched existence for the labourer; if he gave loyal service to a good master he was looked after well. Many of them were given meals or gifts of foodstuff to take home and had gardens and access to the common. Some supplemented their meagre wage with other activities, as in the case of Robert Miller of Caerleon, labourer, 'otherwise known as a miller'.[5]

Most landless workers were farm servants, beginning as such at an early age. George Owen has provided a graphic account of their daily life. Many of them spent their days throughout the year tending cattle, in all weathers. In summer their skins became so brown that they seemed 'like tawny Moors', and in winter they were so tormented with the frost, snow and wind that they might have held 'opinion with the papists that there is a purgatory'. From about the age of 20 their physique became seriously affected by their 'continual labour in tilling of the ground, burning of lime, digging of coal

[1] P. Williams, *Tudor Regime*, p. 177.

[2] J. Guy, *Tudor England* (1988), p. 327.

[3] Palliser, *Age of Elizabeth*, p. 141.

[4] Roll, e.g. Newport, 18, 19, 20; Crick, 4; Abergavenny, 3.

[5] Roll, Crick, 4.

and other slaveries'.[1] Relief from toil and drudgery came on officially recognised holy days when it was customary for people to gather in order to play games, dance and have other forms of recreation. The number of these days was reduced by an Act of 1536 on the grounds that they were hindering agriculture and industry.[2]

Economic necessity compelled the children of the poor, living at the edge of subsistence, to leave their native village to enter service as a domestic servant, if a girl, or as a 'servant in husbandry' if a boy. They were hired by the year, generally at the Michaelmas fairs, or at hiring sessions held under the supervision of the JPs and constables. Single farm servants became part of the family of their employers who became responsible for their training and welfare. They ate with the family and were provided with clothes, which meant they could save their wages in preparation for marriage in their mid-twenties. Married farm workers, living for the most part in squalid one-room cottages, with little furniture, were employed, often irregularly at low wages. Some labourers and other members of the lower orders might have found employment in the new industrial developments of the county, for example, at Tintern, where the wireworks was said to be employing some six hundred men by 1600.[3]

It was once thought that villages were mainly made up of close-knit, kinship-linked communities, where families lived for generations. But historians now conclude that stability in rural communities in the sixteenth century is a myth; our ancestors were mobile.[4] Apart from the gentry, it was only the yeomen and perhaps the most prosperous husbandmen who were likely to stay in the same place for generations. This meant that there was considerable underlying mobility among, for example, maidservants and farm labourers who might move several times during their working lives. As the century progressed, vagrancy also became more common when jobs were harder to find, especially from the mid-century when population growth outstripped economic growth.[5]

---

[1] George Owen, *The Description of Penbrokshire* (ed. H. Owen, 1906), I, pp. 41–4.

[2] E. Duffy, *The stripping of the altars. Traditional religion in England, 1400–1580* (1992), p. 43.

[3] Williams, *Recovery*, p. 399.

[4] M. Stitch, 'Population movement and migration in pre-industrial rural England,' in B. Short (ed.), *The English rural community* (1992), 62–84; N. Heard, *Tudor economy and society* (1992), p. 104; I.K. Ben-Amos, *Adolescence and youth in early modern England* (1994); Ch. 2 and 3.

[5] For destitution and the poor law see below, pp. lxxiii et seq.

4

Government

Central Government

At the centre, the monarch was assisted in governing the realm by the officers of state, Parliament, the Privy Council and the Westminster courts. Central government did not clearly distinguish between its judicial and administrative functions;[1] Parliament and the Privy Council could be regarded as courts as well as legislative and executive institutions, and assize judges also had administrative duties. (As will be seen, the Council in the Marches of Wales was both a judicial and administrative body, and the justices of the peace in the localities were administrative as well as law officials.)

Parliament met only when it was summoned by the monarch, by whom it was also dismissed. Elizabeth called it less frequently than her predecessors; under her there were only thirteen sessions in 45 years and three consecutive years sometimes passed without a meeting.[2] Nevertheless, although the queen insisted on short sessions, an unprecedented number of bills competed for attention. Its chief role was to co-operate with the Crown in passing subsidy bills and other government measures, many of which the local officials were required to carry out.[3]

Unlike Parliament, the Council, to be called the Privy Council in Elizabeth's reign, sat frequently, by the 1590s meeting nearly every day. The size of the Council declined from over 200 members in Henry VII's reign to fewer than twenty under Elizabeth, comprising mainly the great officers of state (especially the Lord Chancellor, the Lord Treasurer — Burghley held this office from 1572 to 1598 — and the principal Secretaries of State) and of the royal household, together with some leading magnates. This body was the foremost instrument of the Tudor government, assisting the monarch in

---

[1] D.M. Palliser, *The age of Elizabeth. England under the later Tudors* (2nd ed. 1992), p. 349.

[2] A.G.R. Smith, *The emergence of a nation state. The commonwealth of England, 1529–1660* (1984), p. 128.

[3] For details of Monmouthshire's county and borough MPs, see *History of Parliament; House of Commons 1509–1558*, I, 146–7; *1558–1603*, I, 203–5.

the formulation of policy, but its most constant preoccupation was with its administrative tasks. It concerned itself with everything that went on in the realm, and its directives to regional and local bodies and officers bear eloquent witness to the diversity of its business. Something of the range of its responsibilities can be gauged from the variety of instructions issued to the Council in the Marches of Wales, for transmission to the shires under its direction, including Monmouthshire, given below.

Many of these tasks were undertaken in the regions and locally but the great central institutions, such as the Westminster Courts, also played a vital role. These may be divided into the equity courts of Star Chamber, Chancery and Exchequer[1] and the common law courts of the Queen's Bench (which heard criminal and civil cases) and Common Pleas (which dealt with civil suits). The former could judge cases on the grounds of equity and thus establish precedent, while the latter group could judge only on precedent.[2] As previously noted, Monmouthshire, unlike the twelve Welsh shires, was placed under the jurisdiction of the Westminster common law courts of Queen's Bench through its inclusion in the Oxford circuit. But, as with the Welsh shires, several other London courts, such as Augmentations and Admiralty also exercised jurisdiction in Monmouthshire, but the most important courts were those of equity and common law. The Exchequer heard suits involving debts and revenues to the Crown, Crown lands and defalcations of officers, but, in practice, its authority was wider. Chancery exercised jurisdiction in civil cases. Star Chamber was much in demand and tried cases of riots, assaults, unlawful assembly and misdemeanours of local officials and gentry; it had the virtues of strength, speed and ability to deal with powerful law-breakers. It heard only a minority of the cases brought to it, the remainder being transferred to other Courts including the Council in the Marches.[3]

The Roll contains three cases of the transfer from the Monmouthshire Quarter Sessions to Queen's Bench, by the writ of *Certiorari*.[4] The writ was usually sued out on slender excuses by defendants seeking to avoid conviction. It could guarantee only a temporary postponement of the case.[5]

---

[1] For Wales, see E.A. Lewis (ed.), *An inventory of the early Chancery proceedings concerning Wales* (1938); I. ab O. Edwards (ed.), *Star Chamber proceedings relating to Wales* (1929); E.G. Jones (ed.), *An inventory of Exchequer Proceedings (Equity) concerning Wales. Henry VIII–Elizabeth* (1938).

[2] G.E. Jones, *Modern Wales, 1485–1979* (1984), p. 77.

[3] P. Williams, *The Council in the Marches of Wales under Elizabeth I* (1958), p. 215.

[4] Roll, Caerleon, 31; Newport, 21; Abergavenny, 36 (see Ch. 2, p. xxxiii, n. 5).

[5] J.S. Cockburn, *A history of the English assizes, 1558–1714* (1972), p. 130.

When the common law judges went on circuit they were armed with four commissions: of nisi prius, authorising them to try civil cases; the two major criminal commissions, of oyer et terminer, which gave them power to hear and determine offences committed within the circuit, and the more important gaol delivery directing them to 'deliver the gaols' to try suspects committed to gaols, or bailed, by the local justices; and of the peace, by which they were included in the commission of the peace of the counties of their circuit, so that they could sit with the county bench in their sessions. As will be seen below, the Roll includes proceedings of two general sessions of the peace at which the judges sat and deliberated with the justices, and each one was followed by a gaol delivery, attended by the justices, but at which the judge alone tried the offences.

The assize judges were also empowered with administrative duties, being required to superintend local government officers, especially the JPs. The Privy Council used the circuit as a channel of communication between the centre and the localities, through which its powers could be brought to bear on local administration. The pre-circuit instructions delivered in Star Chamber to the judges suggested to them the main lines of the charge which they would deliver at the assize, where nearly everyone of importance, especially the sheriff and JPs, would be assembled. The judges were also expected to assess the efficiency of JPs and to report back and to suggest names to include on, or to exclude from, the commission of the peace. Elizabeth complained that many magistrates were 'insufficient, unlearned, negligent and indiscreet'; she enjoined judges to 'look narrowly' into the commission and remove unworthy magistrates.[1] Judges, however, sometimes brought back the prejudiced comments of those among the magistracy to whom they happened to speak or who had lobbied them assiduously on behalf of family or friends. Burghley ordered at least seven purges of the country's commissions of the peace, in spite of which, the chief Monmouthshire families (even well known recusants) continued to be represented on the county bench, with occasional omissions in the 1590s and the rare inclusion of new names, such as those of Henry Billingsley of Penhow, William Rawlins of Wonastow and William Baker of Abergavenny.[2]

The judges were rarely able or willing to perform the supervisory role expected of them. In any case, their flying visits, usually of two or three

---

[1] Ibid., pp. 6–8; J. Guy, *Tudor England* (1988), p. 318.
[2] J.R.S. Phillips, *The justices of the peace in Wales and Monmouthshire, 1541–1689* (1975), pp. 344ff.

days, were much too brief.[1] Also changes of circuit personnel were frequent for many reasons, not the least the hazards of the work; Chief Baron Robert Bell, who presided at the two gaol Deliveries held in Monmouth in February and July 1577,[2] died of gaol fever in the infamous 'Black Assizes' held at Oxford, shortly after leaving Monmouth, in which his junior, Serjeant Barham, the clerk of the assizes, the lord lieutenant, sheriff, coroner and almost 400 others also died.[3]

The Council in the Marches of Wales

Between central government and the local authorities was interposed the Council in the Marches of Wales which had general supervision of seventeen shires (Monmouthshire, the twelve Welsh shires and the border counties of Gloucester, Worcester, Hereford and Shropshire) and sat at Ludlow. We have seen that the need for strong government in Wales and its borders had led to the creation of a Council in 1471, but it was not until the reign of Henry VII that it became a permanent institution and not until the presidency of Lee that its authority became reality. This prerogative court was given statutory recognition by the Act of 1543 and it continued to function until 1689 except for a break between 1641 and 1660.

The powers and duties of this Council were never very clearly defined: the Act of 1543 declared that its President and members were to have 'authority to hear and determine by their wisdoms and discretions such causes and matters as to be or heretofore hath been accustomed and used.'[4] In practice its main functions were twofold, judicial and administrative. As a court, it had a civil jurisdiction roughly corresponding to that of Chancery, a jurisdiction over misdemeanours roughly equivalent to Star Chamber and a criminal jurisdiction over felony and murder.[5] It also had military and police duties, tried to prevent disorder and arrested criminals, including,

---

[1] The largest circuit, Oxford, comprising eight counties, took the judges in the 1580s an average of 28 days to ride from the opening assize to the ending of the last. Cockburn, *Assizes*, p. 25.

[2] Roll, Monmouth I, 1; Monmouth II, 1.

[3] Cockburn, *Assizes*, p. 53. For Bell see *Dictionary of National Biography* and E. Foss, *Judges of England, 1066–1870* (1870), p. 82.

[4] I. Bowen, *The statutes of Wales* (1908), p. 102.

[5] P. Williams, 'The political and administrative history of Glamorgan, 1536–1642', *Glam. County History*, IV (1974), p. 148.

perhaps, those referred by it to the Monmouthshire Quarter Sessions on suspicion of felony.[1]

As an administrative body, one of its main duties was to supervise the activities of the officials of the twelve Welsh shires, especially the sheriffs and JPs, who were chosen on the recommendation of the President and Council, together with the justices of assize[2] and they must have had a major share also in nominating and supervising Monmouthshire officials. It also received instructions from the Crown and a stream of directives from the Privy Council and transmitted copies, where appropriate to the shires under its control, on a range of matters. While certain communications were sent to an individual shire, others were sent to the twelve shires only, some to Monmouthshire and the twelve, but the majority were directed to all seventeen shires. The instructions to Monmouthshire and the twelve were few. One in 1570 required the sheriffs and JPs to undertake a muster inquisition and certify their findings to the Council (but no such certificate was forthcoming from Monmouthshire nor from five Welsh shires). In 1574, on information from the Privy Council that 'sundry quantities of grain and victuals chiefly butter have been taken in Wales and namely in the county of Monmouth under pretence of export to the troops in Ireland but sent elsewhere', Commissioners to make enquiry into the circumstances were appointed in each shire; those for Monmouthshire were Sir Charles Somerset, the sheriff and William Morgan of Llantarnam. In 1585 the Council rebuked the thirteen shires that 'outrageous offences' were being committed, 'especially in parts of South Wales and no correction or punishment used', and required the local officials to go into their various divisions and apprehend the wrongdoers; for every default a fine of £100 would be imposed.[3]

Of the orders from the Council despatched to all seventeen shires, one concerning the excessive number of alehouses draws a distinction between the thirteen shires on the one hand and the four border shires on the other; JPs in all the shires were to meet in their allotted divisions to put the instructions concerning alehouses into force, together with the statutes for the relief of the poor and against vagrancy and notify their proceedings to the Council, but the JPs of the thirteen shires were also to make monthly returns of all murders, felonies and misdemeanours. Letters were also sent to the officials of the seventeen shires to execute the laws and directives against

---

[1] Roll, Monmouth I, 33, 37, 38.

[2] Bowen, *Statutes*, 34 and 35 Henry VIII, c. 26, s. 5. 54–61.

[3] R. Flenley (ed.), *Register of the Council in the Marches of Wales, 1569–1591* (1906), pp. 73, 109, 227–8.

retainers, for the observance of Lent and fish days, restraining the illegal export of corn, and supervising tanning houses (the latter was to be enforced by commissioners — those for Monmouthshire were Sir Charles Somerset, Sir Thomas Herbert, Sir William Morgan and William Morgan of Llantarnam). There were also letters concerning soap-making, the mustering and training of troops, the neglect of archery, a certificate of the number of alehouses and various other responsibilities of the sheriff and JPs.[1]

The Council's Register shows its concern with the internal conditions of various counties. The disorderly condition of Monmouthshire in 1573 caused the Council, 'determined to take measures to restore order there', to order the sheriff and JPs to meet and take measures for the due execution of all statutes and orders against vagabonds and keepers of retainers, and to appoint overseers in every parish for the supervision of butchers and alehouse-keepers. The officials were to meet once a month and send frequent certificates of their work.[2] (There is no record that they did either.) These regulations will give some idea of the extent of the jurisdiction of the Privy Council and of the responsibilities, sometimes more honoured in the breach than in the observance, of the Council in the Marches and of the shire officials.

Monmouthshire received meagre representation on the Council at Ludlow. During the period 1560–1603, for instance, while Shropshire had 22 representatives there were only two for Monmouthshire, Dr David Lewis, Abergavenny, JP and MP for the county, Master in Chancery, Admiralty Judge, Master of Requests and Principal of Jesus College, Oxford, and Edward Somerset, third earl of Worcester. When the latter died in 1589, he was succeeded on the Council by his son Edward Somerset, the fourth earl.[3]

At times there was bitter criticism of the Council's deficiencies. Although its president, Sir Henry Sidney, claimed that Wales was a 'happy place of government', David Lewis, in a report to the government in 1575, referred to the great disorders in Wales, especially in South Wales, and was concerned that 'my country is so far out of order at this time as doth require severe remedy'. He denounced the practices of *cymortha* (a forced payment by lords on tenants) and retaining, and asserted that 'men of no substance nor of credit are made Sheriffs and Justices of the Peace'. For Lewis the only remedy was strict and heavy punishment and a regime similar to Lee's.

---

[1] Ibid., pp. 96, 100, 102–3, 123, 148, 160, 170, 171. Flenley notes that the failure of eight counties (one of which was Monmouthshire) to certify the number of alehouses reflected adversely on the efficiency of the Council and its local administration.

[2] Ibid., p. 102.

[3] P. Williams, *Council in the Marches*, p. 144.

It is possible that his criticisms were aimed at Sidney. Certainly his view concerning the Council's inability to deal with cases with 'speed ... and less charge' was disputed by George Owen who claimed that 'it is the best cheap court in England for fees and there is great speed made in trial of all cases'.[1] Sir William Gerard, a justice of assize and former vice-president of the Council, while aware of the need for reform, also differed from Lewis's view that disorder was rife, claiming that 'in Wales universally are as civil people and obedient to law as are in England.'[2]

There is, however, plenty of evidence in Monmouthshire, as in other counties, to support Lewis's charges concerning retaining. Reference has been made to Star Chamber cases involving the county gentry. Feuds, retaining — even liveried — disorders and riots continued into the reign of Elizabeth and beyond. In 1581, following riots in Abergavenny, the county bench was ordered by the Privy Council to take measures for the 'dispersing of such numbers of men as are retained by the Herbertes, and also that no privie coates or unlawful weapons prohibited by her Majesties lawes and Proclamations be used and worn by anie'.[3] A case in Star Chamber in 1607 involved the Monmouthshire JPs Edward Morgan and Sir William Morgan. Sir William, 'being a great man in his county, upon former malice and quarrel with Edward Morgan had caused a challenge to be sent to him and his sons', that he would disgrace his opponent by a show of force at the Usk Quarter Sessions. William came with kinsmen, friends and hangers-on, some with swords, rapiers, daggers and other weapons, 'in so much as the town was full of weapons and there came 140 to assist'. Edward replied in kind, bringing a strong band of his own men, similarly armed. The balance of terror was effective, and there was only a single minor injury. Three of the judges declared that 'this seeking to be great and bear a side in these countries (i.e counties) especially, is very dangerous'.[4]

As noted above, there was a conflict of views among contemporaries concerning the efficacy of Tudor rule in Wales, but two commentators, Rice

---

[1] G. Owen, *Description of Penbrokshire* (ed. H. Owen, 1906), III, p. 23.

[2] Williams, *Council in the Marches*, p. 259. Williams also cites the opinion of another former vice-president, Paulet, that the trial of murders and felonies committed in Monmouthshire should be held before the Council in Herefordshire. Apparently, Monmouthshire juries could not be trusted to give impartial verdicts.

[3] P. Williams, 'The Welsh borderland under Elizabeth', *Welsh History Review*, 1 (1960–3), 19–36, citing *Acts of the Privy Council 1581–2*, p. 115. The author also gives details of the feuds of the county elite in Herefordshire at this time. Life was no more peaceful on the other side of Monmouthshire, where the gentry of Glamorgan were also engaged in affrays.

[4] A. Fletcher and J. Stevenson (ed.), *Order and disorder in early modern England*, p. 102, citing J. Howarde (ed.), *Les reportes del cases in Camera Stellata*, pp. 312–15.

Merrick of Cottrell, in the Vale of Glamorgan, writing in 1578, and George Owen of Henllys in Pembrokeshire, writing in 1594, both beneficiaries of the new regime, claimed that law and order in the country had been transformed since the Union. Merrick contrasts the 'unorderly' state of Wales before the Tudors with what followed from the 'alteration of government'. Now, he writes, 'life and death, lands and goods rest in the monarchy, and not in the pleasure of the subject. Laws ... are written, and therefore certain to be truly and indifferently ministered. What was justifiable by might ... is now to receive condign punishment by law'. Owen was even more effusive. To him 'the miserable and lamentable' state of Wales 'in former times' was so changed by the 'happy reforming of the ... government in the time of Henry the Eighth by reducing the same into shires and in providing sweet and wholesome laws for the government thereof' that Wales was 'now in far better estate than any other part' of the realm.[1]

The transformation which both so warmly praised had not yet, however, been achieved, not even in their respective counties. In Glamorgan, where Merrick was clerk of the peace, feuding among the leading county families which had been taking place for many years, persisted into the 1570s and beyond. In the 1590s Pembrokeshire, where Owen was a member of the commission of the peace and a deputy lieutenant, was under the control of the Essex faction, whose leading members (the earl, and in his long absences, his uncle, George Devereux, his steward Gelly Meyrick and the latter's brothers) gained so much dominance in county affairs that they were accused of oppression, of influencing appointments to public office in favour of their many followers, and of acquiescing in murder and shielding wrong-doers. Nevertheless, there were now signs of increasingly effective good government in the Welsh counties, including Monmouthshire, and the administrative and judicial changes inaugurated by the Tudors, together with the vigilance of the supervising bodies from the Privy Council down, were bringing real benefits.

One of these bodies, however, the Council in the Marches, was beginning to lose some ground at the end of the Tudor period, possibly because of the long drawn out dispute over the claims to exemption by the four border shires from its jurisdiction. The controversy, begun in Elizabeth's reign, continued until 1624, when they gained exemption, on the ground that they

---

[1] Rice Merrick, *Morganiae Archaiographia. A book of the antiquities of Glamorganshire*, ed. B. Ll. James (S. Wales Record Society, 1, 1983), pp. 67–8; Owen, *Penbrokshire*, III, p. 3.

were 'allwaies meere English Counties, and not part of the Marches'.[1] There
is no suggestion that Monmouthshire was involved in the agitation; its name
is not linked with the four shires seeking to break from the Council's
control. But the claims of the county to exemption were considered;[2] if they
were ever brought to the notice of those in authority they were undoubtedly
rejected on the ground that, whatever might be the position of the four English shires, Monmouthshire was quite clearly part of 'the Marches'.

Local Government: the Shire

Lord and Deputy Lieutenant

Links between central and local government were greatly strengthened in the
later Tudor period with the creation of the office of lord lieutenant. This post
originated to supervise the military organisation in the various shires, at first
on a temporary basis, but it became permanent in 1585, under the threat of
war with Spain and the danger of possible invasion from Ireland. In later
centuries the lord lieutenant advised on the appointment of JPs and other
officials, reported on their activities and was honorary head of the county
bench and custos rotulorum. It is mainly as a military officer, however, that
he emerges in the late sixteenth century, at first helped by commissioners of
musters,[3] but, when the lieutenancy system was made permanent, deputy
lieutenants were also appointed. All local officials — sheriffs and JPs
especially — were to obey and assist the lieutenants, invariably drawn from
the ranks of the aristocracy, and their deputies, chosen from the elite of the
county and most of them already JPs; the deputy lieutenancy was regarded
as superior to the other shire offices.

The first lord lieutenant of Monmouthshire after 1585 was the earl of
Pembroke, who also, by virtue of his office of president of the Council in the
Marches, included all the shires under his presidency (except Gloucester-
shire) in his lieutenancy. His prime responsibility was the shire militia, which

---

[1] The dispute has been traced by P.R. Roberts, 'Wales and England after the Tudor
"Union": crown, principality and parliament, 1543–1624', in C. Cross *et al.* (ed.), *Law and
government under the Tudors* (1988), 111–38.

[2] E. Owen (ed.), *A catalogue of the manuscripts relating to Wales in the British Museum*,
I (1900), pp. 16, 130.

[3] For esample, the 1570 commissioners for Monmouthshire were Charles Somerset,
William Morgan of Pencoed, William Herbert of Coldbrook and William Morgan of Llanthony,
esquires: Flenley, *Register*, p. 69. Commissioners for other purposes were also established from
time to time.

was the only source of men (aged 16–60) for home defence and for wars in
Europe and Ireland; he was to conduct the summer muster at which the
militia assembled and was armed, drilled and equipped and he was also to
choose men for war service. The lieutenant had some hand in the appointment of his deputies. In 1593, when Sir William Herbert of St Julians,
deputy lieutenant of Monmouthshire, and Kennard Herbert, deputy lieutenant
of Montgomery, both died, Pembroke's recommendation of Nicholas Herbert
for Monmouthshire and Richard Herbert for Montgomery was accepted.[1] In
1595, Monmouthshire's sole deputy lieutenant, Thomas Morgan, was joined
by two others, Rowland Morgan and Matthew Herbert.[2] Although the work
carried heavy responsibilities and could be unpopular, there was no shortage
of aspirants for the post because of the prestige and power which went with
it.[3] Both Pembroke and his deputies, in Monmouthshire and the other shires,
were sometimes reprimanded by the Privy Council for malversation and
neglect of duty,[4] with the result that 'unapt and loose persons' were chosen
for service in Ireland, although the Council was prepared to concede to
Pembroke that he could not be 'present in person in all places'.

Through the lieutenancy the Privy Council came to enjoy direct communication with the shires. The majority of its members, like Pembroke, also
served as local lord lieutenants; thus in some cases the top officials of central
and local government were the same people.

One historian has argued that war and the danger of war was a 'significant factor making for the diminution of the effective power of the local
magistracy. Many JPs, no doubt, felt that they were being reduced to the
status of mere administrative assistants to the lieutenancy.'[5]

Sheriff

The shrievalty was an office of great antiquity, its origins as 'shire-reeve'
shrouded in the mists of the pre-Norman era. In the Middle Ages the sheriff
had achieved almost viceregal status as a vital link between central and local
government. Gradually, however, he lost power, as new officials such as JPs
came to encroach on his traditional duties. Despite this decline, he still, in

---

[1] *Acts of the Privy Council, 1592–3*, pp. 277–8. By 1600 there was a formidable list of
Herberts as DLs in various shires, most of them Pembroke's relatives.

[2] *Acts of the Privy Council, 1595–6*, pp. 17–18.

[3] G.E. Jones, *The gentry and the Elizabethan state* (1977), pp. 61–3.

[4] *Acts of the Privy Council, 1588–9*, pp. 328–9; *1599–1600*, pp. 219–21.

[5] R. Ashton, *Reformation and revolution, 1558–1660* (1984), p. 133.

the Tudor period, enjoyed considerable prestige, George Owen saying of him that he was the 'chief officer of trust and credit in the shire and the Prince's lieutenant'.[1]

The office had usually been held for a period of years, but it was open to so much abuse that by the Tudor period the custom had arisen of making annual appointments. The sheriff of Monmouthshire was 'pricked' by the sovereign from a list of three names prepared by the justices of assize, in conjunction with the President of the Council in the Marches, and submitted to the Lord Chancellor or the Lord Keeper, who might alter or add to it. Those nominated were invariably gentry of substance, knights or esquires, and already members of the commissions of the peace (although the sheriff relinquished his membership of that body during his term of office). The newly appointed sheriff had to give bonds to answer his financial obligations to the Crown, obtain his patents of office and take his oaths of office before the President of the Council in the Marches,[2] before a judge of assize, or — and this was the usual procedure — before two or more JPs.[3] He chose a deputy sheriff and a number of bailiffs, normally one for every hundred: a Star Chamber case also refers to the Monmouthshire sheriff's 'especial' bailiff.[4] Like the sheriff, these officers were appointed for one year only and could not be reappointed until two,later three, years had passed (nevertheless there were infringements of the law in the case of bailiffs). The sheriff had to reside in his 'bailiwick' unless he was on official business. The special choice of a gentleman for the office depended less on his ability to carry out his duties — many of which were performed by his deputy — than his capacity to meet the expenses of the office. It is true that the office brought in many exactions and fees for the service of writs and the appointment of subordinates, as well as an annual fee of £5. On the other hand, the sheriff had to spend money on taking up office and in auditing his accounts; he had also to make payments to his subordinates and provide hospitality, especially to the judges of assize and their entourage.

The sheriff's duties, which were wide-ranging, can be grouped under four heads, financial, military, judicial and administrative. His financial duties included the collection of payments due to the Crown, especially the fines

---

[1] J.G. Jones, *Concepts of order and gentility in Wales, 1540–1640* (1992), citing Owen, *Penbrokshire*, III, p. 67.

[2] This could be a long and troublesome journey, 'when the days are most deep, the weather most foul'; B. Howells, 'Government and politics, 1536–1642', *Pembrokeshire County History*, III (1987), pp. 126–58, citing Owen, *Penbrokshire*, III, p. 65.

[3] *Calendar of State Papers, Domestic, 1591*, p. 69.

[4] Edwards, *Star Chamber Proceedings*, p. 97.

imposed by all law courts in his bailiwick. Non-payment of fines and recognisances resulted in distraint of goods by the sheriff, who also imprisoned any unfortunates having neither goods nor chattels. In addition, he was responsible for all felons' goods[1] and distraining the goods of defaulting recusants. He had to render an account of all sums to the Exchequer.

What military duties the sheriff continued to perform, after he had been supplanted in this sphere by the lord lieutenant, were normally done in co-operation with the JPs, deputy lieutenants, vice-admirals and special commissioners. He was also directed to help to levy soldiers for service in Ireland and elsewhere, and to see that the mariners who had 'withdrawn themselves into ... remote places to avoid the prest' were hunted down.[2] By the eighteenth century he had ceased to be a military officer.

His legal work was more extensive. His most ancient judicial duty was to preside over the county and hundred courts and the tourn. The Act of 1543 commanded him to keep the tourn twice a year but there is no evidence to show that the Monmouthshire sheriffs held such a court. Nor is information available on the holding of hundred courts, except that the sheriffs did attempt to hold them for a brief period.[3] Concerning the monthly county court, where, by the Act of 1543, the sheriff was to hold pleas of *Replegiare*[4] and to hear civil suits of less than 40*s*., entries on the Roll show that it sat regularly and that it was also used for the purpose of outlawry. Offenders who had not appeared before the JPs and against whom writs had been issued ordering the sheriff to compel them to appear, were 'exacted' or called upon to appear in the county court. If they failed to appear after being exacted at five successive courts sentence of outlawry was passed upon them by coroners who sat with the sheriff in the county court.[5] Outlawry in the sixteenth century was not as severe in its consequences as it had been in the Middle Ages, when any man could put an outlaw to death. An outlaw in the case of trespass or misdemeanour could be imprisoned if found and forfeit his personal goods. In a felony case the outlaw forfeited his lands and chattels and his outlawry amounted to a conviction for the offence with

---

[1] The Roll shows that in most cases the felons had no chattels, e.g. Newport, 18, 20; Monmouth I, 19, 20, 21, 23.

[2] *Acts of the Privy Council, 1595–6*, pp. 274–5.

[3] W. Rees, 'The union of England and Wales', *Trans. Hon. Soc. Cymmrodorion* (1937), pp. 59–60, citing Owen, *Penbrokshire*, III, p. 64.

[4] A writ empowering a person to recover his goods; Roll, Usk I, 9.

[5] Roll, Caerleon, 3; Abergavenny, 3; Usk II, 3.

which he was charged.[1] Glanmor Williams holds that the outlawry procedure was 'toothless' in Wales and the Marches, where there was little inclination to flee to the woods; instead, men took refuge with their friends at some distance from their homes, lay low during the day and at night ventured to the nearest ale house to 'make merry and wench'.[2]

It was also at the county court that statutes and ordinances were proclaimed. One proclamation which brought it into prominence and gave the sheriff great influence, was the announcement of the elections for Parliament. The writ for the election of members was addressed to the sheriff and was read at the county court and elsewhere in the county; it was there that the election of knights of the shire took place and it was from there that the sheriff also issued instructions to the borough officers to hold their elections, a return of which was to be sent to him.

Although a number of statutes had checked abuses connected with the offiice, Monmouthshire sheriffs, like all others, sometimes continued to interfere with elections, as in 1558, 1559 and 1572. In 1558 Sir William Herbert of St Julians alleged that at the Monmouth county court he and William Morgan, Llantarnam, had been re-elected county MPs but that the sheriff had returned Morgan and Francis Somerset, third son of the earl of Worcester; the dispute was referred to the assizes, where a jury upheld the election of Somerset.[3] In the 1559 election, the candidates were George Kemeys of Troy, William Morgan of Tredegar and Thomas Herbert of Wonastow. The sheriff was Sir Thomas Morgan of Pencoed, whose support was pledged to his relative William Morgan and to Herbert. Kemeys and Morgan were elected but the sheriff substituted Herbert's name for Kemeys. Proceedings were started in the Exchequer court against the sheriff for making false returns, but the result is not known.[4] Perhaps Thomas Herbert remembered the occasion when he was sheriff in 1572 and acted according-ly. The candidates at this election were Charles Somerset (MP in 1571), fourth son of the earl of Worcester, William Morgan of Llantarnam (MP in 1555, 1558 and 1571) and Henry Herbert, son and heir of the sheriff for 1572. As sheriff, Thomas Herbert was prevented from standing but he used his official position to get his son elected 'by a method simple in its

---

[1] W.O. Williams (ed.), *A calendar of the Caernarvonshire quarter sessions records*, I (1956), p. xcviii, citing Halsbury's *Laws of England*. A case in Edwards, *Star Chamber Proceedings*, p. 104, concerned the forcible rescue of the goods of Thomas David Williams, an outlaw of Llanelli, from the 'distraint of the sheriff and his deputy'.

[2] G. Williams, *Recovery, reorientation and Reformation. Wales, c. 1415–1642* (1987), p. 48.

[3] *The House of Commons, 1509–1558*, (ed. S.T. Bindoff), I, 147.

[4] *The House of Commons, 1558–1603* (ed. Hasler), I, 203.

impudence'. Instead of holding the election in the common hall of Monmouth castle, as was customary, and where the Morgan supporters, 900 of them, were congregated, the sheriff held it in an alehouse, where Charles Somerset and Henry Herbert were declared elected by him. In the Star Chamber case brought against him by William Morgan, the sheriff found no excuse for his behaviour.[1]

The sheriff had duties connected with other courts also whether held outside the shire, such as the court of the Council of the Marches and the Westminster courts, or within the shire, that is to say, the assizes and quarter sessions. He had to make arrangements for proclaiming and holding two assizes during his year of office, which meant providing lodgings and entertainment for the two judges and their clerks and 'office staff', producing prisoners, empanelling grand and petty juries, summoning all others required to attend,[2] executing writs and processes, arranging for the collection of fines, and hanging, whipping or otherwise punishing the guilty. He had similar duties for four general sessions of the peace and for any special sessions which might be held. Providing and summoning panels of jurymen was not always satisfactorily performed; the list of those qualified to act was not kept up-to-date, friends were excused from serving, and partial juries were returned. There are numerous instances of the latter abuse[3] and the authorities were constantly concerned to restrain it. Reference has also been made previously to allegedly partial Monmouthshire juries.

The sheriff was a servant of the county magistrates but there were brief occasions when he was raised in power over them, as when the Council in the Marches in 1577, out of patience with the justices for their neglect in certifying to it all offences within twenty days of their being committed, instructed the sheriff to assemble them and bind them by obligation of £100 to certify each offence.[4]

The responsibility for keeping the county and other gaols also fell to the sheriff, who deputed the oversight of the prisoners to a keeper. Gaol was mainly a place where suspects were held before trial rather than a form of punishment in itself. John Hughes, the keeper of the 'common gaol' at Caerleon, was indicted at the gaol delivery for allowing a prisoner to escape,

---

[1] Ibid., p. 204; Edwards, *Star Chamber Proceedings*, p. 205.

[2] The full details of the sheriff's writ of *venire facias* for quarter sessions are to be found in the Roll, Caerleon, 2; similar orders were directed to him at every sessions.

[3] E.g. Flenley, *Register*, p. 209 (partial dealing towards Thomas Powell of Llantillio in a trial for murder); *Acts of the Privy Council, 1592–3*, p. 166; the fear that such a jury would be chosen, or would use more 'partialitie than equitie' in a trial of a certain Romsey, 'allyed to Rowland Morgan, now High Sheriff'. See also Chapter 5, n. 1.

[4] Flenley, *Register*, pp. 177–9.

this prisoner having been accused of stealing a 'brown bay gelding of the value of three pounds', the property of Watkin Williams, *alias* Howells. At the next gaol delivery, 'John Hughes, formerly gaoler of the common gaol at Caerleon' was remanded to prison on a charge of having stolen a bay gelding valued at three pounds, property of Watkin Williams, *alias* Howells.[1] Was the escapee's offence now transferred to the disgraced gaoler?

An important function of the sheriff, and more especially of his subordinates, was the service and execution of writs issued out of the local and central courts; the records show them engaged in this aspect of their work.[2] We are reminded of the dangers involved in this and other unpopular duties of these officers; we learn, for example, of an assault on them while executing a writ at Skenfrith, while attempting to keep the peace, and the forcible rescue of the goods of an outlaw from the distraint of the sheriff and his deputy.[3] Their misdeeds are also recorded. William Morgan and his bailiff refused to arrest a man upon a writ from Chancery.[4] A succession of Elizabethan sheriffs — Rees Morgan, Nicholas Herbert, William Jones and Andrew Morgan — made wrongful use of processes and commissions issued to them out of the Exchequer Court.[5] The sheriff was usually placed at the head of commissions to enquire into recusancy in the county; this was an admirable opportunity for the unscrupulous sheriff, of whom Andrew Morgan was one, for he, out of malice towards Thomas (aged 98) and Herbert Harry of Dingestow, wrongfully inserted their names in the list of recusants, 'lugged and hayled' them to Monmouth goal, seizing their goods and converting them to his own use. Sir William Herbert, his deputy, and the gaoler were accused of various misdemeanours, including an assault on Walter Morgan Wolfe Esq., and imprisoning Wolfe's wife and servant for 70 days, putting them in irons, refusing them bail, beating the servant and putting him in the stocks.[6] In these and other matters the Monmouthshire sheriffs were no worse than their counterparts elsewhere.

It is unlikely that the sheriff's involvement in the affairs of the shrievalty was very great.[7] A county election, the visits of the judges of assize, attend-

---

[1] Roll, Monmouth I, 12; Monmouth II, 62.

[2] Roll, Usk I, 9; Edwards, *Star Chamber Proceedings*, pp. 97, 105.

[3] Roll, Usk I, 9; Edwards, *Star Chamber Proceedings*, pp. 100, 104.

[4] Edwards, *Star Chamber Proceedings*, p. 98.

[5] Jones, *Exchequer Proceedings*, pp. 260–1.

[6] Jones, *Exchequer Proceedings*, pp. 265–6; Edwards, *Star Chamber Proceedings*, p. 115.

[7] T. E. Hartley, 'Under-sheriffs and bailiffs in some English shrievalties, *c.* 1580–*c.* 1625,' *Bull. Inst. Historical Research*, 47 (1974), 164–85.

ance at the assizes and perhaps at quarter sessions would engage his attention, but much of his other work, and especially the details, he would leave to his deputy and bailiffs, whom he appointed, for a fee, from the many supplicants for these offices. If the shrievalty was a burdensome, expensive and unpopular office, this did not deter a number of them from accepting it for a second time.[1] Much depended on their choice of subordinates, with each one of whom they entered a bond to protect them from the consequences of any negligence or illegal act on their part. The deputy sheriff was drawn from lower down the gentry scale[2] than his master (sheriffs and JPs, unless already 'esquires', assumed that style while in office) and perhaps had some legal training. He encountered a number of difficulties, especially of clearing the sheriff's account at the Exchequer, always a problem without the added grievance of having to pay fees to a number of officials there at every turn. There was a strong temptation for him to resort to corrupt practices in order to cover expenses. The responsibility for executing writs and empanelling juries for cases concerning their own hundred was generally passed on to the bailiffs. In spite of the odium and dangers attached to these offices and that of the sheriff, they were sought for financial gain; in the execution of all writs between party and party the officers responsible were entitled to a fee. In short, these officers held 'offices of profit', which they exploited to the full. The nature of their duties was hardly likely to attract the gentlest and most scrupulous spirits. They were frequently regarded by the general public as 'social predators intent on extortion and intimidation'; in the words of Vicar Prichard (in *Canwyll y Cymry*)

> Mae'r shirafiaid a'u depidion
> Yn anrheithio bobl wirion
> Ac wrth rym eu braint a'u swyddau
> Yn eu 'speilio liw dydd goleu.[3]

[1] E.g., Sir Thomas Morgan, Pencoed, 1547–8, 1558–9; William Morgan, Llantarnam, 1567–8, 1572–3; Sir William Herbert, St Julians, 1577–8 (Glam.), 1579–80 (Mon.).

[2] Roll, Newport, 31: Thomas Powell, under-sheriff, styled 'gentleman'.

[3] 'The sheriffs and their cormorant train / On the fleeced populace distrain / And under veil of justice prey / Upon their wealth in open day'. B. Howells, 'Government and politics, 1536–1642', *Pembrokeshire County History*, III (1987), 132. The translation will be found on p. 415, n. 9.

Justices of the peace

Local government and the preservation of law and order in the sixteenth century and later were dominated not by the lieutenant nor the sheriff, however, but by the justices of the peace. In the office of JP, instituted in England in medieval times, and introduced into Wales from 1536, the Tudors found a flexible instrument for carrying on the judicial and administrative work necessitated by its self-government.[1] It was under this dynasty that the office attained the prime position in local affairs that it retained until the late nineteenth century.

To the JPs' primary task of preserving law and order, the Tudors added so many administrative duties that William Lambarde, the Kent JP, in his justices' manual, *Eirenarcha*, depicted them as overburdened with 'not loads but stacks of statutes'. It is claimed, however, that many of the statutes enumerated by him were rarely enforced, and that their 'main task at their quarter sessions was to have cases brought before them by constables and grand juries and not to initiate action themselves, and they did not go out of their way to look for extra work'.[2] The contents of the Roll, together with the often less than zealous response to directives from the Privy Council and the Council in the Marches, reinforce the impression that the justices were not overstretched. Nevertheless, this was an office of authority, which gave the Crown a body of part-time, amateur (some had legal qualifications) and virtually unpaid magistrates-cum-administrators, and it was also one of prestige and much sought after by the gentry. To help amateurs to administer the law, the Tudors, by the quorum clause in the commission, ensured the presence at the sessions and out of sessions meetings of at least one of a small group of experienced or legally qualified justices; by appointing the leading justice as custos rotulorum they aimed to ensure the creation of organisation, the supervision of other justices, and the preservation of court records, and thus help to safeguard legal precedent; and by appointing a qualified clerk of the peace to guide the justices, they provided a professional element.[3]

Rowland Lee had strongly opposed the introduction of the office of JP into Wales and Monmouthshire, reporting to Cromwell that there were few Welsh gentry 'above Brecknock' who had the necessary £20 p.a. property

---

[1] Compare with the writer who saw the wisdom of the action of the Tudors in introducing JPs into Wales: 'Wales is true to the Crown', he wrote in 1542, 'because it is not under one ruler but several in each shire', (*Letters & Papers*, XVII, 68.)

[2] Williams, *Tudor regime*, p. 152; Palliser, *Age of Elizabeth*, p. 356.

[3] G.R. Elton, *The Tudor Constitution* (1982), p. 465.

qualification (which for Wales was waived, in any case); nor did he have much faith in the integrity of the Welsh gentry, dwelling 'nigh the Welshry' as they did, and 'kynned and alyed' in the same.[1] As we have seen, George Owen and David Lewis also expressed concern that some unworthy magistrates were chosen, and to their criticism must be added that of Richard Davies, bishop of St Davids, himself a member of the Carmarthenshire bench, who claimed that JPs 'have not judged rightly, meaning between party and party, but dealt partially and corruptly against the law and conscience ... How think you what it is to commit authority to such men?'[2] Whatever their shortcomings, it was to them that the all-important duties of JPs were entrusted, in the belief that the men who enjoyed the influence and prestige which brought deference and obedience should be given the authority to govern in the localities. The JPs played a prominent role in both law enforcement and county administration.

The Tudors issued *ad hoc* commissions to the gentry on a variety of matters, as we have seen, but the commission of the peace was the most regular and most important. JPs were appointed by the Lord Keeper of the Great Seal or the Lord Chancellor, who relied for their choice on the recommendations of the assize judges, lord lieutenant (from the end of the sixteenth century), territorial magnates and the President of the Council in the Marches. The names and duties of those chosen to be justices of the peace, and those of the quorum, as well as the custos, appeared on the commission of the peace, issued out of Chancery. The term can be used in two senses; it refers both to the royal commission which granted powers to those named to act as JPs within a defined territorial unit, usually a shire or borough, and to the body of justices named in the commission.

The justices' duties came from two sources, statutes and the commission of the peace. By 1603 no fewer than 309 statutes imposed responsibilities on JPs, 176 of these having been passed since 1485. As shown above some statutes were not often activated, but a number of them engaged the increasing attention of the justices as the century progressed, especially those relating to economic regulations, the upkeep of roads and bridges, the relief of poverty, vagrancy, apprenticeships, alehouses and wages and prices, to list only the main items in their local government activities. The commission of the peace authorised them to hold regular sessions, to enquire by jury into a variety of offences and try cases upon indictment. They were to enforce the laws concerning the peace and take sureties for good behaviour. They

---

[1] *Letters & Papers*, XI (2), 453; XI, 1255.

[2] H.A. Lloyd, *The gentry of south-west Wales, 1540–1640* (1968), p. 178

were encouraged to seek the advice of assize judges in difficult cases and, after 1590, were required to transfer to them all felonies.

Whenever a JP was appointed, dismissed (an unusual occurrence) or repositioned on the commission (there was much jostling to move above rival JPs as order of precedence was vital and determined seating at sessions and assizes), a complete new commission had to be issued. The commission was the only formal notification a gentleman had of his appointment or dismissal and doubtless the clerk of the peace bore the main responsibility for notifying the person concerned. No magistrate could take up his duties until he had been sworn in at the assizes, where he had to take the prescribed oaths, of allegiance and impartiality, and subscribe to the Elizabethan Acts of Supremacy and Uniformity; the government generally forbore to scrutinise too closely the observance of the latter acts, and a number of well known Monmouthshire Roman Catholic families continued to be included in the commission throughout the reign, such as the Somersets and the Morgans of Llantarnam. A justice might also be sworn in by other justices or by the clerk, acting in virtue of a writ of *dedimus potestatem*, but this procedure was reserved for justices unable to attend the assizes for whatever reason.[1]

The number of justices, always exceeding the maximum of eight laid down by the Act of 1543, continued to grow throughout the sixteenth century, as also did the number of those of the quorum.[2] This expansion of the quorum did not necessarily signify any marked growth in the number of justices learned in the law.[3] In fact it was probably due to pressure from the justices to obtain the prestige connected with the quorum and perhaps made necessary by the increasing activity of justices out of sessions, which, in most cases, required the presence of two or more justices, one of them to be of the quorum. Those named in the commission fell into two categories. The first consisted of ex-officio justices, such as the principal officers of state, assize judges, the President and members of the Council in the Marches, the bishops and the earls of Worcester and Pembroke; the second section comprised the working commission of resident, or at least partly resident, county gentry.

---

[1] T.G. Barnes and A.H. Smith, 'Justices of the peace, 1558–1688' *Bull. Inst. Historical Research*, 33 (1959), p. 226.

[2] See Monmouthshire Commissions of the peace in Phillips, *JPs in Wales*, pp. 344ff.

[3] Barnes and Smith, 'Justices of the Peace', p. 222, are of the opinion that the quorum in Welsh (including Mon.) counties was rather high, 'perhaps because of a higher proportion of legally qualified gentry in Welsh commissions'.

The justices met in their general sessions of the peace. The meetings were also called 'quarter sessions' because they were held four times a year, in the weeks after Michaelmas (29 September), Epiphany (6 January), Easter and the translation of St Thomas (7 July), but since the latter coincided with the summer assize, the summer quarter sessions was held after the feast of Corpus Christi (60 days after Easter). The Monmouthshire Roll of 18–19 Elizabeth[1] shows that general sessions were held at Caerleon (Tuesday after Michaelmas, 2–3 October 1576, in modern dating), Newport (Tuesday after Epiphany, 8 January 1577), Abergavenny, (Tuesday after Easter, 9 April 1577), and at Usk (Tuesday after Corpus Christi, 11 June 1577). We are left to guess how long each sessions lasted, except in the case of Caerleon, which was of two days' duration,[2] and what accommodation these small market towns could offer to house the court — at an inn, probably — and supply food and lodgings for the concourse of justices, officials, jurors, constables, witnesses, the gaoler and his prisoners, and others called upon to attend.[3] Two gaol deliveries, each preceded by a general sessions of the peace, were held at Monmouth, one beginning on Monday 25 February, 19 Elizabeth, (1577) the other beginning on Thursday 11 July, 19 Elizabeth (1577). The Roll also makes reference to previous sessions and gaol deliveries.

By the 1570s, the volume of business being dealt with by the JPs demanded that their meetings should occur more frequently than once every three months and special sessions came to be arranged between quarter sessions. The Roll shows that special sessions were held at Usk (at which two separate benches sat) on 27 October 1576, at Crick on 13 February 1577, and at Raglan, on 14 March 1577. The Roll also indicates that justices were active out-of-sessions (perhaps in the parlour of one of the justices) in such matters as binding over to keep the peace, committing to gaol on suspicion of felony (there is one instance of the bailiffs of Monmouth having the power) and in enroling indentures.[4] The solitary justice was empowered to conduct the preliminary examination of suspects and witnesses in cases

---

[1] The Roll covers the period 2 Oct. 1576 – 12 July 1577 (the latter date assumes that the assizes lasted two days), i.e. a little over nine months; Elizabeth's regnal year began on 17 November.

[2] Roll, Caerleon, 1. The calling of two grand juries at the quarter sessions held at Usk II, Newport and Abergavenny suggests that these sessions also lasted two (or more) days.

[3] In the 18th century, until a Sessions House was built at Usk in the 1770s, quarter sessions were held at inns: the Three Salmons (Usk), Hanbury Arms (Caerleon), Beaufort Arms (Chepstow), and King's Head (Newport). Sessions and assizes at Monmouth were held in the Grand Jury Room. Gwent Record Office, Quarter Sessions Records.

[4] See Roll, Newport, 13; Monmouth I, 12, 21, 32; Raglan, 5, 6, 7.

of felony, take recognizances, commit felons to prison and bind over the unruly to be of good behaviour. Two or more justices acting together, one of whom was to be of the quorum, had yet wider powers. For instance, they could look into cases of maintenance and riots, fix the poor rates, supervise the repair of highways, take bail, grant alehouse licences and regulate the weights and measures. Not unexpectedly, there are examples of the abuse of their wide powers by some justices, and David Price of Michaelchurch cannot have been the only one to have become a JP for 'greatness sake'. The most blatant abuse concerns the case of Sir William Herbert, as custos, who, when a kinsman accused of murder was indicted at a gaol delivery, prevailed upon the justice of assize to make the indictment null and void.[1]

The Monmouthshire gentry who were included on the commission were drawn from the ranks of the esquires[2] (or they assumed that status on appointment) and above, and the same names recur on successive commissions, such as the Morgans of Tredegar, Machen, Pencoed, Llantarnam and elsewhere; the Somersets of Raglan; the ap Rogers (subsequently known as Progers) of Wernddu; the Watkinses of Caerwent; the Lewises of St Pierre and elsewhere; the Joneses of Treowen and Dingestow; the Powells of Perth-hir and Lanpill (Trellech); the Joneses of Troy; the ap Roberts (Proberts) of Pant-glas; the Kemeyses of Kemeys and Cefn Mably; the Cecils of Allt yr Ynys and Llanthony; the Welshes of Llanwern; and the various branches of the Herberts at Coldbrook, St Julians and elsewhere.

The development of the system of divisions, by which justices took a particular responsibility for a district, usually a hundred, of the shire had some influence on nominations, but in the end an entirely even spread of magisterial oversight was difficult to achieve, since there were forests and uplands where the gentry were thin on the ground. The list of resident justices together with their divisions which the custos, Rowland Morgan, supplied to the Council in the Marches in 1573 was as follows:

Caldicot	William Morgan Kt, William Lewis, Christopher Welshe, Thomas Watkins
Newport	Rowland Morgan, Thomas Morgan, Edward Morgan
Usk	William Morgan of Llantarnam

---

[1] Edwards, *Star Chamber Proceedings*, p. 95 (Price), p. 104 (Herbert).

[2] A list of 1630 gives the number of esquires in the county as 34: Owen (ed.) *MSS in the British Museum*, II, 473.

Abergavenny   William Herbert of Coldbrook

Skenfrith   Thomas Herbert Kt, Harry Herbert

Raglan   Walter Jones

Trellech   George ap Robert

To these three hundreds (Skenfrith, Raglan, Trellech) also are limited Rees Morgan, Matthew Herbert and William John ap Robert in the hundred of Abergavenny. Also the Rt. Hon. William, the Earl of Worcester, Edward, Lord Herbert, Charles Somerset Kt, resident in the shire, do commonly be at the castle in Raglan, William (Blethin) Bishop of Llandaff, lies at his lordship at Malhern (Mathern) in the Hundred of Caldicott, David Lewes, Doctor of Laws, doth lie at his abode in Abergavenny in the Hundred of Abergavenny.

Coroners: William David ap John, William Cockes gent., no deputies.

Clerk of the Peace: John Waters; no deputy.[1]

Thus, with the custos, there were 22 resident justices, but the bishop and David Lewis had duties which took them away from the county.
   More important than the composition and the size of the commission was the number of members who attended to their duties, for it was by these that the county's affairs were controlled. Table I lists attendances by justices at four quarter sessions, three special sessions, and two sessions of the peace and gaol deliveries during the period covered by the Roll.
   The table shows a satisfactory attendance at sessions and assizes, and the justices who attended four or more sessions can be considered active in the execution of their duties. Family and estate ties, absence from home comforts, difficulties of travel, inaccessibility of the place of meetings and the expense involved in entertainment at these meetings could have been some of the reasons for absence. For a few justices, perhaps, county government involved 'policing the parishes nearest one's seat, rather than assiduous attendance at sessions'. Yet every JP must have had a sense of the court's significance. The proceedings of sessions, however humdrum, embodied and gave expression to the rule of law that made possible the

---

[1] Flenley, *Register*, p. 137.

Table 1: Justices sitting in Monmouthshire, 1576–77

Justice	QS Caerleon	QS Newport	QS Aberg.	QS Usk I	Sp.S. Usk II	Sp.S. Crick	Sp.S. Raglan	QS & GD Monm.	QS & GD Monm.	Total
Charles Somerset kt		*						*		2
Rowland Morgan	*	*								2
Wm Morgan, Llantarnam	*	*	*	*	*				*	6
Thomas Morgan		*	*	*				*	*	5
William Lewis	*	*	*	*	*	*				6
William Evans Ll.B.		*								1
Matthew Herbert	*	*	*	*	*					5
William John ap Roger		*		*	*		*	*	*	6
Thomas Herbert kt							*	*	*	3
Wm Herbert, Coldbrook	*			*	*		*	*	*	6
Henry Herbert					*			*	*	3
Thomas Watkins						*				1
Edward, Lord Herbert				*			*			2
William Cecil					*		*		*	3
Walter Jones	*		*	*					*	4
William Powell			*							1
Edmund Morgan	*			*	*				*	4
Christopher Welshe									*	1
Rees (Rice) Morgan					*					1
Total	7	8	6+	9	9	2	5	6+	10+	

Notes: QS = Quarter Sessions; Sp.S. = Special Sessions; GD = Gaol Delivery. (1) This is not a complete list of attendances since the names of some justices who attended at Abergavenny and the two Assizes were not named, but referred to as 'and other their colleagues'. (2) The Roll also shows that most justices attended to their out-of-court duties and were quite active. (3) Two separate courts sat at the Special Sessions at Usk. (4) Christopher Welshe and Rees (Rice) Morgan served the office of sheriff for part of the year. (5) William Evans's Llandaff duties contributed to his poor attendance.

security of property and inheritance and that held together a society that was divided by great differences of wealth. Conrad Russell has suggested that in a gentleman's existence quarter sessions 'was perhaps a more important, because more permanent, symbol of the rule of law than Parliament'.[1]

Of the minor shire officials the most important was the coroner, who represented the interests of the Crown (hence his name). There were two for Monmouthshire, drawn from the 'meaner sort of gentlemen', and chosen by the freeholders meeting in the county court under the sheriff's supervision. They performed a range of duties linked to criminal proceedings such as murder, sudden death and, as we have seen, outlawries. In addition, they enquired into treasure trove and shipwrecks. Secondly, there was the escheator, appointed annually by the Lord Treasurer to administer the Crown rights in feudal land in the county. In Tudor times his duties merged into those of a newer officer, the feodary.

Local Government: the Hundred

The hundred stood between the shire, the largest unit, and the parish, the smallest unit of local administration and law enforcement. It was a unit of considerable vitality and utility. It was a primary division for judicial purposes and later came to be adopted as the unit for petty sessions; it was also employed as a convenient district for taxation, the military levy, for the oversight of public order and for general administration.

The only officer, apart from the sheriff's bailiff, whose area coincided with the hundred, was the Chief or High Constable. By the Act of 1543, 'two substantial Gentlemen or Yeomen' were to be appointed in each hundred to have a 'special regard for the King's Peace'. They were yearly appointed and sworn in by the JPs in quarter sessions from a list drawn up by outgoing constables.

This unpaid post carried heavy duties. It was on them that the shire officers called when they were ordered to raise a tax or loan for the county and the government; they had military duties, especially in connection with the muster; under the JPs they were responsible for the general conservation of the peace and the enforcement of the law in their divisions. They had to attend sessions and assizes, report any violation of the law they knew about, to make arrests and to act as jurors. The high constables also had oversight within their hundred of trade regulations, vagabondage, highways and

---

[1] C. Russell, *Parliament and English politics, 1621–9* (1979), p. 337.

bridges, alehouses and the observance of fish days. They supervised and gave orders to the parochial officers and in their turn were supervised by the JPs.

Their many disagreeable functions led to frequent assaults on them and attempts to obstruct them in the execution of their duty. Serious offences by these officials resulted in their appearing in Star Chamber.[1]

Local Government: the Parish

The parish, with its subdivisions, the townships, hamlets and chapelries, played a prominent role in Tudor local government. Other types of local community overlapped with the parish from time to time. In medieval times, the manor was pre-eminent. The manorial courts, which continued into the sixteenth century and beyond, and through which the lord exercised his jurisdiction over his tenants concerning tenure, inheritance and disputes, also had rights of criminal jurisdiction, dealing with minor misdemeanours; the courts were also involved in such matters as road and bridge administration,[2] which was not, therefore, the preserve of the common law courts.

The parish was further tied into hierarchies of authority by the church-wardens' obligations[3] to report to the archdeacon concerning the state of the church fabric, the conduct of the parson, the attendance at church of the parishioners, their behaviour in and out of church, the conduct of alehouses and cases concerning sexual offences, defamation of character, brawling and disputed wills which were subject to trial in the archdeacon's court,[4] sometimes referred to as the bawdy court. It is claimed for the local church and manorial courts that they had advantages such as speed, cheapness and flexibility over the common law courts and that the 'traditional over-emphasis on the county justices has given a false picture of the actual involvement of courts in the lives of most villagers.'[5]

---

[1] Roll, Crick, 5; Edwards, *Star Chamber Proceedings*, p. 103 (assault on high constable and bailiffs in Usk), p. 95 (James Morgan of Magor, high constable of Caldicot, together with a number of petty constables, accused of corruption and assault), p. 97 (high constable of Wentloog, accused of assault under colour of his office and other offences).

[2] E.g. National Library of Wales, Badminton Collection, 598: Manor of Court Peers; the jury present an encroachment on a bridge called Pont(pis)till; 1529: Manor of Magor and Redwick, when a certificate was produced to the effect that a way leading from Treowen to 'Crosse y Brwde' previously presented to be faulty had been sufficiently repaired.

[3] K. Tiller, *English Local History* (1992), p. 120.

[4] For the ecclesiastical courts, see P. Riden, *Record Sources for local history* (1987), pp. 80–3, 104ff. See also J. Hunt, 'Monmouthshire wills proved in the Prerogative Court of Canterbury, 1414–1560' (Cardiff Local History Dissertation, 1985).

[5] Palliser, *Age of Elizabeth*, pp. 358–9.

The Tudors sought for a local unit through which to transmit their authority to the localities. They chose not the manor but the parish, 'the one organisational mechanism consistently present through existing chains of command and to higher authority'.[1] Thus, the parish, an ancient ecclesiastical division, now also became the basic unit of civil government from the 1530s (and remained so until the early nineteenth century). The law adapted the old parish officers — churchwardens and petty constables — to its use; created new ones — overseer of the poor and surveyor of the highways; and imposed on them and the inhabitants a number of obligations, including the keeping of the peace, the relief of poverty, the suppression of vagabondage and the repair of the highways. One of the first duties, in 1538, required the parson and churchwardens to keep a register of baptisms, marriages and burials in the parish. As in the shire, the distribution of office holding in parish life followed the distribution of wealth; churchwardens, overseers, surveyors and quarter sessions jurymen tended to be drawn from among the minor gentry and the yeomanry, and husbandmen and craftsmen provided the constables; labourers, cottagers and poor craftsmen scarcely ever participated in local administration at all. The whole parish was obliged to join in the 'hue and cry' for suspects and once a year every man had to perform his statute labour on the highway or find a sufficient substitute. There were parish taxes to pay, and the property-less man who escaped these was usually found among the destitute and thus was liable to be confined to his parish for the term of his life, or was sent back there if he became a vagrant.

The parish, enjoying a measure of self-government through its own officers and its vestry meetings, was under the general authority of the JPs. Parish government was to some degree directed by its 'inhabitants in vestry assembled'. Its jurisdiction extended not only to matters relating to church discipline and property but also to all matters of communal interest; in addition it elected one of the two churchwardens — the warden of the 'pentre' (i.e. the village) as he is invariably described in the register of Llanddewi Rhydderch. The vestry claimed some shares too, in the appointment of the other officers, and householders were expected to take it in turns to serve these annually appointed offices, for which they were untrained and unpaid, and often relieved to hand on to their successors.

The oldest and foremost local office was that of petty or parish constable, sometimes referred to as the headborough. He was required to report regularly to the local JPs and to the quarter sessions on public nuisances, sedition, recusancy, drunkenness, injury, homicide, robberies, thefts and tumults. He had wide powers of arrest and could call on the public to help.

---

[1] Tiller, *Local History*, p. 24.

The culprit so arrested might be detained in the stocks, which all the villages were required to 'have, to repair and to maintain',[1] or the parish cage, until he could be brought before a magistrate.[2] The duty of keeping the whipping post fell to him, as well as the task of whipping vagrants on their way to their native village. He was the chief link between parish and hundred and reported to the high constable, and to the JPs on a variety of matters. His varied and responsible duties made great demands on him and sometimes he was a target of assault and accused of misdemeanours.[3] He has not had a good press since Shakespeare's Dogberry but more recent studies suggest that the accepted picture of this official is in need of revision.[4]

We shall meet the other parochial officers in the next chapter.

The Boroughs[5]

The shire town of Monmouth was incorporated by charters of 1447 and 1549; ('the grant of a charter of incorporation was the formal acknowledgement by the Crown of the vesting of power in a small urban elite'). By these charters the burgesses were granted a commonalty from which they chose annually a mayor, coroner, two bailiffs and two sergeants; the mayor and bailiffs were to be justices of the peace within the borough and to hold a 'Hundred Court'.[6] They also had powers of committal to the assizes[7] and supervised the Parliamentary elections, to which the other contributory boroughs sent burgess representatives. The 1549 charter also instituted fifteen capital or chief burgesses. The borough officers, like officers elsewhere, were sometimes assaulted, as two cases on the Roll indicated. William Bunting of Monmouth, yeoman, 'a common rioter, brawler and disturber of the Queen's peace', was found guilty of a series of verbal and physical assaults, including

---

[1] Roll, Usk II, 38.

[2] Roll, Monmouth I, 12.

[3] Edwards, *Star Chamber Proceedings*, p. 103 (assault on Jenkin Morgan, petty constable of Llanfihangel Roggiet in the hundred of Caldicot, as he was bringing the alehouse-keepers of Llanmartin to Chepstow on the orders of the high constable), p. 110 (constable of Grosmont charged with corruption in the levying of soldiers for Ireland, on the orders of the deputy lieutenants).

[4] See J. Kent, 'The English village constable, 1580–1603', *Journal of British Studies*, 20 (1981), 26–49.

[5] See *History of Parliament, 1558–1603*, I, 205; P. Courtney, *Medieval and later Usk* (1994), pp. 117ff. passim.

[6] K.S. Kissack, *Monmouth: the making of a county town* (Chichester, 1975), p. 2.

[7] Roll, Monmouth II, Gaol Delivery, 47–49.

three in the borough court-house, where he attacked one of the town bailiffs, 'there and then doing and executing his duty', assaulted Thomas Williams of Trellech, gentleman, with an iron pike, adding 'many opprobious ... words', and wounded John Morgan of Skenfrith, gentleman, whom he accused of being 'a brybyng thyffe'.[1] The midnight assault on two 'sworn watchmen' of the town reminds us of the system of preventive policing introduced by the Statute of Winchester in 1285 for every parish, but by the sixteenth century increasingly confined to urban areas, where watches patrolled the streets after dark.[2]

Monmouth had long been a possession of the Duchy of Lancaster and the leading local duchy offices of steward and receiver were held during the Elizabethan period by the earls of Pembroke and by a branch of the Herbert family. Sir Thomas Herbert reinforced his authority in the borough and district with 'livery men'.[3]

Monmouth was one of the nine market towns in the county, the others being Abergavenny, Newport, Usk, Caerleon, Chepstow, Raglan, Grosmont and Magor. Apart from Abergavenny, Chepstow and Monmouth ('an indifferent good town') the rest were 'poore and decayed'.[4] The boroughs of Caerleon, Newport, Trellech and Usk, together with the lordships of which they formed part, were granted to William Herbert, first earl of Pembroke (second creation) in the reign of Edward VI. Herbert influence, exercised in each borough through the lord's steward or constable of the castle, was considerable, not least in the appointment of local officials.

Caerleon was governed by a mayor and two bailiffs; it had a 'sessions house' and a 'common gaol'.[5] It was the port on the Usk at which ships unloaded until it was displaced as a port by Newport, which, according to Leland, was a 'myle and more by foot path from Caerleon'.[6]

Newport assumed that name with the development of the new port in medieval times; the Welsh called (and still call) it Cas-newydd (New Castle) because the town owed its origin to the castle which was built there by Robert, earl of Gloucester, in the twelfth century; in Latin deeds and charters

---

[1] Roll, Crick, 3. Abergavenny, 14, records that a William Bunting of Monmouth, yeoman, could not be found to asnwer charges against him.

[2] Roll, Monmouth II, Gaol Delivery, 8.

[3] Edwards, *Star Chamber Proceedings*, p. 112.

[4] Owen, *Penbrokshire*, III, pp. 292, 302.

[5] Edwards, *Star Chamber Proceedings*, pp. 108, 113 and Roll, Monmouth I, Gaol Delivery, 12; Monmouth II, Gaol Delivery, 62.

[6] *The Itinerary in Wales of John Leland* (ed. L.T. Smith), p. 45.

it was *Novus Burgus*, the New Borough.[1] With the granting of a charter in 1314 it became prosperous while Caerleon declined. With Usk and Chepstow, it had a population of about 1,000,[2] but, as with other medieval towns, it suffered contraction and, by the sixteenth century, its population had sunk considerably. Although it was described in 1521 as a 'proper town and goodly haven coming into it, well occupied with small quays', Leland, some twenty years later, found it a 'bigge town' but 'yn ruine'.[3]

In the sixteenth century Newport was governed by a mayor, bailiffs, aldermen and a recorder. (Newport received a charter of incorporation in 1623 instituting 12 aldermen, but deeds show that aldermen were present in the borough in Elizabeth's reign.) The mayor was chosen from three nominated aldermen by the constable of the castle, who was usually a member of the St Julians branch of the Herberts (reference has already been made to the riotous struggle for supremacy between the Herberts and the Morgans of Tredegar). That Sir William Herbert, the constable, did not hesitate to intervene in the affairs of the borough was shown when some burgesses tried to block the election of Miles Herbert to the office of mayor and his friends to other offices, after he had converted the bridge money to his own use.[4] Through the action of the constable 'with force and no free voice, the corrupt officers were re-elected on the council ... and thus enabled to carry out their corrupt schemes'.[5] The bridge fund was never repaid and it was found necessary to petition for an Act of Parliament to repair 'the great bridge of Timber' at Newport, 'fallen to great ruine and decay', together with Caerleon bridge, which was also in ruinous condition. The Act charged the county with their repair. The mayor also was frequently vigorously involved in borough affairs as on one occasion during a disturbance in the borough when the sheriff's officers attempted to make an arrest, the mayor rang the town bell and refused to allow the arrest.[6] Newport had its own commission of the peace by the 1620s and members of the Morgans and Kemeys families had town houses there.

Whereas the other Gwent boroughs were sited at important communication points, such as river crossings and confluences, Trellech is on a plateau and its position was probably chosen to exploit the woods of that area,

---

[1] Bradney, *Monmouthshire*, V (ed. M. Gray, 1993), p. 23.

[2] M. Griffiths, 'Country and Town', in T. Herbert and G.E. Jones (ed.), *Tudor Wales* (1988), p. 76.

[3] Gray, Thesis, p. 48; *Itinerary in Wales*, p. 14.

[4] See below, p. lxxxi.

[5] Edwards, *Star Chamber Proceedings*, p. 103.

[6] Jones, *Newport, 1550–1850*, p. 18; Edwards, *Star Chamber Proceedings*, p. 106.

especially for iron-smelting. It was also a good source of millstones, useful for the farming community, and it had quarries of freestone and limestone, but by the sixteenth century they do not seem to have been in production.[1] By that time it had declined to being a village, although it had at least a mayor, and it soon afterwards ceased to be referred to as a borough.

It was the scene of a violent attack on John Waters, presumably the clerk of the peace, and his son.[2]

The chief officers of the borough of Usk were a portreeve and two bailiffs, former portreeves holding the title of alderman; there was also a recorder and sometimes the lord's steward or an important local personage seems to have acted in that capacity. Court records suggest that at times there were turbulent scenes on the streets of the borough, especially on market-days or during the meetings of the quarter sessions and during these affrays local officials were attacked while trying to keep the peace. On one market-day William Saunders of Llangoven, gentleman, was, with others, the assailant or, alone, the victim of three assaults.[3] In a Star Chamber case, it was said of the same Saunders and a number of other gentlemen that it was useless suing them 'and their people' at the sessions or the Council in the Marches, because of their great influence, although they had terrorised 'the principal fair' at Usk, and had assaulted the portreeve and burgesses of the borough when they issued a proclamation for keeping the peace. When they were due to be tried at the quarter sessions there a large number of their friends 'as well as servants in livery assembled there and the defendants went unpunished'. Another affray involved Thomas Morgan of Tredegar and William Morgan of Machen, both JPs, with their tenants and followers; they were alleged to have assaulted a number of people, including the high constable and bailiffs of Usk and to have held a warlike assembly at a special sessions, which resulted in the break-up of the meeting. A quarrel between the same William Morgan and Henry Morgan of Penllwynsarph JP and their respective servants, led to a 'great assembly' of people in the streets of the borough at sessions time. A member of a prominent Usk family, Watkin John Rumsey, who was clerk of the peace of the county and recorder of the borough, was accused with others of 'murder, perjuries, assaults and other misdemeanours in the neighbourhood of Usk'.[4] Another member of the local elite, Roger Williams, who had built and lived in the Great House in Old Market Street in the borough, later moved to his new

[1] G. Williams, *Recovery*, p. 76.

[2] Roll, Usk I, 3.

[3] Roll, Usk I, 5, 8; Newport, 21.

[4] Edwards, *Star Chamber Proceedings*, pp. 115, 103, 113, 109.

country mansion at Llangybi, after purchasing the lordship of Tregrug in 1555, and he and his descendents became influential figures in county affairs.

Chepstow belonged to the Somersets, the earls of Worcester, and was governed by the lord's steward, his brother usually, and two bailiffs as the charter of 1524 confirms. It did not have a mayor nor an elite of burgesses and aldermen and throughout the sixteenth century was under the firm control of the Somerset family, as the following Exchequer court case in Elizabeth's reign testifies. William Robinson, a messenger of the court, had been sent to Chepstow to arrest two merchants who had evaded the payment of tonnage on wine which had been landed by them at the port. He complained to the court that he was accused by the defendants Thomas Somerset Esq. and Charles Somerset Esq., steward of Chepstow, his brother, of having been sent to cause trouble for merchants trading with 'my lord, his brother's port', where, they claimed, the queen had no authority. The defendants further threatened to put him in the pillory with his ears nailed, and seized his badge of office and the processes. It was only after much entreaty that the messenger was given back badge and processes, but his request to have the two merchants bound for their appearance at the Exchequer Court was refused.[1]

As a port, Chepstow, 'a haven of three fathoms at low water, somewhat dangerous to come to for rocks',[2] exported, mainly to Bristol, local agricultural products, such as hides, skins, leather, wool, cloth, butter and cheese, and imported goods which were in short supply or unobtainable locally; for example, wines, oils, salt, fruit, tar and fine cloth.[3] The 1524 charter described the town as having fallen into indigence, but it recovered during the course of the century. Phaer, in about 1550, called it 'meetly (moderately) well furnished of all manner victuals and other provisions'; Camden, writing in 1586 saw it as a 'town of good note' and George Owen as 'a little Towne and indifferent good'.[4] The bridge over the Wye at Chepstow, which Camden said had been 'built upon piles, and is exceeding high, which was necessary because the tide here rises to a great height',[5] was the subject of a petition to Parliament in 1577 'in the name of the greatest part of the inhabitants of South Wales' which wished to remedy a defect in the Highways and Bridges Act of 1531. That Act, it was claimed,

---

[1] Jones, *Exchequer Proceedings*, pp. 247–8.

[2] Phaer's report on harbours *c.* 1550, cited in M. Griffiths, 'Country and Town', in Herbert and Jones (ed.), *Tudor Wales*, p. 100.

[3] Williams, *Recovery*, p. 77.

[4] Griffiths, 'Country and Town', pp. 100, 91; Owen, *Penbrokshire*, III, p. 302.

[5] Griffiths, 'Country and town', p. 91.

applied only to areas that had been shired and not to marcher lordships, as Chepstow then was. But now that the borough was in shire territory the Act extended the provisions of the 1531 Act to it and placed the responsibility for maintaining Chepstow bridge on the magistrates of the counties of Monmouth and Gloucester jointly.[1]

Abergavenny, a Neville possession, had two bailiffs and a recorder as its leading officials. It finally received a charter of incorporation in 1638, by which it was to be governed by a chief steward, a deputy steward, bailiffs and ten capital burgesses and fifteen inferior burgesses. With Usk, Caerleon, Newport and Monmouth, and other Welsh and English towns, it was included in an Act of 1543 'for the repairing of decayed houses', this being one of a series of such acts at this time for renewing urban fabric throughout the country. Abergavenny, in fact, was a flourishing town, its wealth based in the main on the woollen industry. It was one of the largest Gwent towns, Leland considering it to be 'a faire walled town, meatly well inhabited', while to George Owen, at the end of the sixteenth century, it was 'a Fine Towne wealthie and thryveing, the very best in the shire'.[2] It is described in a Star Chamber case as 'an ancient borough and market town, a place of continuous access and resort and also by reason of the manifold trades and mysteries therein exercised, grown to be of very good wealth and stability, of quiet and orderly demeanour'.[3] According to the records of the same court, the peace was shattered by Matthew Herbert Esq., his kinsmen and followers, on a number of occasions: once, they caused such riots in the borough that the bailiffs failed to secure order and, during these disturbances, a brother-in-law of Dr David Lewis, 'high' judge of the Admiralty, was murdered and Walter Herbert having been arrested on suspicion of committing the crime, was rescued from custody by Matthew Herbert; at another time, they made a 'riotous gathering' of a hundred persons to influence the election of the bailiffs; and John William ap Roger JP, of Wernddu, complained that he had been assaulted by them as he was on his way to Abergavenny to attend to his duties as a justice.[4]

Among the distinguished sons of Abergavenny in this period were Dr David Lewis (d. 1584),[5] and his nephew and godson, David Baker (b.

---

[1] G.R. Elton, 'Wales in Parliament, 1542–1581', in R.R. Davies (ed.), *Welsh society and nationhood* (1984), p. 113.

[2] *Itinerary in Wales*, p. 45; Owen, *Penbrokshire*, III, p. 302.

[3] Edwards, *Star Chamber Proceedings*, p. 102.

[4] Ibid., pp. 108, 106, 109.

[5] David Lewis' will (J.M. Jones, Thesis, No 62) contains various bequests to members of his family in Abergavenny, including a house to his godson, David Baker.

1575), who became recorder of the borough but later took orders as a Benedictine and was henceforth known as Father Augustine Baker.[1] He wrote several religious works, and is recognised as 'a master of the spiritual life'.[2] His father, William Baker, was married to David Lewis's sister, Maud, and was included in a list of the 'chief gentlemen' of Monmouthshire compiled by George Owen for 1602; he and Roger Williams of Llangybi appear on the Roll as parties to a deed of bargain and sale enrolled at the Raglan quarter sessions.

Star Chamber records have been cited above, as elsewhere in this study. It has been claimed that some of the suits before this court — as well as before the other equity courts and the Council in the Marches — were brought out of malice rather than any serious desire to settle disputes. Some cases tried by the court were brought by plaintiffs who 'were already involved in parallel litigation ... and who sought to embarrass their opponents by bringing malicious allegations of riot, assault' and acts of intimidation.[3] The use of force by the gentry began to decline as the resort to litigation increased; the purpose of the latter was not only to harass an enemy but possibly also to impoverish him by dragging him through the courts. The outcome of most of these suits is not known, but the imposition of heavy fines by Star Chamber on some Glamorgan offenders helped to deter other aggressors in the county.[4]

Attendance at Ludlow and reading Elyot's *Governour*, may also have influenced gentry to be more conscious of their responsibilities in promoting the 'public weal'. Most of them were 'no longer prepared to endanger a structure (i.e. the Tudor settlement) that they had helped to create and from which they had benefited so much'.[5]

---

[1] Bradney, *Monmouthshire*, I, p. 177.

[2] Williams, *Recovery*, p. 438.

[3] J.A. Sharpe, *Crime in early modern England* (1984), p. 96.

[4] Williams, *Tudor regime*, p. 124.

[5] J.G. Jones, *Early modern Wales, c. 1525–1640* (1994), p. 121.

5

Quarter Sessions
and Gaol Delivery

As the previous chapter explained, the Roll comprises the proceedings of
quarter and special sessions, and of gaol deliveries. Quarter sessions, as
Beattie points out, were more flexible than the assizes, in that, although they
were required to meet at particular times of the year, these meetings could
last as many days as were needed to complete the business in hand; in
addition, special sessions could be called, if necessary. The assizes were held
by judges of the Westminster Courts and took place between the terms of
these courts when the judges were free to go on circuit. They worked to a
tight schedule, which set out the few days when they would be at a
particular town, where they would work at speed to clear the gaol before
moving on to the next centre on their circuit. (It has been noted elsewhere
in this essay that the largest circuit, Oxford, comprising eight counties,
including Monmouthshire, took the judges an average of twenty-eight days
to ride.) Procedure in the quarter sessions followed, in the main, that of the
assizes. The assizes and quarter sessions held twice a year were major events
in the life of Monmouth, as, to a lesser extent, were the quarter sessions held
once a year at the other small market towns of the county in their turn, and
were a significant boost to the local economy.

This chapter discusses the work of the two courts, beginning with the
justices' sessions. The JPs, in their quarter sessions, received professional
guidance from the clerk of the peace; the holders of this office in Monmouthshire in the sixteenth century were Hugh Huntley (1540–43), John
Waters (1544–65 and 1569–76), Richard Hoskyns (1566–67 and possibly
also (1567–69) and Walter Rumsey (1581–1609).[1] None had a deputy.

From 1545 there was statutory provision for the appointment of the clerk
of the peace by the custos rotulorum. The clerk's duties were to assist the
justices 'in drawing up their indictments, in arraigning their prisoners, in

---

[1] I. ab Owen Edwards (ed.), *Catalogue of Star Chamber proceedings relating to Wales*
(1929), p. 109; 'Watkin Jno. Rumsey, Clerk of the county and Recorder of Usk', and others,
were accused of murders, perjuries and assaults in the neighbourhood of Usk, and of illegal
levying of fines on petty constables. See also p. liii, n. 3.

joining issue for the Crown,[1] in entering their judgements, in awarding their process and in making up and keeping their records.'[2] In addition, the administrative functions which were being increasingly acquired by the justices made quarter sessions 'not merely a criminal court for the county, but also a governmental assembly, a board with governmental and administrative powers',[3] the whole of the office work for which fell on the clerk, who could thus be considered the chief executive officer of his county. He was the county's only professional officer until full-time treasurer, surveyor and bridge-masters were appointed in the eighteenth century.[4]

The following sections will be concerned with those administrative duties of the JPs which are recorded on the Roll — poor law, vagrancy, alehouses and highways — together with some related functions.

Poverty and Vagrancy

Of the many causes of distress and unemployment, leading to poverty and vagrancy which gave concern to the government in the sixteenth century, the basic underlying factors were inflation, worsening economic conditions and demographic pressure. Many of those, male and female, who were unable to find employment in the countryside or the towns were forced to move from their homes to seek work, and if they could not find it, joined the growing ranks of migrants. They were thought to be a threat to social order, health and morality. They were said to form themselves into large bands of professional and potential criminals, were seen as carriers of disease and responsible for outbreaks of plagues. The authorities took the view that they were idle and delinquent, preferring begging and stealing to a hard day's work, migrating not to seek employment but to take advantage of urban and parish welfare. However, it is now claimed that most vagrants were children and young people aged about 14 to 25, unable to find employment in service or apprenticeship and forced to leave home to seek work. (Of the only group of migrants brought before a Monmouthshire bench in 1576–77, a party of

---

[1] Roll, Caerleon, 33.

[2] E. Stephens, *The clerks of the counties* (1961), p. 36.

[3] F.W. Maitland, *The constitutional history of England* (1908), p. 223.

[4] See B. Howell, 'Local administration in Monmouthshire, 16th–19th centuries' (Unpublished University of Wales [Cardiff] M.A. Thesis, 1951) for the history, until the early 19th century, of all aspects of the Monmouthshire JPs' administrative duties and the gradual creation of a professional staff.

four, three of them were under 14 years of age.)[1] Child labour was an essential and acceptable part of the domestic economy and long periods away from the parental home, from the ages of seven or eight, were part of the common experience of youth. One in five children lost their father by the age of ten, and a quarter of all children were fatherless by the age of fifteen. Even where both parents survived, the experience of most adolescents was of long periods away working as servants or apprentices in other households. Sixteenth-century conditions forced many children and teenagers to join migrants genuinely seeking casual or longer-term work, but often unable to find it. Although there was crime, it is now considered to have been mainly pilfering in dearth years, rather than the work of organised gangs of criminals.

There were two basic types of poverty. The first was of the impotent poor, the pauper, and this represented 'deep' poverty. This group was made up of the very young and the old, and consisted of the disabled, widows, widowers, the sick, deserted wives, broken families with small children; a wide gap separated them from those in employment. By the end of the Tudor period there was a young population; it is estimated that 40 per cent of the population were children and about 45 per cent of them were below the age of ten. The second group were the 'shallow' poor, comprising, in the main, the increasing number of cottager and labouring families living on the edge of poverty. Illness, injury, a bad harvest, a trade slump — any of these could plunge such families into poverty. In addition, many other families had scarcely enough income to buy the necessities of life, which brought them near or over the poverty line.[2]

From medieval times the poor had been relieved by individual and community action, as Scripture commanded. They depended in the main on the religious houses (the end of monastic charity in the 1530s left 'a real vacuum'); hospitals (e.g. medieval Usk had a hospital and almshouse);[3] parish and municipal welfare (there were few, if any, of these in Wales, but London, Bristol and the border towns attracted a number of Welsh, including Monmouthshire, migrants); the *plastai*; and gifts of food and other necessities from neighbours. People also left money in their wills for works of mercy designed to relieve the poor.[4] By one of Elizabeth's Injunctions

---

[1] See below, p. lxxvii.

[2] N. Heard, *Tudor economy and society* (1992), p. 109

[3] P. Courtney, *Medieval and later Usk* (1994), p. 101.

[4] E.g. Bradney, *Monmouthshire*, I, p. 300; IV, p. 28–9; V, p. 6: J. Hunt, 'Monmouthshire wills proved in the Prerogative Court of Canterbury, 1414–1560' (Cardiff Local History Diploma Dissertation, 1985), Nos 26, 114, 118; J.M. Jones, 'Monmouthshire wills proved in the

(1559), clergy were to discourage dying parishioners from making any religious obit other than bequests to the poor — and for the upkeep of highways.[1]

Tudor attempts to grapple with the twin problems of poverty and vagrancy led to the passage of a number of Acts. One in 1531 distinguished between the impotent poor, who were to be allowed to beg within their own community, after obtaining a licence from the JPs, and the sturdy unemployed, who were to be whipped, put in the stocks and returned to their homes; no allowance was made for the able-bodied unemployed who genuinely wanted to work. Five years later an Act ordered the parish to be responsible for the relief of the impotent poor, money for the purpose to be raised by voluntary means in each parish. The sturdy poor willing to work were to have work provided for them, but the indolent poor were to be punished. Except that it did not levy a compulsory poor rate — that came later — this Act, recognising as it did that the poor fell into three categories, the very young, infirm and aged, who required outdoor relief, the industrious poor for whom work should be found, and the sturdy rogue, who was to be punished, contained all the essentials of the more famous Elizabethan Poor Law at the end of the century. Other Acts followed, such as the barbaric (and fortunately short-lived) Act of 1547 by which vagrants were to be branded and enslaved, and the Statute of Artificers of 1563. But the statute with which the Monmouthshire justices of 1576–77 were mainly concerned was one passed in 1572. The Privy Council and the Council in the Marches, it will be recalled, frequently exhorted the magistrates to execute the vagrancy laws. Perhaps it was in response to one such letter that the JPs acted at their Abergavenny sessions held on the Tuesday after the close of Easter, 1577, to enforce the statute of 1572 which ordered that any person

> being sound and able in body and capable of ... working, not having land or master and ... practising any lawful trade, craft or office and who ... may be caught begging in any part of the realm, wandering about and misbehaving themselves ... are to be arrested ... styled ... vagabonds[2]

and were to undergo the penalties provided by the Act. Those over the age of 14 were to be grievously whipped and bored through the gristle of the

---

Prerogative Court of Canterbury, 1560–1601' (Unpublished University of Wales [Cardiff] M.A. thesis, 1990), Nos 124, 128, 138, 139, 149.

[1] Below, pp. lxxx et seq.

[2] 14 Eliz. c. 5.

right ear 'to be made with a hot iron of the compass of an inch about';
vagrants under 14 were to be whipped. That was the punishment meted out
to four vagrants (three of whom were below 14 years of age) who appeared
before the bench at Abergavenny.[1]

The 1572 Act also stated that for a second offence the vagrant would be
judged a felon unless he could find someone to stand surety for him, which
involved a person taking the vagrant into service. Such a vagrant, at the first
Monmouth Gaol Delivery (the Act in the entry on this Roll being referred
to as the 'Statute of Rogues'), for a second default was taken into service
and had to appear before the justices at the end of two years, binding the
master in the sum of £10.[2] For a third offence, a vagrant would be treated
as a felon, without benefit of clergy.[3] The penalties of ear boring and death
for a vagrant were lifted in 1593. The Roll contains one further reference to
a vagrant, from Somerset, taken at Abergavenny 'wandering and begging'
and committed by three JPs.[4]

Acts of 1598 and 1601 consolidated Tudor legislation concerning the
relief of the poor. The parish was retained as the lowest unit of the poor law
and on it was placed the financial burden. Parish execution of the law was
placed in the charge of the newly created overseers of the poor (usually
two), who were nominated yearly by two JPs from among the parish
householders. The overseers and the churchwardens were to make and collect
a poor rate, to apprentice pauper children, to distribute relief to the needy
and supply material for the employment of the poor. The work was to be
supervised by the JPs, who were to require strict accounts from the
overseers. In addition, the justices were empowered to provide in each
district a house of correction, where the idle were to be 'straitly kept' as well
as in work'.[5] They also had the power to arrest any wandering idler, have
him whipped until 'the blood came', and then sent back to the place of his
birth, or to the parish through which he had last passed without punishment.
Acts for the erection of hospitals and for the supervision of charitable trusts
were also passed in 1598 and 1601. Elizabethan legislation remained the
basis of the Poor Law until the Poor Law Amendment Act of 1834, although
other Acts were passed in the intervening period, notably the Act of

---

[1] Roll, Abergavenny 31.

[2] Roll, Monmouth I, Gaol Delivery, 40.

[3] Below, pp. xcii et seq.

[4] Roll, Monmouth II, Gaol Delivery, 51.

[5] Monmouthshire had only one house of correction, at Usk. Its origin can be traced no
further back than 1630; Bradney, *Monmouthshire*, III, p. 23. Sir Charles Somerset in 1598
bequeathed £40 to build a house of correction at Chepstow: Jones, Thesis, No 139.

Settlement and Removal of 1662, which took up much quarter sessions time in the eighteenth century.

One of the major duties of the justices in connection with the poor was to assist the government in the proper distribution and price of food, mainly corn and bread, especially in time of dearth. Scarcity of corn meant also a deficiency of, and the discouragement of, the eating of meat, the encouragement of the eating of fish, and the control of butchers and of the number of alehouses (which otherwise might result in the excessive consumption of barley). The government sought to prevent the export of grain overseas in times of shortage and to ensure that all corn should be brought to the markets and sold at a fair price. 'Badgers' (corn merchants) were to be licensed by JPs, who were also to prevent the most common offences against the marketing of food; that is 'engrossing', the cornering of excessive quantities of grain; 'forestalling', buying up the grain while it was still in the field or before it came to market; and 'regrating', the purchase of corn for resale at a profit. The sheriff's *venire facias* required him to summon a grand jury 'to make enquiry concerning ... regrating, forestallings, ... ', but there is no record in the Roll of any such cases.

The Tudor directives bearing on these problems were committed to the care of JPs and other local officials. To judge from Privy Council correspondence these requirements were nowhere strictly enforced. The Monmouthshire justices held meetings to make arrangements for the better furnishing of the markets with grain; they informed the Council in a letter from Usk, dated 7 June 1586, that the markets were reasonably well provided, but that the quantity in store was not sufficient to last until the harvest. The Council, however, continued to complain that, in all counties, too many badgers were being given licences and too many ill-disposed persons (including some JPs), 'without any charitable respect to the sustentation of their neighbours', were going unpunished.[1]

Alehouses

There was no social institution that caused more heart-searching in the Elizabethan period than the alehouse.[2] No-one doubted that they were

---

[1] *Calendar of State Papers, Domestic, 1581–90*, CXC, 9; R. Flenley (ed.), *Register of the Council in the Marches of Wales, 1569–1591* (1906), p. 123.

[2] There were three types of victualling house, in declining order of size and status: the inn, offering wine, ale or beer, together with elaborate food and lodging to wealthier travellers, and a place for the upper classes to 'meet, trade, politick and get drunk' — and hold quarter sessions; the tavern, selling wine, etc, and food to the more prosperous, but without the

necessary. Their role in the economy of the poor was vital; their recreational function was generally accepted. The mass of the population depended on ale and beer as a chief source of nourishment. Ale, wrote John Taylor, was the poor man's comfort, assuaging hunger and cold; 'it is the shepherd, the mower, ploughman and blacksmith's most esteemed purchase, the tinker's treasure, the pedlar's jewel, the beggar's joy and the prisoner's loving nurse'.[1] Alcohol, according to Keith Thomas, was a narcotic which anaesthetized people against the strains of contemporary life. It was extensively used in Elizabethan prisons and flowed freely at times of plague.

The alehouse provided news of work, social intercourse, an atmosphere of warmth, hospitality and entertainment and was a lodging house for the migrant poor. But to those in authority alehouses represented a major threat to public order and morality (and to barley supplies, already noted), they were 'nests of Satan', 'nurseries of all riot and excess' and the resort of 'loose idle persons'. An Act of 1552 denounced the proliferation of popular drinking houses and required that all alehouse-keepers should be licensed by JPs on bonds and backed by sureties, in the interests of preventing 'hurts and troubles ... abuses and disorders'. The objections of the government were contained in letters from the Privy Council via the Council in the Marches; for example, one dated 25 March 1573, directed to Monmouthshire and the twelve shires. By it the JPs were urged to control the number of alehouses, of which there were an excessive number,

> many in desert and secret places, and the number still increasing by the obtaining of licences from JP's who are far away from the affected places and ignorant of the character of the applicant or the needs of the locality. As by these felonies are increased, thieves, murderers and women of light conversation are har-boured, rogues and vagabonds maintained, whoredom and detestable life, unlawful games as ... Dice, Cards, Bowls, Kayles (i.e. ninepins), Quoits ... commonly exercised.[2]

JPs and other local officers were required to amend their ways, divide them-selves into their allotments and carry out all laws concerning the excessive

---

extensive accommodation of the inn; and the alehouse, with smaller premises, serving ale or beer and providing basic food and lodging to the lower orders. P. Clark, *The English alehouse* (1983), p. 10.

[1] Cited in A. Fletcher, *Reform in the provinces* (1986), p. 229, and K. Thomas, *Religion and the decline of magic* (1971), p. 23.

[2] The government's objection to gambling — 'another escape from reality' (Keith Thomas) — was that it led to disorder.

number and licensing of alehouses, especially those in 'suspect or remote' places, as well as the laws for the punishment of vagrants, relief of the poor and the abolition of unlawful games.[1] Other legislation fixed the price of ale and beer, and forbade drunkenness and 'tippling' (sitting drinking in an alehouse for more than one hour in the individual's home parish).

There is no record that any Monmouthshire alehouses were suppressed but the Roll testifies that a number of alehouse-keepers in 1576–77 (most described as yeomen, some 'spinsters', one tailor, one corvisor, one labourer) were presented or fined for selling ale, or selling bread, ale or other victuals without a licence, some having committed the offence more than once; the fine varied between 1s. and 2s.[2]

Highways

The care of the highways was, from the sixteenth century, an obligation of the parish. The statute of 2 & 3 Philip and Mary, c. 8 (1555), with amendments, formed the basis of road maintenance for nearly three hundred years. By it the parish had to provide an annually appointed surveyor of the highways from among its inhabitants, who, in their turn, supplied the necessary manual labour (later converted to a highway rate); the justices were to exercise a general supervision over the system. From a list presented by the parish they were to appoint a new surveyor, to hear pleas for non-fulfilment of statute labour and issue warrants to levy penalties imposed under the Act.

The parishioners' burden embraced both landowners and labourers. Every person for every ploughland in tillage or pasture that he occupied in the parish, and every person keeping a draught of horses or plough in the parish was to provide a waggon or cart with oxen or horses and two able men for four (later six) days' service on the parish highways. In addition to being responsible for the upkeep of that section of the road which adjoined their land, every householder, cottager or labourer, 'able to labour and being no hired servant' was either to work himself on the roads for the statutory period or supply one 'sufficient labourer' in his place. All these teams and labourers had annually to appear on the roads on the date and time fixed by the parish surveyor, who was to give sufficient notice, there to work under his direction for eight hours for the requisite number of days.

---

[1] Flenley, *Register*, p. 102.

[2] Roll, Newport, 55–57; Abergavenny, 37–47, 62, 64–67; Usk, 39.

This statute labour seems to have been performed with the 'utmost remissness', the roads suffering accordingly.[1] The labour was inadequately distributed and six days once a year were not sufficient to maintain the roads in even moderate repair. The surveyor was not trained for his duties, was often reluctant to undertake the work, and even the most enthusiastic and painstaking officer could accomplish little in a year. Few of the JPs realised that they had administrative obligations for the maintenance of the highways, regarding quarter sessions as a purely judicial tribunal, which took action concerning roads only when presentments were made. That was how the roads were administered, by the cumbersome judicial processes of the common law, under which it was open to anyone, 'in his view and proper knowledge', to present, at sessions, assizes or, as we have seen, manorial courts, parishes or individuals, whenever a 'common and ancient King's highway became ruinous, miry, deep, broken ...'.

At the sessions a fine was imposed on defaulting parishes but was usually deferred for three months; if, meanwhile, the repairs were undertaken and certified by JPs the fine was excused. How ineffective the administration or jurisdiction of quarter sessions was in the sixteenth century may be gauged from the repeated non-appearance of parishes, to show reason why their roads had not been repaired, or of individuals why they had not undertaken their statute labour. For instance, a number of parishes, and a few individuals, did not appear at the Caerleon, Newport, Abergavenny and Usk sessions, the fine for parishes being successively reduced from 8s. to 6s. 8d. to 3s. 4d., and for individuals remaining at 2s.[2]

The charge against William Yoroth, a yeoman of Llanarth, that he 'did with force and arms ... enclose and obstruct the Queen's highway' took up much of the JPs' time. Indicted at the spring (1576) quarter sessions at Abergavenny, he attended the summer sessions at Monmouth where he 'put himself on the country' (i.e. pleaded not guilty) and was finally tried — and acquitted — by a jury at the autumn sessions at Caerleon.[3]

As noted above, one of Elizabeth's Injunctions referred to the making of bequests to the poor, and the highways. Since the Middle Ages a significant number of wills left money not only for the relief of the poor but also for more general and apparently more secular purposes. The upkeep of roads, causeways and bridges was one of the commonest forms of such secular bequests. Testators providing for such works made no distinction

---

[1] S. and B. Webb, *The story of the King's highway* (1929), p. 20.

[2] Entries on the Roll concerning the upkeep of roads and non-appearance are as follows: Caerleon, 40–45; Newport, 36–44; Abergavenny, 56–61; Usk II, 40–51, 72–78.

[3] Roll, Caerleon, 33.

between them and works of mercy, with which indeed they frequently join them. Those who provided money for such purposes thought themselves to be performing a religious act. 'All contributions to the comfort of neighbours were understood as a dimension of the promotion of charity', and in medieval times indulgences were granted to those who contributed to these projects.[1]

There is no reference to bridges in the Roll. To our ancestors, accustomed to ride through water and to cross rivers by fords, a bridge was an unusual phenomenon, often coming into existence and being maintained from bequests. By a statute of 1531, the county became responsible for their maintenance, decayed bridges being dealt with much as defective highways were, by presentment. By the Act, the magistrates were to enquire, hear and determine at quarter sessions, 'all manner of annoyances of bridges broken in the highways', the expense of the repairs was to be met out of a county rate'.[2] Thus the county rate, levied in the first place for bridge repairs, preceded the parish highway rate by a century and a half.

Information on the administration of the county's bridges is extremely scanty before the eighteenth century. The first Public Act relating to the county was one passed in 1577 for repairing of Chepstow Bridge, which was replaced by another of 1603, 'for the new making and keeping in Reparation' of Chepstow Bridge, which was to be maintained jointly by the magistrates of Monmouthshire and Gloucestershire. An Act of 1597, noting that 'a certain great bridge of Timber called Newport bridge is standing over the river of Uske [and is] fallen into ruine and decay ... ', required the JPs to repair and maintain both this bridge and that at Caerleon.[3]

With what diligence the Monmouthshire justices discharged their bridge obligations in the sixteenth century we can only guess. We know of a meeting of JPs in 1582 to arrange for the rebuilding of the 'greet bridge of wood of 15 arches over the Uske called Newport bridge', although there was no county rate to meet the expenditure and it was decided to appeal for subscriptions. Miles Herbert JP was made the manager of the fund, with a view to obtaining the strong support of the Herberts, but Miles behaved 'contrary

---

[1] E. Duffy, *The stripping of the altars. Traditional religion in England, 1400–1580* (1992), pp. 367ff. For Monmouthshire bequests for the repair of bridges, roads and causeways see Hunt, Dissertation, and Jones, Thesis, passim.

[2] Webb, *King's highway*, p. 89. It was not until the end of the 19th century that any statute made the building of bridges part of the common duty of any public authority and then it was entrusted to the new county councils.

[3] 39 Eliz. c. 23; Bradney, *Monmouthshire*, V (ed. M. Gray), p. 36.

to expectations and converted the gifts to his own account and implicated other burgesses in his corruption'.[1]

Various documents might be enrolled, registered or deposited with the clerk of the peace, and the enrolment of some deeds of bargain and sale, one of them relating to the Tredegar estate, appear on the Roll, as required by an Act of 1535.[2]

Although the justices' administrative duties were growing apace, they were viewed mainly as conservators of the peace by the mass of the population; the bards made little mention of their patrons as administrators, but rarely failed to pay tribute to their qualities as preservers of law and order in the community. Much of the Roll is taken up with their duties in the latter capacity and, together with the work of the assize judges, will be the concern of the next section.

Judicial Functions of Justices and Judges[3]

Crime in our generation is an everyday cause of serious concern — indeed, some claim that the growth in crime in recent years has been unprecedented — and we sometimes wonder whether previous ages were as alarmed by the problem. But our ancestors were also preoccupied with lawlessness and certainly in the sixteenth century there was a prevalence of crime and disorder, an experience shared by other European countries.[4] Nevertheless, although we have a broad impression of wrongdoing there is little precise information from court records, certainly in the case of Monmouthshire. Assize records of the Oxford circuit have not survived before the 1640s, and the only record of the proceedings of this court is that of the two gaol deliveries included in the Roll, which also contains the only extant quarter sessions records for Monmouthshire before the eighteenth century.[5]

---

[1] Edwards, *Star Chamber Proceedings*, p. 103.

[2] Roll, Raglan 5, 6, 7; Usk II, 87.

[3] Much of this section is based on J.M. Beattie, *Crime and the courts in England, 1660–1800* (1986) (sections of which relate to the 16th century); J.S. Cockburn, *A History of English Assizes, 1558–1714* (1972); idem (ed.), *Crime in England, 1500–1800* (1977); 'Introduction' in idem (ed.), *The Calendar of Assize Rolls* (1985); J.A. Sharpe, *Crime in early modern England* (1984); idem, *Judicial punishment in England* (1990); W.O. Williams (ed.), *A Calendar of the Caernarvonshire Quarter Sessions records*, I (1956), 1544–1558.

[4] J.S. Cockburn, 'The nature and incidence of crime in England', in idem (ed.), *Crime in England*, 49–71.

[5] A bill of 1566 sought to set up record offices in every Welsh shire, an excellent proposal, whose failure the historian must deeply regret: G.R. Elton, 'Wales in Westminster, 1541–1581', in R.R. Davies et al. (ed.) *Welsh society and nationhood* (1984), p. 117.

The Roll, recording as it does the activities of both quarter sessions and assizes over a period of less than a year, sometimes in cryptic and tantalisingly sparse terms, lacks both the extent and the wealth of detail of similar Caernarvonshire records.[1] Nevertheless, it provides us with some knowledge of the extent of crime in Monmouthshire forty years after the Union. But any quantification of crime is a risky enterprise, because of the existence of the 'dark figure', that body of criminal behaviour never presented nor recorded.[2] The claim of Edward Hext, a Somerset JP, that 'the fyveth person that comytteth a felonye' was never brought to trial, has been interpreted by J.S. Cockburn to mean that 80 per cent of all criminals evaded trial, while D.M. Palliser's view is that Hext meant 20 per cent were not tried.[3] Whatever the difference, the comment does point to a discrepancy between actual and indicted crime, as is the case today.[4]

In an age when the decision to prosecute often lay with the person offended against, the trouble — in a small community, a court case might seriously affect social relations — and the cost involved, such as the prosecutor's own expenses, loss of earnings, payment of witnesses and court expenses (the clerical staff of the court depended on fees for a living) acted as a disincentive to the victim to take the case to law. Hext explained that 'the symple man that hath lost hys goods, he ys many times content to take hys goods and lett them slypp, because he will not be bound to give evidens at the assises to hys trouble and chardge'.[5] The victim might also be reluctant to be the cause of inflicting the severe penalties prescribed by law on the offender, if found guilty. Again, neighbourliness, the social ostracism or public humiliation of the accused, family ties, the prompting of friends and the weight of local custom emphasised informal settlement or arbitration of differences; there were practised mediators in most districts, such as the local gentry and the priest, to urge settlement. In addition, in that age of 'two

[1] The only other Welsh county whose 16th-century quarter sessions records have survived is Caernarvonshire.

[2] Sharpe, *Crime*, p. 42.

[3] Cockburn, *Crime*, p. 50; D.M. Palliser, *The Age of Elizabeth. England under the later Tudors, 1547–1603* (2nd ed. 1992), p. 365.

[4] Cf. *Daily Telegraph*, 29 Oct. 1992: 'The British Crime Survey, issued yesterday, for which Home Office researchers interviewed 10,000 people, showed that for every offence recorded by the police, two more crimes went unreported ... many victims either thought certain crimes were too trivial or that there was no point in reporting them because the police could not do anything about them'.

[5] Cited in K. Wrightson, *English society, 1580–1680* (1982), p. 156.

concepts of order',[1] that of the state and that of the village, central
government control over the localities ultimately depended on the parish
constable, who could often find the laws he was expected to enforce at odds
with local ideas and the best interests of his fellow villagers. Much of his
work lay in the traditional area of keeping the King's peace and this
consisted to some extent of defusing problems.[2]

Binding over by the justices to keep the peace, or to be of good
behaviour, often prevented serious crime. Recognisances were widely used
in proceedings against potential malefactors.[3] Surety for the peace was
granted against those who threatened the person or the property of another.
The complainant would go to the local justice to declare on oath that he was
in physical danger or that his goods were threatened. After taking depositions, the justice might bind over the alleged wrongdoer to the quarter
sessions to answer to the charge, together with the complainant and
witnesses and all were required to give financial guarantees of attendance.
When neighbours quarrelled, more often than not they came before a justice
and entered into recognisances and sureties, to keep the peace toward each
other, or to be of good behaviour, and to appear at the next sessions. The
sessions records show a number of breaches of the peace and numerous
failures to bring offenders to their trial, but the recognisances indicate that
some people were amenable to the law.[4] The taking of recognisances was
a very important part of the work of JPs; the system of binding over
constituted a cheap and effective method of curbing interpersonal violence.[5]

If a victim wanted to proceed and press charges he would normally take
his complaint to a JP, assuming he could find one, since JPs were sometimes
not distributed evenly around the county. How the justice was to proceed
was largely governed by the Marian Statutes of 1554 and 1555, which
required him to take the depositions of the prosecutor and his witnesses in
writing and to examine the accused and reduce his statement to writing. All
concerned — prosecutor, witnesses and suspect — were bound over to
appear at the appropriate court, quarter sessions or assizes. By these statutes
the examination of the accused was intended to be a thorough searching out

---

[1] K. Wrightson, 'Two concepts of order: justices, constables and jurymen in seventeenth-
century England,' in J. Brewer and J. Styles (ed.) *An ungovernable people* (1980), pp. 21–46.

[2] Conrad Russell, 'The bourgeois revolution: a mirage?', *History Today* (Sept. 1990), p.
9, claims that C. Herrup's work on 17th-century justice 'has shown that the justice actually
administered was that of local people administering local values.'

[3] Roll, Caerleon, 12–21; Newport, 13, 14; Abergavenny, 18, 19; Usk II, 18–21.

[4] Of those bound over, one failed to appear at the sessions (Abergavenny, 19); his £10 and
surety's £10 were forfeit to the court.

[5] Sharpe, *Crime*, p. 36.

of the evidence that would lead to a conviction. The Tudor magistrates were not being asked to act impartially at this stage; indeed they were forbidden to discharge anyone brought before them accused of committing a felony. All suspects were to be sent on trial and the magistrates' task was to ensure that the strongest evidence of their guilt would be contained in the depositions that they were required to send on to the court. They were not forbidden to report information that was in the prisoner's favour, but nor were they expected to search for such evidence 'as maketh against the King'.[1] In Marian legislation, the prisoner had few rights at this stage in the investigation. He was not to be told precisely what the evidence was against him, nor to be present when the depositions of the prosecutor and witnesses were taken. What was sought was a trial in which the complainant would present his case in such a way that the issues would be reached quickly and the accused forced to reply, directly and unaided by a lawyer, the court judging him by the sincerity of his denials. At the conclusion of the trial enquiry the magistrate was required to grant the accused bail or to commit him to gaol, there to await trial by the circuit judges. A single justice was forbidden to grant bail in a case of felony (i.e. any capital offence) lest he be tempted by corruption. But two justices, one of whom was to be of the quorum, sitting in open court, could bail for any offence except treason, murder or arson, so long as the guilt was not virtually certain (as when the accused had confessed, or had been caught red-handed).[2]

The chain of proceedings leading to trial in either court, therefore, began with the magistrates' examination and they were required to ensure that the prosecutor, witnesses and accused would appear for trial at quarter sessions or assizes. A clear division of work between the two courts was beginning to develop in Elizabeth's reign, by which quarter sessions dealt with misdemeanours and increasingly left felonies to the assize judges — although the Roll shows that in the 1570s such a serious offence as murder was still being dealt with by quarter sessions.[3] Concerning the cases of those bound over to appear at quarter sessions, the justices who had directed the initial examination did not conduct the prosecution; that was done by the clerk.[4] At the assizes the proceedings were controlled by the judge; there was no counsel. In general, trial judges were critical of the local justices for their failure to take adequate examination and sureties for appearance, which sometimes brought delay to trials. Examining magistrates were required to

---

[1] Beattie, *Crime*, p. 271, citing Michael Dalton, *The Countrey Justice* (1618).

[2] Roll, Usk II, 22, 23.

[3] Roll, Usk II, 26.

[4] Roll, Caerleon, 33.

attend the trial to certify any pertinent evidence and supporting documents.[1] In any case, all members of the county bench were obliged to attend assizes to learn from the professionally trained judge, and the Roll shows that they were reasonably well attended, especially the summer assizes;[2] unexcused absences rendered justices liable to amercement at the judges' discretion. One judge conducted the criminal trials, usually at speed, while the other concerned himself with the *nisi prius* (civil) cases; there is no record of the latter on the Roll.

The law recognised two categories of criminal offences, felonies and misdemeanours.felonies, capital offences which could lead to a convicted offender being hanged, included murder (killing with 'malice aforethought'), manslaughter (killing without premeditation), infanticide, rape, counterfeiting, burglary, arson and theft of goods worth one shilling or more (grand larceny). Violence was commonly experienced in sixteenth-century society and there was a high tolerance of violent behaviour; the family was the scene of much of it, and its use by the state in combating crime by public hangings and whippings led to crowds of people witnessing it.[3] Some people tended to be volatile and quarrels could degenerate into violence. Nevertheless, 'petty crime was more common, more typical, and in many ways more entitled to be described as "real" crime then was the serious offence'.[4] Misdemeanours included trespass, riot ('the committing of an unlawful act by three or more persons assembled for the purpose', a legal definition which meant that comparatively petty offences could be subsumed under the term),[5] affray, assault (the most common form of violence brought before the courts), vagrancy, illegal assembly, forcible entry, contempts and the theft of goods worth less than one shilling (petty larceny). Such offences were punished by whipping, being put in the stocks or pillory, imprisoned, fined, mutilated, or a combination of any of these.

Juries played a central role in both courts. The sheriff, by his writ of *venire facias*, was required to call twelve 'knights as other free and loyal men', usually interpreted as 40s. freeholders (raised to 80s. in 1585), 'from the body of the county' to form the grand jury; some twenty or more were called, of whom fifteen or sixteen were sworn and at least twelve were empanelled to act as the jury of enquiry. The charge to the grand and other juries was made by the judges at the assizes and by the senior justice at

---

[1] Cockburn, *English assizes*, p. 102.

[2] Roll, Monmouth I, 1; Monmouth II, 1.

[3] Beattie, *Crime*, pp. 74ff.

[4] Sharpe, *Crime*, p. 5.

[5] Wrightson, *English society*, p. 173.

quarter sessions. The main purpose of the charge was to refresh the jurors' memory on the main parts of the law relating to their immediate business but it was customary for them to preface this with a preamble on the connection between crime and immorality (already probably emphasised in the assize sermon), and to give details of recent changes in government policies and remind the juries of the importance of their work in law enforcement.[1] The best surviving collection of such preambles was that written by Lambarde in the late sixteenth century. The importance of the grand jury, in his eyes, is summarised thus: 'As it pleaseth her Highness to use us [JPs] as the mouth of her laws ... so also she appointeth you that be jurors in place of the eyes of the same laws'. He goes on to say that the laws could not be 'discreetly applied by us without the aid of you'.[2] This jury could present offences of their own knowledge, but the bulk of their findings was based on presentments or draft indictments (called 'bills') prepared by the clerk on behalf of the prosecution, and in their power of preliminary enquiry and discretion they held the key to all Crown proceedings. In considering bills they heard only Crown evidence, since their task was not to convict but to decide whether there was a case to answer. If they concluded that there was a case, they found the bill 'true' and endorsed it '*billa vera*'; the bill then became an indictment. When they were not satisfied, they endorsed it '*ignoramus*' ('we do not know').

The petty or trial jury consisted of twelve men, drawn in the main from the ranks of the yeomen, husbandmen, tradesmen and craftsmen. A trial jury was empanelled when a prisoner pleaded not guilty, and desired to be tried by 'God and the Country', the indictment being marked 'po[nit] se [super patriam]', 'he puts himself [on the country]'. When the jury considered its verdict, three alternatives were possible, guilty, not guilty or find the prisoner guilty of a reduced charge (a 'partial' verdict). The trial jury thus had discretionary power to apply the law as they thought fit in particular cases. If the verdict was 'guilty', the jury was asked to say what property the convicted person had, so that it could be seized by the state; the reply was 'None to our knowledge', because, in fact, the enquiry would be carried out by the sheriff. The clerk then wrote 'po[nit] se [super patriam] cul[pabilis] ca[talla] nul[la]' ('he puts himself on the country, guilty, no chattels') and sometimes added the dread words 'sus[pendatur] per coll[um]' ('let him be hanged by the neck').[3] If the verdict was 'not guilty', the clerk was asked

---

[1] Sharpe, *Crime*, p. 158.

[2] C. Read, *William Lambarde and local government* (1962), p. 69.

[3] Roll, e.g. Newport, 18.

if the accused had fled (as some did, as will be seen) to which a similar answer was given. The clerk then noted, 'po[nit] se [super patriam] non cul[pabilis] nec re[traxit]' ('put himself on the country, not guilty, did not flee'),[1] or 'Non cul[pabilis] nec re[traxit] I[de]o ex[oneratur]' ('not guilty, did not flee, therefore he is acquitted').[2]

Juries played a significant part in shielding prisoners from the severity of the criminal code. It has been suggested that in 'cases of blood' — felonies punishable in the last resort by the death penalty — grand juries sometimes preferred to reject a bill outright rather than hazard the life of the accused by sending him to trial.[3] The contribution of the trial jury in mitigating the full rigours of the law could be decisive in either of two ways; to find the accused not guilty or in under-valuing stolen goods in order to reduce the offence from grand larceny, for which the penalty was death, to petty larceny, the penalty for which was public whipping.[4]

There were also other juries, such as the coroners' and hundredal juries. Members of the latter presented to the court details of any offences committed in their district and a number of these jurors were fined for non-attendance.[5] The attendance of jurors was difficult to enforce and there was sometimes reluctance to accept unpaid responsibility.[6] The Crown tried to ensure that juries were made up of the more substantial persons, prosperous enough to withstand bribery. Sheriffs, however, were said to omit the better-off from panels and 'return the poorer and simple sort, least able to discern the causes in question'.[7]

As the Roll amply demonstrates, when charges were made and process issued against an accused person, in the absence of a paid professional police force he was not easily brought to court. Sheriffs and their officers sometimes felt they were too distant to bother to serve writs and warrants, and were often content to report simply that a defendant could not be found.[8] The accused might flee to the hills or the forests of the county,[9] or

---

[1] Roll, e.g. Monmouth I, 22.

[2] Roll, e.g., Abergavenny, 49, 50.

[3] Cockburn, *Assizes*, p. 129.

[4] Roll, e.g., Monmouth I, 6; Abergavenny, 23; Usk II, 28; Monmouth II, 28. A person at the second Monmouth Gaol Delivery (42) charged with 'the shearing of sheep to the value of 12d.' was found guilty of petty larceny.

[5] Roll, e.g. Usk II, 68–70.

[6] Roger Llyder, who was a member of the grand jury at both the Usk I (7) and Newport sessions (27) was not reluctant to serve, but had an unfortunate name for a juror; his surname closely resembles the Welsh word for 'thief' (lleidr).

[7] P. Williams, *The Tudor regime* (1977), p. 228.

[8] Roll, e.g. Caerleon, 3–33; Newport, 3–8; Usk II, 7–10.

gain the sanctuary of consecrated ground[1] or attach himself to a band of 'followers' or retainers, of which there were still a number in the county, as we have seen; and bailiffs were not above taking bribes. Process issued to the sheriff to procure their attendance at court consisted of a series of writs issued one after another, from sessions to sessions, until those named had come to court to stand trial, or, as previously noted, until outlawed.[2] It would appear from the Roll that process was a slow and cumbersome method of bringing persons to trial. Perhaps in some cases offenders were never brought to trial.

When a transgressor was finally brought to court, and found guilty, his punishment depended on his offence. The sixteenth century possessed a variety of punishments, the broad intention behind them being deterrent and retributive. The insistence on the public nature of punishment, such as hanging, whipping and the pillory, would impress upon the community that wickedness was receiving its just deserts, would shame the offenders and deter potential wrongdoers,[3] and beyond that it performed the wider function of reaffirming the moral boundaries of the society, the watching crowd 'participating in condemning the unacceptable'.[4] The penalties recorded in the Roll are whipping, hanging, branding, imprisonment and fining; the stocks are also mentioned.

The Roll shows that the most common punishment was fining, for a variety of offences, such as defaulting jurors (3s. 4d. each), selling ale without a licence (12d.), the non-appearance of parishes (8s. each) concerning the repair of highways, and individual defaulters on their statute labour (12d. a day). Fines were also imposed for assault (2s.), assault and affray (3s. 4d.), riot and unlawful assembly (2s.), resisting arrest (2s.), and forcible entry (2s.).[5] Fines, together with the valuation placed on stolen goods and murder weapons, were almost always in shillings and pence, although the pound and the mark (13s. 4d.) were occasionally used. The fines were paid to the clerk or sometimes to individual justices.

---

[9] R.R. Davies, *Conquest, coexistence and change. Wales, 1063–1415* (1987), p. 141, refers to the 'daunting' forests of Chepstow, Trellech and Wentwood and to clumps of deciduous trees covering many square miles of upland country south of Usk, which existed in medieval times and undoubtedly were still there in the 16th century.

[1] A criminal taking such refuge had to abjure the realm after 40 days or stand trial; Williams, *Tudor regime*, p. 227.

[2] See Williams, *Caernarvonshire quarter sessions*, pp. xcvii et seq.

[3] Sharpe, *Punishment*, p. 26.

[4] Beattie, *Crime*, p. 469; Sharpe, *Punishment*, pp. 32–3.

[5] Roll, e.g. Newport, 50, 52; Caerleon, 46; Usk II, 81.

Another punishment frequently used was whipping. The penalty was against those found guilty of petty larceny and vagrancy (in a previously cited case one of the vagrants was also branded), although unmarried mothers, and other offenders against sexual morality, might also suffer it. It was carried out in public, usually on market day; the offender was tied either to a whipping post or to the end of a cart, and the punishment was made severe enough to draw blood. Public whipping continued to be ordered until the end of the eighteenth century.

Stocks, which, as previously noted, the law required every village to have, repair and maintain, and which Skenfrith 'has for a long time not had and still has not',[1] was a wooden structure which held the feet of the offender, thus immobilising him, and subjecting him to the public gaze, perhaps ridicule or assault. Its purpose was similar to all other public punishments, to punish, to deter and to give recognition that community values had been transgressed. It was used mainly for minor offences, petty thefts, cheating at cards, excessive drinking, and false accusation. It was also used to hold vagrants before being sent back to their native parish and, if there was no local lock-up, to keep prisoners until they could be taken to the county gaol.

Custody in a gaol was very rarely employed as a form of punishment in itself. A gaol was mainly used as a place to which those suspected of felony were committed by JPs, to await trial by the circuit judges. An instance is recorded in the Roll where the judges committed a convicted prisoner to gaol 'for certain reasons and considerations until they might wish to be further advised thereon', an example, perhaps, of sixteenth-century judges considering any extenuating circumstances in the case, (the prisoner, however, escaped with the alleged connivance of the gaoler).[2] The judges also remanded to prison a number of prisoners 'in the matter of good behaviour',[3] or 'of keeping the peace'; in addition, prisoners sent by the Council in the Marches on suspicion of felony were imprisoned to await trial.[4] Even the briefest stay in prison could be very unpleasant because of gaol fever, plague and other diseases; prisoners lived in cramped and insanitary conditions, were ill-fed and often at the mercy of an unscrupulous gaoler, who was dependent on fees from the prisoners. The general conditions and low level of security resulted in escapes and rescues from

---

[1] Roll, Usk II, 38.
[2] Roll, e.g. Monmouth I, 10.
[3] Roll, e.g. Monmouth I, 16.
[4] Roll, Monmouth I, 33.

prison.[1] There is some evidence, however, that prison was beginning to be seen as a means of punishment in its more modern sense. In 1576 judges were given the option of imprisoning for a year persons to whom benefit of clergy (see below) had been granted. There were, moreover, isolated instances in which a term of imprisonment might be inflicted on convicted offenders, there perhaps to await hanging.[2] The house of correction, most of whose inmates were vagrants or the disorderly local poor who might be amended by its regime of hard labour and correction, was the institution which bore some resemblance to what prisons later became.

Capital punishment took a variety of forms: peers were beheaded; traitors, for acts against the Crown, including counterfeiting the coinage — of which there is an example on the Roll — were hanged, drawn and quartered: for the petty treason of killing his master, a man was drawn on a hurdle and hanged; women, guilty of treason, or petty treason for killing their husband, master or mistress, were burnt at the stake. But the most common form of capital punishment for convicted felons was public hanging. The offences punishable with death at common law were added to in the sixteenth century. The custom of allowing a prisoner to make a gallows speech, in which he expressed his guilt and contrition, and for a clergyman to be present at the execution, to give the prisoner spiritual comfort in his last moments, began in the sixteenth century.

There were a number of 'escape routes' for convicted felons, one of which was by claiming 'benefit of clergy', after conviction but before sentencing. Originally this resulted from the claims of clerics to be subject to the jurisdiction of the church courts (where the penalties were less severe than those of the king's court), even for secular offences; this had resulted in a compromise by which criminous clerics were to be tried in the king's court, but if convicted were to be allowed to claim benefit of clergy and be transferred to the ordinary to be punished. By the later Middle Ages the privilege had been extended to laymen who could pass a literacy test; a felon might escape the gallows if he could 'prove' his clerical status by reading the first verse of the Miserere (Psalm 51, vi). This was the 'neck verse' which the criminal class presumably learnt by rote. Laymen could claim clergy once only and to prevent a second attempt, a statute of 1487 provided for 'felonious clerks', other than real priests, to be branded on the brawn of the left thumb with a 'T' (for thief) or 'M' (murderer) and then turned over to the ecclesiastical authorities. The successful pleading of benefit of clergy

---

[1] Edwards, *Star Chamber Proceedings*, p. 113, assembling of friends by a son, hewing down the door of the county gaol at Caerleon and rescuing the father, committed there by a JP.

[2] Roll, Monmouth I, 14, 18.

is entered on the Roll as 'Po[nit] se [super patriam] cul[pabilem] ca[talla] null[a], legit ut clericus. I[de]o ardetur in manu sua sinistra' ('Puts himself on the country, guilty, no chattels, reads as a cleric. Therefore he is branded on his left hand').[1] The three on the Roll who successfully pleaded clergy, thus passing the literacy test, and escaping hanging, were a glover (grand larceny), a labourer (offence not specified), and a tailor (murder). A statute of 1576 abolished the requirement of being sent to the ordinary; the successful pleading of clergy could be followed by discharge, but the judge, if he saw fit, could send a clergied prisoner to gaol for up to a year. This statute, together with the fact that forbidding clergy to second offenders was not applied consistently, added to the discretionary authority of the judges.[2] The literacy test for benefit was abolished in 1706.

The Tudor period saw a hardening of the criminal code and especially the denial of benefit of clergy for an increasing number of felonies, including burglary, robbery, breaking into a house at night (when there was someone in the house 'put in fear'), murder and rape.[3] The theft of a horse, frequently recorded on the Roll,[4] was regarded as a particularly heinous crime and ineligible for clergy. We learn that among those persons who committed non-clergyable offences more convicts than not escaped the gallows but most horse thieves were hanged.[5] Horse thieves were distinguished from other felons because it was difficult for them to claim that they had stolen out of economic need; the obligation to excuse those who stole from hunger dated from the early Middle Ages. Herrup states that a defence of need could be extended to thefts of livestock that could be eaten,[6] but since horses were not regarded as food, nor even necessarily farm animals (oxen were used for ploughing heavy soil), horse thieves were shown little mercy. The offence was denounced, alone among serious crimes, because it was profitable; the thief had no difficulty in making a profitable sale, and it was felt that his felony had been based on 'calculation and greed'. Common law emphasised the importance of *mens rea* (the intention of the mind) in determining

---

[1] Roll, Monmouth I, 28; Monmouth II, 34, 48.

[2] Beattie, *Crime*, p. 142.

[3] Roll, Newport, 17; Usk II, 26; Monmouth I, 12, 18.

[4] Roll, e.g. Caerleon, 29; Newport, 20; Monmouth I, 7, 8; Abergavenny, 24.

[5] C.B. Herrup, 'Law and morality in seventeenth-century England', *Past and Present*, 106 (1985), 102–23.

[6] However, the Roll records that the death sentence was passed on felons for the theft of two heifers and a cow; Monmouth I, 5, 26. (Beattie, *Crime*, p. 170, claims that sheep and cattle stealing became a capital offence only in the 18th century).

felony.[1] Among other factors which determined criminality was whether an individual had travelled from outside the county, his presence assuming planning that weakened any claim to mercy; however there is nothing on the Roll to suggest that strangers accused of crime were more harshly dealt with than inhabitants of the county.[2]

Justices of the peace in quarter sessions, as well as judges in assizes, had the power to inflict capital punishment. The following felons were sentenced to death during the period covered by the Roll: at Newport quarter sessions, John Lewis and George Baker, labourers, for stealing a purse containing £3 (18), Jevan John, labourer, for stealing a bay gelding valued at four marks, (20); at the first Monmouth Gaol Delivery, Jevan ap Rees, labourer, for the theft of two heifers, each valued at 20s. (5), John ap John Tryley, butcher, for the theft of a heifer (21), Roger Williams, tinker, for the theft of a mare, (23), Thomas Griffith, butcher, for the theft of a cow (26), William Rosser, labourer, guilty on two accounts (not specified) (31); at the second Usk sessions John Williams the elder of Estavarney, yeomen, for the murder by stabbing of John Williams the younger (26). Lewis and Baker appear twice, at Newport and Monmouth (perhaps their sentence at the sessions had to be confirmed at the assizes), as does Jevan Rees, but at the same session (Monmouth I), which may be a clerical error.

Most of these felonies were of grand larceny; there were also a number of cases of petty larceny.[3] Some crimes of violence, too, are recorded, in addition to Williams above. Williams also appears on the calendar of the second Monmouth Gaol Delivery, indicted this time for the same crime (19), together with Matilda ferch William, spinster, (his daughter?), also for the same crime (35). At the same assizes, Watkin John Rosser, labourer, 'not having, in his cups, any fear of God, but seduced by the instigation of the devil', assaulted a man with a 'pyked staffe', from which blow the man died (3). Roger Harry, yeoman, aided and abetted Rosser in the assault, and Harry also harboured him afterwards, knowing him to have committed murder. Harry, at the same assizes, was charged with murder (39). Hugh John Thomas of Rockfield, weaver, was charged with the murder of Hopkin Lace (47), and Thomas John Thomas of Rockfield, tailor (perhaps his brother) was found guilty on the same charge, but escaped the gallows by successfully pleading benefit of clergy (48). At this assizes, also, William George, labourer, was charged with murder by striking his victim on the head with

---

[1] Herrup, 'Law and morality', p. 109.

[2] Roll, e.g. Caerleon, 29, 46; Newport, 17, 20; Monmouth I, 28; Abergavenny, 21, 25; Monmouth II, 51.

[3] Larceny was the taking of property without the threat of violence.

a stone (65). There were, in addition, numerous cases of assault and affray, forcible entry, riot and unlawful assembly, trespass, riot and rout, and the like, with varying degrees of violence, sometimes involving a number of persons and a variety of weapons.

One such incident, an attack on the sheriff's officers, was led by Charles and Hugh Cockes of Skenfrith, gentlemen, with a number of supporters armed with staves, knives, daggers, swords, pikes, lances, bows and arrows and other offensive weapons.[1] There are also references to assaults by a'bastinade', a pike called 'a bearing Bill', an iron pike and a 'pyked staffe'. (there is no mention of firearms). A dagger or knife was frequently used and most people seemed to carry one; but not too much should be made of this since it was needed to cut food and was therefore a necessity.[2] Some twenty persons (most of them labourers), led by Arnold Welshe of Llanwern, gentleman, detained a widow in a house at Dinham, and when the chief constable of the hundred of Caldicot came to arrest them Welshe urged on his followers with the words, 'Kyll hym, kyll hym, thruste hym throwe'.[3] As noted above, violent offences were committed by men under the influence of drink; William ap William *alias* William Grosmont, of Monmouth, cutler, and John Watkins of Llansoy, tailor, at 'about twelve o'clock in the night ... after taking drink', assaulted two Monmouth watchmen.[4] A few clerics were involved in assaults, as victims or assailants.[5] Market-day at Usk seemed to be an occasion for paying off old scores.[6] William Bunting was guilty of a series of assaults and common brawling, mainly in the Monmouth court-house.[7]

The Roll presents a problem in the case of Thomas ap John, *alias* Mason of Brecon, mason, found guilty of 'felony and treason' by counterfeiting

---

[1] Roll, Usk I, 9. Usk II, 81 shows that they were fined 2s. each, Charles Cockes, no longer listed among the defendants, standing surety for them all.

[2] N. Powell, 'Crime and community in Denbighshire', in J.G. Jones (ed.) *Class, community and culture in Tudor Wales* (1989), pp. 261–94.

[3] Roll, Crick, 4, 5. Abergavenny, 14, records that Arnold Welshe of Llanwern, gentleman, could not be found to answer charges against him.

[4] Roll, Monmouth II, 8.

[5] Roll, Caerleon, 30; Abergavenny, 34. Edwards, *Star Chamber Proceedings*, contains five cases of assault on members of the congregation in churches, the most intriguing of which (p. 108) was on a Thomas Pritchard of Llanmartin, gent., by a high constable and others at Llanmartin parish church, the officers refusing to allow the service to commence and forcing the minister and parishioners to depart: the defendants 'claimed that they were attempting to execute a warrant from the sheriff, which they read to the complainant in Latin, English and Welsh'.

[6] Roll, Usk I, 5, 8; Newport, 21.

[7] Roll, Crick, 3.

coinage at the first Monmouth gaol delivery and not guilty, as Thomas ap Mason, at the second.[1] The only case of poaching, by a yeoman, a labourer and 'others unknown', involving taking salmon belonging to the earl of Worcester from several reaches of the River Usk, suggests the existence of an organised gang, poaching possibly for their immediate needs, but more probably to sell on the black market.[2] We are reminded of another sixteenth-century country pursuit in the case of three men entering a wood belonging to William Morgan of Llantarnam and stealing therefrom three 'sparo-hawkes' in a nest.[3]

Many fewer women than men appear on the Roll: perhaps they were considered to be a less serious threat to lives, property and order and victims were more reluctant to charge them than men. Nevertheless, a number of women appear in court, most of them as defendants (sometimes with their husbands), some as assailants (some, too, as victims of assault or rape), some on suspicion of felony, one of 'felony and murder' and committed to prison to await trial. A few women failed to attend court to answer concerning trespass. The term 'spinster' is often used of any women not a widow, including in one instance of girls under fourteen.[4]

The fate of the convicts sentenced to be hanged in 1576–77 is not known; perhaps they were fortunate enough to be among those who escaped hanging. It is possible that the discretionary powers of the judges extended to their granting reprieves to some convicted prisoners at the end of an assize, and of recommending criminals for the sovereign's pardon. The judge might reprieve those who, in his view, had been wrongly convicted by the jury, or any prisoner on whose behalf local gentry and other influential people had interceded. Evidence of this in the sixteenth century is difficult to come by, although something like the eighteenth-century situation, described by Denis Hay and others, where only a minority of criminals ended on the gallows, originated as far back as the fifteenth century.[5]

The felons sentenced to be hanged in Monmouthshire courts in 1576–77 were drawn from the lower orders — most of them were labourers — and the great majority of the offenders who appeared before the sessions and assizes came from the same section of the community. But one should not be tempted to conclude that crime was an activity carried out only or mainly

---

[1] Roll, Monmouth I, 2; Monmouth II, 21.

[2] Roll, Newport, 26.

[3] Roll, Monmouth II, Gaol Delivery, 7.

[4] Roll, e.g. Caerleon, 5, 8; Abergavenny, 31; Monmouth II, Gaol Delivery, 60.

[5] D. Hay, 'Property, Authority and the Criminal law', 17–63, in D. Hay et al. (ed.), *Albion's Fatal Tree* (1975); Sharpe, *Crime*, p. 69.

by the lowest social classes; law-breaking was not the monopoly of the poor. We have seen that some members of the sixteenth-century equivalent of those social groups which were to become 'the backbone of public respectability' were still given to lawless behaviour and not always setting an example of restraint to the middle and lower ranks of the community.

It is as magistrates, however, that the county elite, esquires and above, appear on the Roll (what criterion did the clerk adopt in deciding between the justices he referred to by name in his record of those who attended and the nameless 'other their colleagues'?)[1] Lesser gentry appear as grand jurors and also as defendants. Petty jurors, local minor officers and the majority of the defendants were drawn from the ranks of the lower orders.

In the sixteenth century procedure in criminal trials, some details of which have already been discussed elsewhere in this essay, was much the same in both sessions and gaol delivery.[2] After various preliminaries, the grand jury was sworn, its members taking the oath to 'diligently inquire and true presentment make of all such matters and things as shall be given you in charge ... you shall present no man for envy, hatred or malice ... but in all things you shall present the truth, the whole truth and nothing but the truth'. The jury was charged by the judge in the assizes, and by the chairman in the sessions. There is no mention of the chairman as such on the Roll and in the absence of the custos the chair was taken by the senior justice present. No specimen charge delivered in the Monmouthshire quarter sessions has survived; perhaps it was along similar lines to those delivered by Lambarde in Kent, or to that contained in a late sixteenth-century Hengwrt MS, which explained that their 'matters of charge are ordinarily divided into towe parts': (a) ecclesiastical causes: depraving the sacrament, recusancy and the like; and (b) temporal causes: murder, manslaughter, burglary, the relief of the poor and so on.[3]

After the charge, the grand jury, with the presentments and bills of indictment which had been prepared by the clerk, went to their room, followed by the prosecutor and his witnesses, after they, too, had been sworn. The jury listened to the evidence against each prisoner presented verbally by the prosecutor and witnesses. The accused was not present, nor was he represented. Assize judges and the sessions clerk controlled the flow

---

[1] Roll, e.g., Monmouth I, 1; Abergavenny, 1.

[2] In Elizabeth's reign, Monmouth castle was occasionally delivered at Abergavenny, and the Council in the Marches, as well as circuit judges, delivered Monmouth gaol: Cockburn, *Assizes*, pp. 36–7.

[3] 'A brief discourse of the ordinary charge given to the juries at quarter sessions': K. Williams-Jones (ed.), *A calendar of the Merioneth quarter sessions rolls*, I (1733–65), p. xxxvii.

of evidence to these jurors. On the basis of the prosecution evidence, the jury decided whether a bill of accusation was to be marked '*billa vera*' or '*ignoramus*'. The grand jurors' decision was thus a matter of vital significance. Besides having the major task of deciding whether or not a case should go for trial, this jury also had certain subsidiary duties. They were to consider any presentments made by the hundredal juries, such as that a road was in need of repair. Sometimes they might make a presentment of their own as 'the jury for the body of the county' — as they were sometimes referred to on the Roll — and as such having the right to present the inhabitants of the county for some fault, for example, a bridge in any locality; in this respect they were acting as the 'authentic and legitimate voice of county opinion'.[1] They were mainly concerned, however, with considering all presentments and bills which had been submitted to them by the clerk, and when they had done this, they returned to the court and presented any true bills, which then became indictments. Only rarely was a person against whom an indictment had been made actually present, in custody or in court, and therefore most trials took place at the next sessions, when he heard the charge and was required to plead. If he pleaded 'not guilty', it was usually not until the following sessions that he was tried by a jury; he thus had time to prepare an adequate defence.[2] If the offence was a felony, trial at the assizes followed immediately upon arraignment on the grounds that the accused had been bailed to appear or, more usually, had been in custody. Knowing from his commitment what charge he faced and why he had been brought to court on a particular day, he too had time to think of a defence.

As soon as possible, the person indicted was arraigned before the court. The clerk read the indictment to him, paraphrasing it into English. 'It was obligatory that the indictment be in Latin, but the prisoner was not entitled to have it read in Latin, nor to have a copy of the original, unless he could point out some error in law upon hearing it. This ... was to prevent trifling exceptions to grammar or form.'[3] The clerk then asked him how he pleaded; the court was supposed to ensure that a prisoner did not plead from fear or ignorance, and in cases of doubt to persuade him to plead not guilty. Sometimes, there was plea-bargaining, that is the practice of accepting a half-confession by which a prisoner, protesting his innocence, put himself on the king's mercy in return for a reduced penalty. If the prisoner pleaded 'guilty', the court could pass sentence forthwith, but if he pleaded 'not guilty', to the clerk's next question, 'How wilt thou be tried?', the law

---

[1] Beattie, *Crime*, p. 320.

[2] Roll, Caerleon, 33; Abergavenny, 48–51.

[3] J.H. Baker, 'Criminal Courts and Procedure', in Cockburn (ed.), *Crime*, p. 34.

permitted but one answer, 'By God and the country'. If the prisoner refused to plead or refused to use the required formula or was inclined to be evasive, he was warned of the fate of those who stood 'mute of malice'. In cases of petty larceny and misdemeanour, this led automatically to conviction and judgment followed accordingly; in cases of felony the prisoner was condemned to receive the *peine forte et dure* (abolished in 1772), whereby he was pressed with a gradually increasing weight of iron until he agreed to plead or he died. Some prisoners chose to die in order to protect their dependents from the forfeiture of goods which normally followed conviction.

After a prisoner put himself 'on the country', he was entitled to have any irons removed, for at common law he was to be free from any forcible restraint during his trial. There was no rule that each prisoner should have a separate jury — although at the Abergavenny Quarter sessions, separate juries were sworn for three trials[1] — and the usual practice in the assizes was to arraign about six prisoners at a time for the same jury to try them separately. When enough prisoners had been arraigned the jury was empanelled and sworn: 'You shall well and truly try and true deliverance make between our sovereign lord the King and the prisoners at the bar whom you shall have in charge, and a true verdict give according to your evidence. So help you God'. The prisoner was given an opportunity to challenge the jury, after which he was asked to raise his hand for identification and he was then given into their charge, with the words, 'Look upon the prisoner you that be sworn, and hearken to his cause. You shall understand that he is here indicted' (explaining the indictment in English, that he pleaded not guilty and that they were charged to inquire whether he was guilty or not) ... 'Hear your evidence'. The trial could then begin.

During the trial prisoner could comment on the evidence of witnesses for the prosecution and mount a defence, although it was not until the end of Elizabeth's reign that witnesses in his favour were allowed, but their evidence was heard unsworn. How far a prisoner, perhaps dirty, under-fed and ill after languishing in gaol, was able to present his case successfully depended on his ability to address the jury effectively and cross examine the witnesses, in an unfamiliar and possibly intimidating setting and on whether he had friends on the outside who would be able to arrange for witnesses to be present to speak on his behalf. If he was indicted for felony he was denied the assistance of counsel, unless a point of law arose upon the evidence. It was thought that counsel would 'shadow the matter with words', but if the prisoner defended himself perhaps he might show by the quality and character of his reply to the evidence, facial expression or gesture

---

[1] Roll, Abergavenny, 49–51.

whether he was innocent or guilty. 'That put emphasis on the prisoner's active role. He was very much in the position of having to prove that the prosecutor was mistaken.[1] In any case it was thought that the evidence against a prisoner was so indisputable that it could not be refuted; presumption of innocence had not yet been formulated (not until the end of the eighteenth century). The admission and presentation of evidence, in the absence of counsel (until the end of the seventeenth century), was organised in the sessions by the clerk and in the assizes by the judge. The latter personally cross-examined witnesses and the prisoner and directed comments to the jury during the trial; he thus felt that even if time permitted, a summing-up was not necessary. Most criminal trials were conducted with great rapidity — in part because the judge kept the witnesses to the immediate evidence that related to the issue at hand — during very long sittings in each of the few days assigned to each county, starting early and finishing late.

At the end of the trial, the jury, huddled together in a crowded courtroom, normally brought in a verdict after consulting only briefly. If they wished to retire to consider further, they were put in charge of a jury bailiff who was sworn to keep them without fire or refreshment and free from outside interference.[2] If, on their return, the verdict was 'not guilty', the prisoner was made to kneel and the bench or judge pronounced him to be discharged on paying his fee; despite acquittal he might be bound to good behaviour, if it appeared from the evidence that he had misbehaved. If all members of the jury agreed that he was guilty, the prisoner stood convicted and was led away by the gaoler. Judgement was not given at once, but at the end of the sessions or assizes. Before judgement was given in cases of treason or felony, there was an interval known as the *allocutus*, during which the prisoner was brought to the bar and asked why, when he had been found guilty according to law, he should not have judgement to suffer death. This gave the prisoner, if he so wished, an opportunity to make a speech of mitigation and most especially to make a prayer of clergy, a prayer to allow a pardon, or a prayer for respite of a pregnant woman.[3] All this, together with the judge's wide discretion to reprieve convicted felons, even after sentence, helped to offset those aspects of criminal proceedings which were weighted heavily against the prisoner.

---

[1] Beattie, *Crime*, p. 341.

[2] See M.Ll. Chapman, 'A 16th-century trial for felony in the Court of Great Sessions for Montgomeryshire', *Montgomeryshire Collections*, 78 (1990), 167–70, for the prosecution of the jury for perjury after the return of a perverse verdict, and other interesting aspects of this trial.

[3] Baker, 'Criminal courts and procedure ', in Cockburn, *Crime, 1550–1800*, p. 41.

Until the middle of the sixteenth century, justices in quarter sessions possessed a criminal jurisdiction which rivalled that of the judges of assize, but from then on limitations came to be placed on it.[1] This development began with the two Marian statutes, noted above, by which justices of the peace were to examine suspected felons, commit them to prison, or to bail, to await trial at the assizes, which witnesses for the prosecution were bound over to attend. The justices were to certify depositions concerning felonies to that court. A reduction of their criminal powers continued under Elizabeth, although, as the Roll indicates, they still had authority in the 1570s to hear and determine indictments for felonies brought before them. Assize judges sometimes passed to the clerk of the peace a file of indictments, the majority for misdemeanours, but normally including a few felonies, for decision by quarter sessions. Increasingly, however, quarter sessions were sending the most serious cases to the assizes, and, after about 1590, felonies, were being reserved to the circuit judges, local magistrates concerning themselves mainly with the trial of non-capital offences, their time henceforth being taken up more and more with administrative matters.

---

[1] Cockburn, *Assizes*, p. 90.

6

Conclusion

The government, lacking a standing army and a professional police force, had only 'limited coercive powers';[1] for the implementation of its system of local administration and law enforcement introduced by the Acts of Union, it depended to a great extent on the co-operation and zeal of largely amateur local officials, ranging from sheriffs and justices of the peace of the county to the high constables of the hundreds and the petty constables and other officials of the parishes and townships. The system was working with reasonable efficiency in Monmouthshire in the 1570s, the records showing that the assizes and quarter sessions were meeting regularly (although the proceedings of the latter were occasionally interrupted by riotous assemblies in the streets). There were, however, weaknesses: some hundredal jurors absented themselves from the sessions, an appreciable number of accused persons fled and were not brought to trials, and of those who came before the courts, it is difficult to assess the effectiveness and justice of the trials. Criminal cases in the assizes, and possibly in quarter sessions, were usually dealt with at speed, and it has been claimed that trial and grand juries were 'capricious', that the attitude to evidence was at times 'cavalier', that justices were 'not inhibited from partiality', and that judges made 'little pretence at impartiality', although at times showing mercy.[2] Nevertheless, the assize court was a 'neat means of enforcing the royal law in the localities',[3] and the records of quarter sessions in the county of Monmouth, together with other evidence, demonstrate a general willingness among members of the community to participate in local government and justice.

Local administration was largely dependent upon unpaid, annually appointed and part-time amateurs, which, in spite of complaints about some factious and venal justices and ineffectual officers of the hundreds and parishes, brought certain advantages. One benefit was that the gradations of office-holding corresponded to the social hierarchy, and was suited to a society in which obedience and degree, together with obligations to those below and deference to those above were emphasised, and, at least partly, accepted.[4] A major feature of the system, therefore, was its broad participa-

---

[1] K. Wrightson, *English society, 1580–1680* (1982), p. 149.

[2] P. Williams, *The Tudor regime* (1979), p. 231.

[3] Sharpe, *Crime*, p. 39.

[4] Ibid.

tory base. Thus, not only the higher echelons of society, but its minor gentry, yeomen, husbandmen and artisans, in various capacities, regularly took part. These classes also had important duties in the legal process. In contrast to the magistracy, confined to a comparatively few upper gentry, minor offices, such as membership of the various juries, were dispersed as widely as possible among those eligible, because to depend frequently on a few men was considered to be burdensome to the few and not conducive to good government. Legal service was thus a familiar obligation for many, and certainly for most freeholders.

Similarly, legal authority over criminal matters in the sixteenth century was shared among various groups within the community. Some victims of crime preferred not to prosecute, but for those who did, from their first laying a complaint against a person to the local magistrate to his being sentenced, some two or three dozen men had taken part in the decision-making process, the options of judges or JPs in sentencing being limited by earlier decisions made by others.[1] The system sometimes worked to the advantage of the accused, who often escaped the full rigour of the law. It is an exaggeration to depict the sixteenth century as a brutal age, where life was cheap.

Underpinning the local system of administration of law and order were the justices of the peace, upon whom the energies of the government were centred to ensure that they played their crucial part; most of the Monmouth-shire justices were active in and out of sessions. They were directed and exhorted by the Privy Council and reported on by the Council in the Marches, the lord lieutenants, the bishops and the judges. The result of this sustained pressure was a gradual quickening of county administration. At a more local level, the justices were obliged to rely for the enforcement of the law and co-operation in administration, upon the readiness of individuals to bring breaches of the law to their attention and upon the officials of the county sub-divisions. These officers sometimes felt that preserving good relations with neighbours was more important than the strict enforcement of the law. Lawlessness was not at once eliminated; there was still a tendency to violence in all sections of the community, possibly by the end of our period less among the gentry than the 'ungentle' classes. Nevertheless, there was an increasing ultimate respect for law and order, and, in spite of the frailty of the means of control, the Tudor settlement resulted in a more stable society than had previously existed.

---

[1] Herrup, 'Law and morality', p. 107.

Bibliography

Primary Sources

Manuscript

National Library of Wales: Tredegar Park Manuscripts and Badminton Collection.
Gwent County Record Office: Monmouthshire Quarter Sessions Records.

Printed

Acts of the Privy Council, I–XLIII (1542–1625) (1890–).
Bowen, I., *The statutes of Wales* (1908).
Calendar of State Papers, Domestic, I–XII (1547–1625) (1856–).
Edwards, I. ab O. (ed.), *Catalogue of Star Chamber proceedings relating to Wales* (Cardiff, 1929).
Ellis, H. (ed.), *Original letters illustrative of English history*, 3rd series, III (1861).
Flenley, R. (ed.), *Register of the Council in the Marches of Wales, 1569–1591* (1906).
Jones, E.G. (ed.), *An inventory of Exchequer proceedings (Equity) concerning Wales, Henry VIII–Elizabeth* (Cardiff, 1938).
The itinerary in Wales of John Leland (ed. L.T. Smith, 1906).
Letters and Papers, Foreign and Domestic, Henry VIII, I–XXI (1864–).
Lewis, E.A. (ed.), *An inventory of the early Chancery proceedings concerning Wales* (Cardiff, 1938).
Owen, E. (ed.), *A catalogue of the manuscripts relating to Wales in the British Museum* (Cymmrodorion Record Series, 1900–03).
Phillips, J.R.S., *The Justices of the Peace in Wales and Monmouthshire, 1541–1689* (Cardiff, 1975).
Pugh, T.B., *The Marcher lordships of South Wales, 1415–1536. Select documents* (Cardiff, 1963).
Williams, W.O. (ed.), *Calendar of the Caernarvonshire quarter sessions records. I. 1541–1558* (Caernarfon, 1956).
Williams-Jones, K. (ed.), *A calendar of the Merioneth quarter sessions rolls. I. 1733–65* (Dolegllau, 1965).

Secondary Sources

Ashton, R., *Reformation and revolution, 1558–1660* (1984).

Batho, R., 'Noblemen, gentlemen and yeomen', in J. Thirsk (ed.), *Agrarian history of England and Wales*, IV (Cambridge, 1967), 276–306.

Barnes, T.G. and Smith, A.H., 'Justices of the Peace, 1558–1688', *Bulletin of the Institute of Historical Research*, 33 (1959), 221–42.

Beattie, J.M., *Crime and the courts in England, 1660–1800* (1986).

Ben-Amos, I.K., *Adolescence and youth in early modern England* (New Haven, Conn., 1994).

Bradney, J.A., *A history of Monmouthshire from the coming of the Normans into Wales down to the present time*, I–IV (1904–33).

Bradney, J.A. (ed. M. Gray), *A history of Monmouthshire. V. The Lordship of Newport* (South Wales Record Society, 1993).

Chapman, M.Ll. (ed.), 'A 16th-century trial for felony in the Court of Great Sessions for Montgomeryshire', *Montgomeryshire Collections*, 78 (1990), 167–70.

Clark, P., *The English alehouse* (1983).

Cockburn, J.S., *A history of English assizes, 1558–1714* (Cambridge, 1972).

(ed.), *Crime in England, 1500–1800* (1977).

'Introduction', in idem (ed.), *Calendar of Assize Rolls* (1985).

Courtney, P., 'The rural landscape of eastern and lower Gwent, 1070–1750' (University of Wales [Cardiff] Ph.D. thesis, 1983).

Medieval and later Usk (Cardiff, 1994).

Cross, C. *et al.* (ed.), *Law and government under the Tudors* (Cambridge, 1988).

Davies, J.C., 'Report on the records of the county of Monmouth' (Typescript in Gwent County Record Office, 1939–40).

Davies, R.R. et al (ed.), *Welsh society and nationhood* (Cardiff, 1984).

Conquest, coexistence and change. Wales. 1063–1415 (Oxford, 1987).

Dictionary of National Biography (1885–1900).

Dictionary of Welsh Biography (1959).

Duffy, E., *The stripping of the altars. Traditional religion in England, 1400–1580* (New Haven, Conn., 1992).

Elton, G.R., *The Tudor constitution* (Cambridge, 1982).

Emery, F., 'The farming regions of Wales', in J. Thirsk (ed.), *Agrarian history of England and Wales*, IV (Cambridge, 1967), 113–60.

Fletcher, A., *Reform in the provinces* (1986).

Fletcher, A. and Stevenson, J. (ed.), *Order and disorder in early modern England* (Cambridge, 1984).

Fletcher, J.K., *The Gwentian poems of Dafydd Benwyn* (Cardiff, 1909).

Foss, E., *Judges of England* (1870).

Fox, C. and Raglan, Lord, *Monmouthshire Houses* (Cardiff, 1951–54).

Gray, M., 'The dispersal of crown property in Monmouthshire, 1500–1603' (University of Wales [Cardiff] Ph.D. thesis, 1984).

'Change and continuity: the gentry and the property of the Church in south-east Wales and the Marches', in J.G. Jones (ed.), *Class, community and culture in Tudor Wales* (Cardiff, 1989).

Griffiths, M., 'The emergence of the modern settlement pattern, 1450–1700' in D.H. Owen (ed.), *Settlement and society in Wales* (Cardiff, 1987), 225–48.

'Country and town', in T. Herbert and G.E. Jones (ed.), *Tudor Wales* (Cardiff, 1988).

Griffith, W.P., 'Beth oedd y dyn Tuduraidd?' in D.G. Jones and J.G. Jones (ed.), *Bosworth a'r Tuduriaid* (Caernarfon, 1985), 31–39.

Guy, J. *Tudor England* (Oxford, 1988).

Hale, J. *The civilization of Europe in the renaissance* (1993).

Hartley, T.E. 'Under-sheriffs and bailiffs in some English shrievalties, *c*.1580–*c*.1625', *Bull. Inst. Historical Research*, 47 (1974), 164–85.

Hay, D. *et al. Albion's fatal tree* (1974).

Hayes, H. *Cymru a'r Dadeni* (Bangor, 1987).

Heard, N. *Tudor economy and society* (1992).

Herbert, T. and Jones, G.E. (ed.), *Tudor Wales* (Cardiff, 1988).

Herrup, C.B. 'Law and morality in seventeenth-century England', *Past and Present*, 106 (1985), 102–23.

Howell, B. 'Local administration in Monmouthshire, 16th–19th centuries' (University of Wales [Cardiff] M.A. thesis, 1951).

Howell, B.'Local administration and law enforcement in 16th-century Monmouthshire.' (University College, Cardiff, Local History Diploma dissertation, 1991).

Howell, R. *A history of Gwent* (Llandysul, 1988).

Howells, B. 'Society, 1536–1642', *Pembrokeshire County History*, III (Haverfordwest, 1987), 32–59.

'Government and politics, 1536–1642', *Pembs. County History*, III, 126–58.

'The lower orders', in T. Herbert and G.E. Jones (ed.), *Tudor Wales* (Cardiff, 1988), 41–66.

'The lower orders of society', in J.G. Jones (ed.), *Class, community and culture in Tudor Wales* (Cardiff, 1989), 237–59.

Hunt, J. 'Monmouthshire wills proved in the Prerogative Court of Canterbury, 1414–1560' (University College, Cardiff, Local History Diploma Dissertation, 1985).

Jenkins, G.H. *Hanes Cymru, 1530–1760* (Cardiff, 1983).

Jones, B.P. *From Elizabeth I to Victoria. Newport, Mon., 1558–1850* (Newport, 1957).

Jones, F. 'Welsh genealogy', *Trans. Hon. Soc. Cymmrodorion* (1948), 303–466.

Jones, G.E. *The gentry and the Elizabethan state* (Swansea, 1977).

Modern Wales, 1485–1979 (Cambridge, 1984).

Jones, J.G. *Wales and the Tudor state* (Cardiff, 1989).

Y Morganiaid o Dredegyr (Casnewydd, 1988).

(ed.). *Class, community and culture in Tudor Wales* (Cardiff, 1989).

'Hanfodion undod gwladwriaethol cyfraith a threfn yng Nghymru cyfnod y Tuduriaid, tystiolaeth beirdd yr uchelwyr', *Llên Cymru*, 15 (1984–86), Rhif 1–2, tt. 24–105.

'Concepts of continuity and change after the Act of Union, 1536–1603', *Anglesey Antiquarian & Field Club Transactions* (1990), 22–57.

Concepts of order and gentility in Wales, 1540–1640 (Llandysul, 1992).

Cymru a'r Tuduriaid (Aberystwyth, 1993).

Early modern Wales, c. 1525–1640 (1994).

Jones, J.M. 'Monmouthshire wills proved in the Prerogative Court of Canterbury, 1560–1601' (University of Wales [Cardiff] M.A. thesis, 1990).

Kent, J. 'The English village constable', *Journal of British Studies*, 20 (1981), 26–49.

Kissack, K. *Monmouth. The making of a county town* (Chichester, 1975).

Lloyd, H.A. *The gentry of south west Wales, 1540–1640* (Cardiff, 1968).

Maitland, F.W. *Constitutional history of England* (Cambridge, 1908).

Martin, G.H. and Spufford, P. *The records of the nation* (Woodbridge, 1990).

Merrick, R. *Morganiae Archaiographia* (ed. B.Ll. James) (South Wales Record Society, 1983).

Miller, A.C. 'William Morgan of Pencoed', *Welsh History Review*, 9 (1978–79), 1–31.

Owen, G. *Description of Penbrokshire*, III (ed. H. Owen) (Cymmrodorion Record Series, 1906).

Owen, G.D. *Elizabethan Wales* (Cardiff, 1962).

Palliser, D.M. *The age of Elizabeth. England under the later Tudors, 1547–1603* (2nd ed. 1992).

History of Parliament. The House of Commons, 1509–1558 (1982); *The House of Commons, 1558–1603* (1981).

Pound, J. *Poverty and vagrancy in Tudor England* (1971).

Powell, N. 'Crime and community in Denbighshire', in J.G. Jones (ed.), *Class, community and culture in Tudor Wales* (Cardiff, 1989), 261–94.

Pugh, T.B. 'The ending of the Middle Ages, 1485–1536', in *Glamorgan County History*, III (Cardiff, 1971), 555–87.

Read, C. (ed.), *William Lambarde and local government* (Ithaca, N.Y., 1962).

Rees, W. 'The Union of England and Wales', *Trans. Hon. Soc. Cymmrodorion*, 1937, 27–100.

Reeves, A.C. *Newport lordship, 1317–1536* (Newport, 1979).

Riden, P. *Record sources for local history* (1987).

Roberts, P.R. 'Wales and England after the Tudor Union: Crown, Principality and Parliament, 1553–1624', in C. Cross *et al.* (ed.), *Law and government under the Tudors* (Cambridge, 1988).

'The Welsh language, English law and Tudor legislation', *Trans. Hon. Soc. Cymmrodorion* (1989), 19–75.

'The Union with England and the identity of "Anglican" Wales', *Trans. Royal Historical Soc.*, 5th series, 22 (1972), 49–70.

'The Welshness of the Tudors', *History Today* (Jan. 1986), 7–13.

Robinson, W.R.B., 'Patronage and hospitality in early modern Wales: the role of Henry, earl of Worcester, 1526–1549', *Bull. Institute of Historical Research*, 51 (1978–79), 20–36.

'The officers and household of Henry, earl of Worcester, 1526–49', *Welsh History Review*, 8 (1976), 26–41.

'The *Valor Ecclesiasticus* of 1535 as evidence of agrarian output', *Bull. Inst. Historical Research*, 56 (1983), 16–33.

Russell, C. *Parliament and English politics, 1621–9* (Oxford, 1979).

'The bourgeois revolution: a mirage?', *History Today* (Sept. 1990), 7–9.

Sharpe, J.A. *Crime in early modern England* (1984).

Judicial punishment in England (1990).

Smith, A.G.R. *The emergence of a nation state. The Commonwealth of England, 1529–1660* (1984).

Somerville, R. *The Duchy of Lancaster. I. 1265–1603* (1953).

Stephens, E. *The clerks of the counties* (Warwick, 1961).

Stitch, B. 'Population movement and migration in pre-industrial rural England', in B. Short (ed.), *The English rural community* (Cambridge, 1992).

Stone, L. *The crisis of the aristocracy* (1965).

Tate, W.E. *The parish chest* (Cambridge, 1967).

Thomas, K. *Religion and the decline of magic* (1971).

Tiller, K. *English local history* (Gloucester, 1992).

Webb, J.G. 'Parliamentary taxation in Monmouthshire' (University of Wales [Cardiff] M.A. thesis, 1987).

Webb, S. and B. *English local government. V. The story of the king's highway* (1929).

Whittle, E.H. 'The sixteenth- and seventeenth-century gardens at Raglan Castle', *Monmouthshire Antiquary*, 6 (1990), 159–93.

Wiliam, E. 'Domestic architecture', in J.G. Jones, *Class, community and culture in Tudor Wales* (Cardiff, 1989), 159–96.

Williams D. *A history of modern Wales* (1977).

'A note on the population of Wales, 1536–1801', *Bull. Board of Celtic Studies*, 8 (1937), 359–63.

Williams, D.H. 'Monmouth Priory at the suppression, 1534–37', *Monmouthshire Antiquary*, 3 (1970–78), 186–91.

Williams, Glanmor. *Recovery, reorientation and Reformation. Wales 1415–1642* (Oxford, 1987).

'The economic life of Glamorgan, 1536–1642', *Glamorgan County History*, IV (Cardiff, 1974), 1–72.

'Glamorgan society, 1536–1642', *Glamorgan County History*, IV (Cardiff, 1974), 73–141.

Williams, G.J. *Traddodiad llenyddol Morgannwg* (Caerdydd, 1948).

Williams, Penry. *The Tudor regime* (1979).

The Council in the Marches of Wales under Elizabeth I (Cardiff, 1958).

'The Welsh borderland under Elizabeth I', *Welsh History Review*, 1 (1960–63), 19–36.

'The political and administrative history of Glamorgan, 1536–1642', *Glamorgan County History*, IV (Cardiff, 1974), 143–201.

Williams, W.O. 'The survival of the Welsh language', *Welsh History Review*, 2 (1964), 67–93.

Wrightson, K. *English society, 1580–1680* (1982).

'Two concepts of order: justices, constables and jurymen in seventeenth-century England', in J. Brewer and J. Styles (ed.), *An ungovernable people* (1980), 21–46.

A Calendar of the Monmouthshire Quarter Sessions and Gaol Deliveries Roll of 18–19 Elizabeth I (1576–77)

The Roll

The Roll is to be found among the Tredegar Manuscripts and Documents in the National Library of Wales, where it is scheduled as Tredegar 148. It consists of 25 membranes, each closely written on both sides in Latin (except for three deeds in English, and a sprinkling of English words and phrases); the membranes measure 231 mm. in width and vary in length between approximately 700 and 800 mm. The document is written throughout in the same hand, except where otherwise indicated in the calendar.

An unusual feature of the Roll is that it contains the proceedings of both quarter sessions and gaol delivery. The records of the two courts, each of which had its own clerk, were usually kept on separate files, but as the two courts were complementary in various ways, occasionally gaol delivery proceedings are to be found among quarter sessions records, as for instance in both Staffordshire and Essex.[1] It is, however, exceptional, if not unique, for the records of the two courts to be on the same roll, as is the case in the document calendared here.

A note, written in a modern hand, enclosed with the Roll explains that it was found among some old documents in the study at Tredegar House. It was the only document of its kind there, and was probably preserved by having come into the custody of the Tredegar family from the fact that it contained, in the records of the Usk Quarter Sessions, held on 11 June 1577, the enrolment of a deed of bargain and sale relating to the Tredegar estate, as required by law.[2]

---

[1] In response to an enquiry, the Staffordshire Record Office stated that amongst that county's quarter sessions rolls there are 'occasional proceedings of Gaol Delivery with particular sessions, e.g. Epiphany 1608–09, and a few documents relating to gaol delivery or assizes have been bound up with the quarter sessions rolls'. F.G. Emmison, *Guide to the Essex Record Office* (1969), p. 4, explains that among that county's QS records are two assize rolls (1565) and occasional documents emanating from assizes.

[2] See below, pp. 78–80.

In an age when there was considerable negligence and indifference by county and other officials in obligations towards the proper care of records, Arthur Agarde, *c.* 1600, regarded as 'the father of modern archival practice', wrote that there were four causes of 'wrack to records ... fire, water, rats and mice and misplacing', all of which could be prevented by 'diligence', but there was a fifth, even greater danger to records and that was the 'plain taking of them away'.[1] If the latter is what the Tredegar family did with the Roll of 1576–77 then it helped to preserve, not to lose, the document. Indeed, in the seventeenth century there are two examples in Wales of the preservation of county records by their inclusion in the archives of prominent county families: in the muniments of the Vaughans of Llwydiarth there are a number of Montgomeryshire Quarter Sessions rolls for the period 1614–20, and the Chirk Castle papers of the Myddletons contain the Denbighshire Quarter Sessions rolls for 1643–99.[2]

Monmouthshire shared in the general improvement in the care and custody of county and other official records which began in the eighteenth century and its virtually unbroken run of quarter sessions documents begins in 1719.[3]

Editorial Method

As in all documents of this class, there is much repetition of identical Latin phraseology for similar types of entries. It seemed pointless to repeat this in full each time and thus generally one example is given in full of the original Latin but only a summary of other entries of a similar nature.

The abbreviated Latin of the original text has been extended. The extensions are not indicated except in some of the marginal notes in the text, where square brackets are used. Round brackets are used for other explanatory matter.

Quotations from the original text are enclosed in double inverted commas, translation in single inverted commas.

The entries for each sessions have been given serial numbers to facilitate reference.

---

[1] E.M. Hallam, 'Nine centuries of keeping the public records', in G.H. Martin and P. Spufford (ed.), *The records of the nation* (1990), p. 23.

[2] K. Williams-Jones (ed.), *A calendar of the Merionethshire quarter sessions rolls. Vol. I. 1733–65* (1965), p. xxiii.

[3] W.H. Baker, *Guide to the Monmouthshire Record Office* (Newport, 1959), p. 16.

The spelling of place-names as in the original document has been retained throughout, but this seemed less appropriate in the case of personal names. In view of the original writer's invariable habit of Latinising the first of a series of Christian names and of surnames, it has been thought better to subject both Latin and English forms of personal names to the same treatment by representing them all by the recognised modern equivalent, as far as possible. Even so, some have been retained in the form found in the Rolls, including unusual names such as Alsona and Ssela and 'trade' names such as Sayre, Bochor and Ygove (*Y gof*, smith). Only an arbitrary choice can be made between Jacob and James for Jacobus, Hugh and Hugo for Hugo, or Anne and Anna for Anna. The Roll shows that many people were still using Welsh patronymic names.

During 1576–77 the court sat at Caerleon (pp. 5–21), Usk (pp. 22–26), Newport (pp. 27–37), Monmouth (also gaol delivery) (pp. 39–47), Crick (pp. 48–49), Raglan (pp. 50–51), Abergavenny (pp. 52–63), Usk again (pp. 64–80) and Monmouth again (once more including a gaol delivery) (pp. 81–90). The Crick sessions preceded the first Monmouth sessions and gaol delivery but is entered after it in the original text.

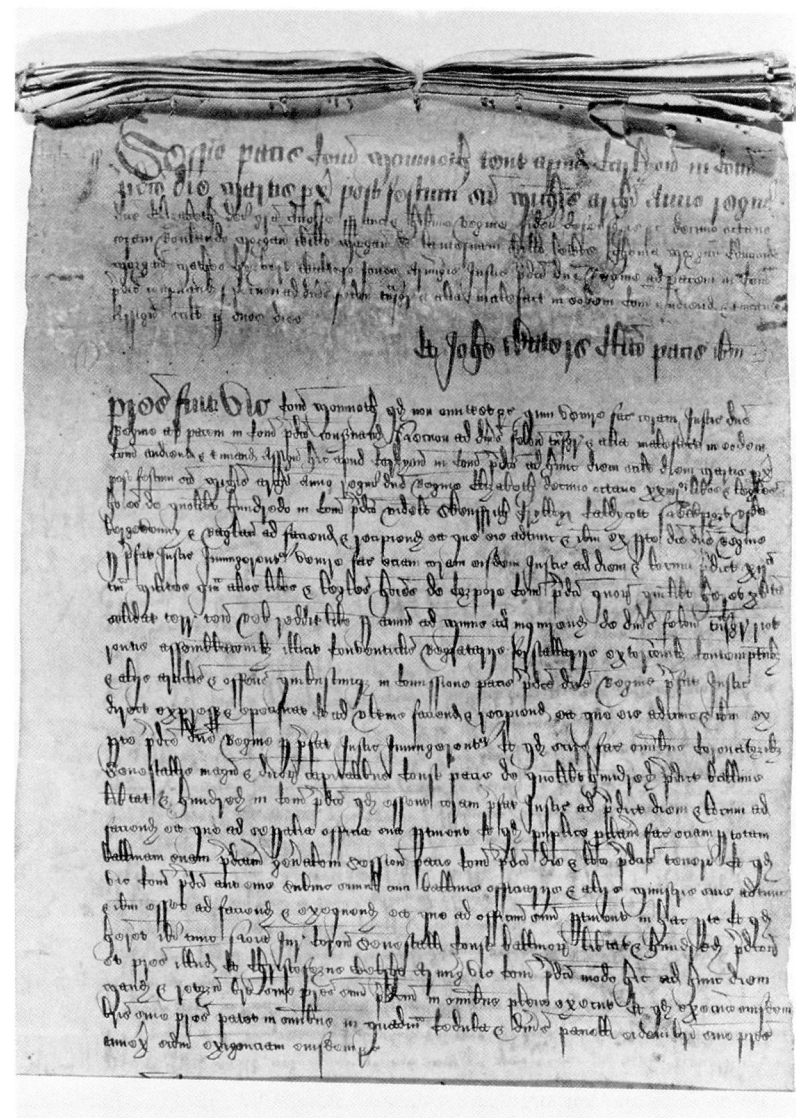

Plate 1. The first two entries of the Quarter Sessions held at Caerleon, the first sitting of the justices entered on the Roll. See opposite for a transcript and translation.

4

Caerleon

Left hand margin: "Carlyon"
1. "SESSIO PACIS Comitatus Monmoth tenta apud Carlyon in Comitatu predicto die Martis proximo post Festum Sancti Michaelis Archangeli anno regni Domine Elizabeth Dei gratia Anglie ffrancie et Hibernia Regine, Fidei Defensoris, etc. decimo octavo coram Roulando Morgan, Will Morgan de Lanternam, Williamus Lewys, Thoma Morgan, Edmundo Morgan, Matheo Herbert, Waltero Jones, armigeris, Justiciariis predicte Domine Regine ad pacem in Comitatu predicto conservandam Necnon ad diversas felonias, transgressiones et alia malefacta in eodem Comitatu audienda et terminanda assignatis, scilicet per duos dies,
   Et JOHANNE WATERS, Clerico Pacis ibidem."

'SESSION OF THE PEACE of the County of Monmoth held at Carlyon in the aforesaid county on the Tuesday next after the Feast of Saint Michael the Archangel in the eighteenth year of the reign of our Sovereign Lady Elizabeth, by the grace of God of England, France, and Ireland Queen, Defender of the Faith, etc., before Rowland Morgan, Williarn Morgan of Lanternam, William Lewis, Thomas Morgan, Edmund Morgan, Mathew Herbert, Walter Jones, Esquires, Justices of the aforesaid Sovereign Lady the Queen assigned to preserve the peace in the aforesaid County and also to hear and determine divers felonies, trespasses and other misdemeanours in the same County, that is to say for two days,
   And (before) John Waters, Clerk of the Peace of the same place'

2. "PRESCRIPTUM FUIT VICECOMITI Comitatus Monmoth quod non omitteret etc. quin venire faceret coram Justiciariis Domine Regine ad pacem in Comitatu predicto conservandam Necnon ad diversas felonias, transgressiones, et alia malefacta in eodem Comitatu audienda et terminanda assignatis hic apud Carlyon in Comitatu predicto ad hunc diem, scilicet diem Martis proximum post Festum Sancti Michaelis Archangeli anno regni Domine Regine Elizabeth decimo octavo, xxiiij liberos et legales homines de quolibet Hundredo in Comitatu predicto, videlicet Skenffrith, Trylleg, Caldycott, Newport, Uske, Bergevenny, et Raglan ad facienda et recipienda ea que eis adtunc et ibidem ex parte dicte Domine Regine per prefatos Justiciarios inungerentur: Venire faceret etiam coram eisdem Justiciariis ad diem et locum predictos xij tam milites quam alios liberos et legales homines de corpore comitatus predicti quorum quilibet haberet xls. solidate terre

tenementorum vel redditorum libere per annum, ad minus, ad inquirendum de diversis feloniis, transgressionibus, riotis, routis, assembacionibus illicitis, conventiclis, regratariis, forstallariis, extorcionibus, contemptubus, et aliis articulis et offensis quibuscunque in commissione pacis predicte Domine Regine per prefatos Justiciarios directis expressis et specificatis, et ad ulterius faciendum et recipiendum ea que eis adtunc et ibidem ex parte predicte Domine Regine per prefatos Justiciarios iniungerentur: Et quod scire faceret omnibus coronatoribus, senescallis magnatorum et dominorum, capitalibus constabulariis pacis de quolibet Hundredo predicto, quod essent coram prefatis Justiciariis ad predictum diem et locum ad faciendum ea que ad separalia officia sua pertinent et quod puplice (*sic*) proclamacionem faceret etiam per totam ballivam suam predictam generalem Sessionem pacis Comitatus predicti die et loco predictis teneri et quod Vicecomes Comitatus predicti aut eius subvicecomes simul cum ballivis, officiariis, et aliis ministris suis adtunc et ibidem esset ad faciendum et exequendum ea que ad officium suum pertinent in hac parte et quod haberet ibi tunc nomina juratorum, coronatorum, senescallorum, constabulariorum, ballivorum libertatum et Hundredorum predictorum et prescriptum illud. Et Christoferus Welshe, armiger, Vicecomes Comitatus predicti modo hic ad hunc diem mandat et retornat breve sive prescriptum suum in omnibus plene executum, Et quod executio eiusdem brevis sive prescripti patet in omnibus in quadam cedula et diversis pannellis eidem brevi sive prescripto annexis secundum exigenciam eiusdem etc."

'ORDER HAS BEEN MADE to the Sheriff of the County of Monmoth that he should not fail etc. to cause to come before the Justices of the Sovereign Lady the Queen assigned to preserve the peace in the aforesaid County, And also to hear and determine divers felonies, trespasses, and other misdemeanours in the same County, here at Carlyon in the County aforesaid on this day, that is to say the Tuesday next after the Feast of Saint Michael the Archangel in the eighteenth year of the reign of the Sovereign Lady Elizabeth, 24 free and loyal men from each Hundred in the aforesaid County, namely Skenffrith, Trylleg, Caldycott, Newport, Uske, Bergevenny, and Raglan to do and to receive those things which then and there might be enjoined on them by the aforesaid Justices on the behalf of the said Sovereign Lady the Queen; And that he should cause to come also before the same Justices on the day and to the place aforesaid 12 as well knights as other free and loyal men from the body of the aforesaid County of whom each should have at least 40*s.* of freehold land, tenements, or rents freely per annum to make enquiry concerning divers felonies, trespasses, riots, routs, unlawful assemblies, conventicles, regratings, forestallings, extortions, contempts, and other articles and offences whatsoever directed, expressed and specified by the aforesaid Justices in the commission of the peace of the aforesaid Sovereign Lady the Queen; And further to do and receive those things which then and there might be enjoined on them by the aforesaid Justices on the behalf of the aforesaid Sovereign Lady the Queen. Further that he should make known to all coroners, seneschals of magnates and lords, chief constables of the peace of every Hundred aforesaid, and bailiffs of liberties and Hundreds in the aforesaid County, that they should be before the aforesaid Justices on the day and in the place aforesaid to do those things which appertain to their several offices and that he should also publicly make proclamation throughout his bailiwick that the aforesaid general Session of the peace of the aforesaid County is to be held on the day and in the place aforesaid; and that the Sheriff of the aforesaid County or his deputy together with his bailiffs, officers, and other servants should then and there be present to do and to execute those things which appertain to their office in this behalf, and that he should have there then the names of the jurors, coroners, seneschals, constables, and of the bailiffs of the liberties and Hundreds aforesaid and that order. And Christopher Welshe, Esquire, Sheriff of the aforesaid County, now here on this day delivers and returns his writ or order fully executed in all points and (declares) that the execution of the same writ or order is set forth in all points in a certain schedule and in the divers lists annexed to the same writ or order in accordance with the requirement of the same etc.'

3. L.H. Margin: "Carlyon"
"PRESCRIPTUM FUIT ETIAM eidem Vicecomiti quod exigi faceret Williamum Jenkyn nuper de Llanvapley in Comitatu Monmoth, yoman, de Comitatu in Comitatum quousque etc. utlageretur. Si non etc. Et si etc. tunc eum caperet et salve etc. ita quod haberet corpus eius coram Justiciariis Domine Regine ad pacem in Comitatu predicto conservandam Necnon ad diversas felonias, transgressiones, et alia malefacta in eodem Comitatu audienda et terminanda assignatis ad hanc generalem Sessionem pacis hic apud Carlyon in Comitatu predicto ad hunc diem, scilicet diem Martis proximum post Festum Sancti Michaelis Archangeli anno regni Domine Regine Elizabeth decimo octavo ad respondendum eidem Domine Regine de quibusdam feloniis et raptis de quibus ipse indictatus existit. Et Vicecomes Comitatus predicti, videlicet Christoferus Welshe, armiger, non misit neque retornavit breve sive prescriptum predictum. Et ipse non venit. Ideo prescriptum est eidem Vicecomiti sicut alias quod de novo exigi faciat predictum Will Jenkyn de Comitatu in Comitatum quousque etc. utlagetur. Si non etc. Et si etc. tunc eum capiat et salve etc. ita quod habeat corpus eius coram prefatio Justiciariis ad proximam generalem Sessionem pacis Comitatus predicti proximam post Festum Pasche proximum futurum

tenendam, ubicunque etc. ad respondendum Domine Regine in forma
predicta.

per breve IX Novembris anno regni
Regine Elizabeth XVIj."

L.H. Margin at end: "Ex[igi] de novo," 'to be summoned again.'

'ORDER HAS ALSO BEEN MADE to the same Sheriff that he should
cause William Jenkins late of Llanvapley in the County of Monmoth,
yeoman, to be summoned from County-court to County-court until etc. he
should be outlawed. If not etc. And if etc. then he should take him and
safely etc., so that he might have his body before the Justices of the
Sovereign Lady the Queen assigned to preserve the peace in the aforesaid
County and also to hear and determine divers felonies, trespasses, and other
misdemeanours in the same County, at this general Sessions of the peace
here at Carlyon in the aforesaid County on this day, that is to say the
Tuesday next after the Feast of Saint Michael the Archangel in the
eighteenth year of the reign of the Sovereign Lady Elizabeth, to answer to
the same Sovereign Lady the Queen concerning certain felonies and thefts
of which he stands indicted. And the Sheriff of the aforesaid County, namely
Christopher Welshe, Esquire, has not sent nor returned the aforesaid writ or
order. And he himself (i.e. the defendant) has not come, etc. Therefore order
is made to the same Sheriff that he shall cause the aforesaid William Jenkins
to be summoned anew from County-court to County-court until etc. he be
outlawed. If not etc. And if etc. then he shall take him and safely etc. so that
he may have his body before the aforesaid Justices at the next general
Sessions of the peace of the aforesaid County to be held after the Feast of
Easter next following, wheresoever etc., to answer to the Sovereign Lady the
Queen in the form aforesaid.

By writ of the 9th November in the 17th year
of the reign of the Queen Elizabeth.'

4. The Sheriff reports (in a form identical with that of No 3 above) that,
acting on a writ, he failed to find Thomas Baker late of Bergevenny,
labourer, and Nicholas Thomas of Comeyoy, husbandman, required to
answer concerning certain felonies and murders. He makes return that 'they
have not come etc.' The Justices direct a new order, that the offenders
should appear before them at the next Easter Session.

Similar reports of the Sheriff from Nos 5–11 (incl.):

5. In the case of Katherine Jenkin, wife of Thomas William John, late of Pennalth, "spynster" required to answer concerning a certain trespass. A new order for her appearance at the next Epiphany Session.
By a writ of 12th March, 18 Elizabeth.

6. In the case of William Morgan John of Pennecoyde, John Richards of Aberustoyth, Charles Watkin of Llandylowe Barthalowe, William John Philips of the same town, Reginald John ap Jenkin of Aberustoyth, all yeomen, William Herbert of Llanvehangell Cylcornell, gentleman, John Philip Thomas, of Comeyoy, yeoman, David Williams of Llanveyre Kylgedyn, tinker, John Mathew of Llannyssen, otherwise called John Mathew of Rompney, gentleman, Morgan Spriggin of Llannyssen, yeoman, and John Miller of Bethowesnewyth, required to answer concerning certain trespasses and contempts. A new order for their appearance at the next Epiphany Session.
Original writ; Epiphany 18 Elizabeth.

7. In the case of Philip Edwards of Uske, John Edwards of Uske, Dionina ferch Jenkin wife of the aforesaid Philip Edwards, spinster, Reginald Roberts of Comeyoy, labourer, Rees ap Jenkin of Bergevenny, corvisor, Robert James of Llantellyo Cryssenny, glover, George Thomas of Treergayre, Rees David Sant of Grussemont, James (or Jacob) David Williams of the same town, John Harries of Saynt Moughan, Richard Sadde of the same town, Henry Wilcocke, of Llangewa, John ap Jenkin of Dyngestowe, John Parke of the same town, Jenkin ap John of Llangattock Vybon Avell, Philip Jenkin Apowell Williams of Llantellyo Cryssenny, Stephen ap Rees of Llanvehangell Ystemllewren, Watkin Howell Thomas of Llantellyo aforesaid and Richard ap Jenkin of Bergevenny, corviser, (all yeomen except otherwise stated) required to answer concerning certain trespasses and contempts. A new order for their appearance at the next Epiphany Session.
Original writ; Easter 18 Eliz.

8. In the case of Margaret ferch Hopkin of Aberustoyth, widow, required to answer concerning certain trespasses and 'entry where entry is not allowed by law.' He makes return 'that he has nothing in his bailiwick by which she can be attached.' A new order for her appearance at the next Epiphany Session.
Original writ; 27th July, 18 Elizabeth.

9. In the case of William Hughes of Monmoth, John Morris of Carlyon, John William Hughes of Uske, William Morris Hughes of Uske, all yeomen, Thomas Roberts, Dyngestowe, gentleman, and Rees Jenkins of the town of Newport, tanner, required to answer concerning certain trespasses and contempts. A new order for their appearance at the next Epiphany Session. Original writ; Trinity, 18 Elizabeth.

10. In the case of John Morris of Carlyon, yeoman, otherwise called John Hughes of Carlyon, yeoman, John William Hughes of Uske, yeoman, John Morris Hughes of Uske, tailor, William Morris Hughes of Uske, tanner, James Hughes of Uske, labourer, and Rees Jenkins of the town of Newport, tanner, required to answer concerning certain divers trespasses and contempts. A new order for their appearance at the next Epiphany Session.[1] Original writ; Trinity 18 Elizabeth.

11. In the case of Philip ap David of Llangom, weaver, Jenkin David of the town of Monmoth, labourer, and Rees Jenkins of the town of Newport, tanner, required to answer concerning certain trespasses and contempts. A new order for their appearance at the next Epiphany Session.

12. L.H. Margin: "Relaxatio [securitatis] pacis."
"Ad hanc Sessionem venit Georgius Harryes et gratis remisit et relaxavit securitatem pacis quam prius habuit versus Howellum Williams de Llansoy in Comitatu Monmoth, yoman. Ideo ipse de ulteriore securitate pacis invenienda versus predictum Georgium Harryes exoneratur."

'To this Session came George Harries and freely remitted and released the security of the peace which he formerly held against Howell Williams of Llansoy in the County of Monmoth, yeoman. Therefore he (i.e. Howell Williams) is released from finding further security of the peace towards the aforesaid George Harries.'

13. L.H. Margin: identical with No 12.
Meredith John Nicholas of Ytton and Anna his wife, bound over to keep the peace towards John Morgan Ll'en (Llewelen) by Thomas Watkin, Esquire, are released from their recognisances.

---

[1] The formula of the Sheriff's return reads 'quod non sunt inventi in balliva sua per quod possunt attachiari.' Clearly, 'et nihil habent in balliva sua' is required before 'per quod'.

14. L.H. Margin: identical with No 12.
Morris Gwilym of Rochefyld, bound over to keep the peace towards Walter
Jones, *alias* Spicer, and Thomas Spicer at the last Easter Session, is released
from his recognisances.

15. L.H. Margin: identical with No 12.
Llewelen Bochor (no town given) relinquishes the security which he held
against Rees Jenkins of Newport, who is accordingly released from his
recognisances.

16. L.H. Margin: identical with No 12.
John Jones of Llandylowe Barthalowe, clerk, John William Philip Nicoll of
Comeyoy, Henry John Philip Nicoll of Comeyoy, and Nicholas ap Robert of
Comeyoy, all yeomen, bound over at the preceding Corpus Christi Session
to keep the peace towards John Thomas, are released from their recogni-
sances.

17. L.H. Margin: identical with No 12.
John Thomas of Comeyoy, bound over at the preceding Corpus Christi
Session to keep the peace towards the above-mentioned John Jones, William
Philip Nicoll, Henry John Philip Nicoll, and Nicholas ap Robert, is released
from his recognisances.

18. "AD HANC SESSIONEM Morgannus George de Llanbadock in
Comitatu Monmoth, yoman, in propria persona sua venit coram prefatis
Justiciariis, Et manucepit pro Henrico Howells de Llanbadock, laborer, Et
idem Henricus assumpsit pro seipso quod ipse gereret pacem versus Thomam
Laborer de Llansoy durante vita naturali ipsius Thome Laborer, Ita quod
dampnum vel malum aliquod eidem Thome Laborer de corpore suo vel
mutilacionem membrorum suorum non faciat nec fieri procurabit quovis-
modo, videlicet predictus Morgannus George sub pena decem librarum, Et
predictus Henricus manucepit pro seipso sub pena decem librarum. Quam
quidem summam decem librarum predictus Morgannus George ac dictam
summam decem librarum predictus Henricus recognoverunt et concesserunt
se Domine Regine debere et de bonis et catallis, terris et tenementis suis, ad
opus et usum ipsius Domine Regine levari si contingat in premissis seu in
aliquo premissorum predictorum deficere et inde legittimo modo convinci,
etc."

'AT THIS SESSION Morgan George of Llanbadock in the County of
Monmoth, yeoman, came in his own proper person before the aforesaid
Justices and stood surety for Henry Howells of Llanbadock, labourer, and the

same Henry undertook on his own behalf that he would keep the peace towards Thomas Labourer of Llansoy for the duration of the natural life of the same Thomas Labourer so that he would not cause any loss or ill to the same Thomas Labourer in respect of his body or mutilation of his limbs, nor would he in any way procure the same to be done; that is to say, the aforesaid Morgan George, under penalty of ten pounds. Also the aforesaid Henry stood surety in his own behalf under penalty of ten pounds. Which sum of ten pounds the aforesaid Morgan George and the said (other) sum of ten pounds the aforesaid Henry acknowledged and admitted that they owed to the Sovereign Lady the Queen and that (these sums) should be levied from their goods and chattels, their lands and holdings, for the purpose and use of the same Sovereign Lady, if it should happen that the same Henry should in the foregoing matters or in any one of the foregoing default and thereafter in legal manner be convicted, etc.'

19. L.H. Margin: "M[emorandum] pro pace; r[emandatus] post Fest[um] Trin[itatis]."
Thomas Jones of Uske, gentleman, is bound over to keep the peace with Reginald Hughes and to appear in person at the next Trinity Session. Charles Herbert of Monmoth, gentleman, and Leonard Jones of Llangeby, yeoman, stand surety each in the sum of a hundred shillings and Thomas Jones himself in the sum of ten pounds.

20. L.H. Margin: identical with No 19.
Morgan Howell of Uske, yeoman, is bound over to keep the peace with Reginald Hughes and to appear in person at the next Trinity Session. Thomas Jones of Uske, gentleman, and Leonard Jones of Llangeby stand surety each in the sum of a hundred shillings and Morgan Howell himself in the sum of ten pounds.

21. (No marginal note.)
David Williams of Rompney, yeoman, is bound over to keep the peace with Joanna Thomas and to appear at the next Epiphany Session. Morgan David ap John of Henllys and Arthur Williams of Rompney stand surety each in the sum of a hundred shillings and David Williams himself in the sum of ten pounds.

22. L.H. Margin: "Magna Inquisitio", 'Grand Jury'.

Roger Williams, gentleman	James Harry
John Powell Llewelen	Jenkin Morgan
Morgan David ap John	Morgan Parry
John George	Thomas Poyrkin
John William Tanner	Robert Lace
David Reynolds	

Rees ap Jenkin
David William Thomas
John Tanner
Maurice Powell Vachen
Thomas James[1]

23. L.H. Margin: "Felonia."

"QUI DICUNT super sacramentum suum quod Johannes Davyd Powell Davyd nuper de Bergevenny in Comitatu Monmoth, tinker, in Festo Sancti Bartholomei Appostoli (*sic*) anno regni Domine Elizabeth, Dei gratia Anglie ffrancie et Hibernie Regine, Fidei Defensoris, etc. decimo octavo vi et armis etc. apud Bergevenny in Comitatu predicto unam peciam panni Wallici vocati Welshe fryse coloris nigri ad valenciam xlvj*s*. viij*d*. de bonis et catallis cuiusdam Thome Sadler tunc et ibidem inventam felonice furatus fuit cepit et asportavit contra pacem Domine Regine coronam et dignitatem suas."

'WHO DECLARE on their oath that John David Powell David, late of Bergevenny in the County of Monmoth, tinker, did on the Feast of Saint Bartholomew the Apostle, in the eighteenth year of the reign of the Sovereign Lady Elizabeth, of England, France and Ireland Queen, Defender of the Faith etc. with force and arms etc. at Bergevenny in the aforesaid County feloniously steal, take, and carry off a piece of Welsh cloth called "Welshe fryse" of black colour to the value of 46*s*. 8*d*. from the goods and chattels of a certain Thomas Sadler then and there found, against the peace of the Sovereign Lady the Queen, her crown and dignity.'

Note written over the name of John David Powell David: "po[nit] se [super patriam] non cul[pabilem] nec re[traxit]"; 'Puts himself (on the country), not guilty, did not flee.'

---

[1] Each column is bracketed on the right-hand side to the word "Jur[atus]", 'sworn.' This is so in the case of every jury-list in the Roll.

24. L.H. Margin: "Insultum et affraia." 'Assault and affray.'
A similar indictment against Thomas John of the town of Uske, gentleman, and Walter Williams of the same town, yeoman, who on the 6th March of the same year 'by force and arms broke and entered at Uske the close of a certain Reginald Hughes and made assault and affray against the aforesaid Reginald Hughes being then and there in the peace of God and of the aforesaid Sovereign Lady the Queen and then and there struck the same Reginald on the left arm and then and there grievously wounded and maltreated him so that his life was despaired of.'

25. L.H. Margin: 'Riot and Rout.'
And that William Prees of Llanwenarth, yeoman, Thomas William Jenkins of Llanbeder in the County of Brecon, yeoman, and William Be'an (Bevan?) ap Rees of Llanbeder aforesaid, on the 6th of August of the same year at Llanwenarth 'unlawfully and riotously assembled and gathered themselves together and made assault on a certain Edward Lewis and a certain Philip Watkin Jenkins.'

26. L.H. Margin: 'Assault and affray.'
And that Rees Jenkins of Newport, tanner, made an assault on a certain Gwen Meredith on 8th September of the same year at Newport.

27. L.H. Margin: 'Trespass, riot and rout.'
And that Owen Sayre, yeoman, Rees Owen Sayre, corvisor, and James Owen Sayre, labourer, all of Monmoth, unlawfully and riotously assembled and entered a close belonging to Thomas Herbert, Knight, in the occupation of William Catchmay, and stole therefrom 14 cows, black, red and "pyed" of the goods and chattels of the said William Catchmay.

28. L.H. Margin: "Secunda Inquisitio."

Philip Howell Wyllym	Lewis Morgan.
William John Thomas	Morgan William Thomas
Richard Cradock	John William Meyrick
Morgan Williams	John Howell Jones
Morgan Watkins	

William Roberts
Richard Durban
Morgan Llewelen Gruffyth
Philip John Morris
Lewis David
Jenkin Thomas

29. L.H. Margin: 'Felony.'
Indictment that Mathew Llewelen of Newport, yeoman, John Booker of
Minsterwood (*sic*; *recte* Minsterworth?) in the County of Gloucester,
labourer, and David John of "Tylo" in the County of Glamorgan, on 31st
August of the same year broke and entered the close of John William
Vaughan, gentleman, at Carlyon and stole a grey horse value five pounds.

30. L.H. Margin: 'Assault and affray.'
And that Henry Phillips, *alias* Williams, of Matharne, yeoman, and Thomas
Prichard of Llanmarten, gentleman, on 17th October of the preceding year
assaulted Andrew Voyne, clerk, at Chepstowe 'with a certain staff called a
"bastinado" and with a dagger.'

31. L.H. Margin: 'Extortion.'
And that William Watkin of Sherenewton, bailiff of William, Earl of
Worcester, of the manor of Newton, did on 28th September of the same year
take by extortion "colore officii sui" ('under colour of his duty') two shovels
of the goods and chattels of George David.

Between this and the entry next following is inserted, in another hand: "Et
postea Justiciarii pacis Comitatus predicti miserunt indictamentum predictum
coram Domina Regina in Bancum suum termino Hillarii anno regni sui xix
virtute brevis dicte Domine Regine de Certiorari prefatis Justiciariis directi,
etc." 'And afterwards the Justices of the peace of the aforesaid County sent
the aforesaid indictment before the Sovereign Lady the Queen to her Bench
in the Hilary Term in the 19th year of her reign in virtue of a writ of
Certiorari of the said Sovereign Lady the Queen directed to the
aforementioned justices etc.'

32. L.H. Margin: 'Assault and affray.'
And that Philip Meyrick Naysshe, yeoman, and Agnes his wife assaulted
Roger ap Richard at Naysshe on 10th May of the same year.

33. L.H. Margin: "Carlyon."
"AD GENERALEM SESSIONEM pacis Comitatus Monmoth tentam apud
Bergevenny ... die Martis proximo post Clausum Pasche anno regni Domine
Elizabeth ... decimo octavo coram Edwardo Domino Herbert, Williamo
Morgan de Lanternam, Williamo Herbert de Colbroke, Thoma Morgan,
Riceo Morgan, armigeris, et aliis sociis suis, Justiciariis predicte Domine
Regine ... per sacramentum xij juratorum presentatum fuit quod Williamus
Thomas John Yoroth de Llanarth ... yoman, vicesimo die ffebruarii anno
regni predicte Domine Regine, xviijº apud Bethowesnewyth ... vi et armis

etc. regiam viam ducentem de Kemys Brydge versus Monmoth ... inclusit et obstupavit et eandem viam sic inclusam et obstupatum adhuc custodit ad grave dampnum omnium vicinorum suorum ibidem viam predictam transmissorum et contra pacem predicte Domine Regine. Et postea, scilicet ad generalem Sessionem pacis Comitatus predicti tentam apud Monmoth ... die Martis proximo post Festum Corpus (*sic*) videlicet vicesimo sexto die Junii anno regni predicte Domine Regine nunc xviij° coram Edwardo Domino Herbert, Carolo Somersett, milite, Thoma Herbert, milite, Williamo Herbert de Colbroke, Thoma Morgan, armigeris, et aliis sociis suis ... venit predictus Williamus Thomas John Yoroth in propria persona sua et lecto indictamento predicto allocatum est ei qualiter se de transgressione et obstupacione vie predicte acquietare velit. QUI dicit quod ipse in nullo est inde culpabilis. Et de hoc ponit se super patriam. Et Johannes Waters qui pro Domina Regina in hac parte sequitur pro eadem Domina Regina scilicet. Ideo prescriptum est Vice-comiti Comitatus predicti quod venire faciat coram prefatis Justiciariis ad proximam generalem Sessionem pacis Comitatus predicti die Martis proximo post Festum Sancti Michaelis Archangeli proximum futurum apud Carlyon ... tenendam, xij etc. per quos etc. Et qui nec etc. ad triandum exitum predictum quia tum etc. Idem dies datus est prefato Williamo ibi etc. AD QUAM QUIDEM generalem Sessionem pacis ... tentam apud Carlyon predictam ... coram Williamo Morgan de Lanternam, Williamo Lewys, Thoma Morgan, Edmundo Morgan, Matheo Herbert, Waltero Jones, armigeris, et aliis sociis suis... venit tum predictus Johannes Waters qui pro Domina Regina in hac parte sequitur quum predictus Williamus John Thomas Yoroth in propriis personis suis. Et Vicecomes Comitatus predicti, videlicet Christoferus Welshe, armiger, modo retornavit breve sive prescriptum suum predictum in omnibus plene executum et servitum, scilicet pannellum de xxiiij nominibus eidem brevi sive prescripto annexum. SUPER QUO juratores jurate predicte exacti fuerunt, quorum quidem xij, videlicet Williamus John Watkin, Henricus Howells de Llangattock, Thomas John Howell, Rosser Thomas de Llangattock, Howellus ap Jenkyn de Rewlace, Davidus Thomas Agwyllym de Trostrey, Johannes Roberts de Aberustoyth, Morganus Howell de eadem, Rosser Davyd Howell de eadem, Hugo John Williams de Llannarth, Philippus William Adam de Raglan, et Williamus Richard Morgan de Mamhylad venerunt. QUI AD VERITATEM de premissis dicendam electi, triati, et jurati dicunt super sacramentum suum quod predictus Williamus Thomas John Yoroth non est culpabilis de transgressione et obstupacione vie predicte nec de aliqua inde parte modo et forma prout per indictamentum."

'AT THE GENERAL SESSION of the peace of the County of Monmoth held at Bergevenny ... on the Tuesday next after the Close of Easter in the

eighteenth year of the reign of the Sovereign Lady Elizabeth ... before
Edward Lord Herbert, William Morgan of Lanternam, William Herbert of
Colbroke, Thomas Morgan, Rees Morgan, Esquires, and other their
colleagues, Justices of the aforesaid Sovereign Lady the Queen ...
presentment was made on the oath of 12 jurors that William Thomas John
Yoroth of Llanarth, yeoman, did on the 20th February in the eighteenth year
of the reign of the aforesaid Sovereign Lady the Queen at Bethowesnewyth
with force and arms etc. enclose and obtruct the Queen's highway leading
from Kemys Bridge towards Monmoth ... and still keeps the same road thus
enclosed and obstructed to the grave hurt of all his neighbours there passing
along the aforesaid road and against the peace of the aforesaid Sovereign
Lady the Queen. And afterwards, that is to say at the general Session of the
peace of the aforesaid County held at Monmoth ... on the Tuesday next after
the Feast of Corpus (Christi), namely the 26th day of June in the 18th year
of the reign of the aforesaid Sovereign Lady the Queen, before Edward Lord
Herbert, Charles Somerset, Knight, Thomas Herbert, Knight, William Herbert
of Colbroke, Thomas Morgan, Esquires, and other their colleagues ... the
aforesaid William Thomas John Yoroth came in his own person and the
indictment aforesaid having been read it was put to him how he wished to
acquit himself concerning the trespass and the obtruction of the aforesaid
road. AND HE declares that he is in no wise guilty thereof, and accordingly
puts himself on the country. And John Waters who prosecutes for the
Sovereign Lady the Queen in this behalf represents the same Sovereign Lady
the Queen. Therefore order is given to the Sheriff of the aforesaid County
that he shall cause to come before the aforesaid Justices at the next general
Session of the peace of the aforesaid County, to be held at Carlyon on the
Tuesday next after the Feast of Saint Michael the Archangel next following,
12 etc. by whom etc. and who neither etc. for trying the aforesaid issue,
because then etc. The same day was appointed for the aforesaid William,
there etc. TO WHICH THE GENERAL SESSION of the peace held at
Carlyon aforesaid ... before William Morgan of Lanternam, William Lewis,
Thomas Morgan, Edmund Morgan, Mathew Herbert, Walter Jones, Esquires,
and other their colleagues, came both the aforesaid John Waters who
prosecuted for the Sovereign Lady the Queen in this behalf and the aforesaid
William Thomas John Yoroth in their own proper persons. And the Sheriff
of the aforesaid County, namely Christopher Welshe, Esquire, has now
returned his writ or order fully executed and served in all respects, and also
a list of 24 names attached to the same writ or order. Upon which the jurors
of the aforesaid jury have been summoned, of whom furthermore 12, namely
William John Watkins, Henry Howell of Llangattock, Thomas John Howell,
Rosser Thomas of Llangattock, Howell ap Jenkin of Rewlace, David Thomas
ap Gwilym of Trostrey, John Roberts of Aberustoyth, Morgan Howell of the

same place, Rosser David Howell of the same (town), Hugh John Williams of Llanarth, Philip William Adam of Raglan, and William Richard Morgan of Mamhylad have come, WHO having been chosen, tested, and sworn to speak the truth concerning the foregoing matters state on their oath that the aforesaid William Thomas John Yoroth is not guilty of the trespass and obstruction of the aforesaid road, nor any part thereof, in the form and manner as by the indictment.'

34. L.H. Margin: "Carlyon."
A record, identical in form with that immediately preceding, of the indictment at the same three Sessions of one John Rees ap Howell Gronowe of Llangattock Llyngoyed, yeoman, that he on 25th April of the same year broke and entered the close of a certain James John Richards at Llangattock and with animals of his, viz. a horse and a mare, grazed, trampled and consumed grass belonging to the said James and inflicted other enormities on him to the grave hurt of the said James.

The final sentence is not found in the preceding account. "Ideo concessum est per curiam quod predictus Johannes Rees Apowell Gronowe de transgressione predicta eat quietus et sine die etc." 'Therefore it is granted by the court that the aforesaid John Rees ap Howell Gronowe shall go acquitted of the aforesaid trespass and 'sine die' etc.'

"FFINES EXACTA AMERCIAMENTA AD SESSIONIS PREDICTE"
'Fines, charges, amercements of the aforesaid Sessions'

35. "AD HANC SESSIONEM Watkyn Morgan, generosus, Richardus Herbert de Llanwenarth, generosus, Thomas William Watkyns, de eadem, Lodovicus Jenkyns de Aberustoyth, Walterus Williams de Llanvesseryng, generosus, Howellus Aphowell de eadem, Philippus Watkyns de Mamhylad, Johannes Thomas Llewelen de Llanarth et Henricus Davyd de Llanwenarth, quidam juratores impannellati ad eandem Sessionem ad inquirendum pro Domina Regina pro Hundredo de Bergevenny, non comparuerunt coram prefatis Justiciariis ad diem et locum predictos quando exacti fuerunt sed defaltum fecerunt, ita quod pro defalto illo separatim mulcta prout per prefatos Justiciarios assessata est, videlicet super eorum quemlibet iij$s$. iiij$d$., sic in toto ...

R.H. Margin: xxx$s$.

'AT THIS SESSION Watkin Morgan, gentleman, Richard Herbert of Llanwenarth, gentleman, Thomas William Watkins, of the same town, Lewis Jenkins of Aberustoyth, Walter Williams of Llanvesseryng, gentleman,

Howell ap Howell of the same town, Philip Watkins of Mamhylad, John Thomas Llewelen, of Llanarth and Henry David of Llanwenarth, certain jurors empanelled for the same Session to make enquiry for the Sovereign Lady the Queen for the Hundred of Bergevenny, did not appear before the aforementioned Justices at the day and place aforesaid when they were summoned but made default, so that for that default a fine was assessed severally as by the aforementioned Justices, namely upon each of them 3*s*. 4*d*. thus in all ...'

R.H. Margin: 30*s*.

36. Similar record of fines, all of 3*s*.4*d*., imposed on defaulting jurors from the Hundred of Skenffrith; Howell ap Watkin, gentleman, Edward Mason, William John ap Philip, John David Thomas, Thomas William David ap Adam, John David Thomas of Dyngestowe, and Richard Woore. "Sic in toto ..." (but no entry in R.H. Margin).

37. Similar record of fines on defaulting jurors from the Hundred of Uske; John ap Morgan of Llangeby, Thomas ap Thomas of Llandenny, William Thomas "Agllm" (ap Gwilym?) of the same town and George Thomas Cradock.

R.H. Margin: 13*s*. 4*d*.

38. Similar record of fines on defaulting jurors from the Hundred of Trilleg; Walter John ap Rosser, gentleman, Thomas Harry of Llanyssen, William Hopkins of Llansoy, John Egham of Comvagor, Thomas John of Wolfes-newton, David Jenkins of Llannyssen, Edmund Nicholas of Kylgornick, John Worley of Llandogo, John Thomas Turner of Comkarvan, and Thomas William Weaver of Micheltroy.

R.H. Margin: 33*s*. 4*d*.

39. Similar record of fines on defaulting jurors from the Hundred of Caldycott; Henry Lewis of Matharne, gentleman, Morgan Rees of Porte-skewett, John Rees of Wondye, Adam ap Jenkin of the same town, John Bettyngs of Naysshe, senior, Robert Johns of Penhowe, James Morgan of the same town, Rees Jeyn of Naysshe, Richard Wyllym of Redwyck, David ap Jenkin of the same town, and John ap Jenkin of Caldycott.

R.H. Margin: 36*s*. 8*d*.

40. "AD HANC SESSIONEM tenentes et inhabitantes de Llanhenock ... non venerunt neque comparuerunt coram prefatis Justiciariis ad respondendum Domine Regine nec ostendendum quare ipsi non emendaverunt neque reparaverunt altam viam infra parochiam de Llanhenock predictam ducentem

de villa de Carlyon versus villam de Uske ... prout debent unde indictati sunt. Ideo ipsi fierunt exacti per Vicecomitem Comitatus predicti modo super eos retornantem, videlicet – viij*s*."

'AT THIS SESSION the freeholders and inhabitants of Llanhenock ... did not come nor appear before the aforementioned Justices to answer to the Sovereign Lady the Queen and show why they have not mended or repaired the high road within the parish of Llanhenock aforesaid leading from the town of Carlyon towards the town of Uske ... as they are bound to, of which (offence) they are indicted. Therefore they have been charged by the Sheriff of the aforesaid County now making return on them, that is to say – 8*s*.'

41. Similar charge imposed on Tredonock in relation to the road leading from the town of Carlyon towards the town of Uske.

R.H. Margin: 8*s*.

42. Also on Llantryssen in relation to the road leading from Llanllowell towards Pull Baugh.

R.H. Margin: 8*s*.

43. Also on Chrystchurche in relation to the road leading from Chryst-churche towards "Stonen Brydge" on the outskirts of Somerton.

R.H. Margin: 8*s*.

44. Also on Pantege in relation to the road leading from Bergevenny towards Newport.

R.H. Margin: 8*s*.

45. Also on Lewis John Treharon of Chrystchurche, yeoman, Thomas Williarns of Westercoyde, yeoman, and Lewis James of Chrystchurche, yeoman, in relation to a road leading towards their lands within the parish of Chrystchurche leading from Chrystchurche towards Llanwerne. Fine: 2*s*. each.

R.H. Margin: 6*s*.

46. "AD HANC SESSIONEM venerunt Williamus Prees de Llanwenarth, ... yoman, Thomas William Jenkyn de Llanbeder in Comitatu Brecon, yoman, et Williamus ap Jenkyn ap Rees de Llanbeder predicta ... yoman, indictati de insultu et affraia ad eandem generalem Sessionem pacis. Et admittuntur ad ffines suas cum Domina Regina pro indictamento predicto faciendo. Et ffinis eorum cuiuslibet assessatur per prefatos Justiciarios at iij*s*. iiij*d*., sic in

toto x*s*. Plege pro ffinibus suis Johannes James de Llandylowe Barthalowe in Comitatu predicto et predictus Williarn Prees. – x*s*."

'TO THIS SESSION came William Prees of Llanwenarth ... yeoman, Thomas William Jenkins of Llanbeder in the County of Brecon, yeoman, and William ap Jenkyn ap Rees of Llanbeder aforesaid ... yeoman, indicted for assault, and affray at the same general Session of the peace, And are admitted to their fines with the Sovereign Lady the Queen for carrying out the aforesaid indictment, And the fine of each of them is assessed by the aforementioned Justices at 3*s*. 4*d*., thus in all 10*s*. Surety for their fines; John James of Llandylowe Barthalowe in the aforesaid County and the aforesaid William Prees.'

R.H. Margin: 10*s*.

47. Similar record of admission to a fine for assault imposed at the preceding Epiphany Session on William Morgan John of Pennecoyde, yeoman; James Cockes of Monmoth, gentleman, stands surety. (The formula begins AD ISTAM SESSIONEM instead of the otherwise universal AD HANC SESSIONEM.)

R.H. Margin: 3*s*. 4*d*.

48. "AD HANC SESSIONEM venit Georgius Thomas de Treergayre ... yoman, indictatus de insultu et affraia ad generalem Sessionem pacis Comitatus predicti tentam die Martis proximo post Clausum Pasche ultimum preteritum. Et dat Domine Regine de fine pro indictamento predicto exonerando prout per prefatos Justiciarios assessatum est, videlicet ijs. qui soluti fuerunt ad manus Johannis Waters, Clerici pacis ibidem in parte solucionis vadiorum suorum huius sessionis, – 2*s*."

'TO THIS SESSION came George Thomas of Treergayre ... yeoman, indicted for assault and affray at the general Session of the peace of the aforesaid County held the Tuesday next after the Close of Easter last past. And gives to the Sovereign Lady the Queen as a fine for release from the aforesaid indictment as has been assessed by the aforementioned Justices, that is to say 2*s*. which have been paid into the hands of John Waters, Clerk of the peace of the same place, in charge of the payment of fines of this Session, – 2*s*.'

49. Record of admission to a fine imposed on John Thomas of Kemys Comaunder and Anna his wife for assault. John Thomas ap Rosser of Goytre stands surety.

R.H. Margin: 6*s*. 8*d*.

Usk I

1. SESSION OF THE PEACE held at Uske on the 27th October in the 18th year of the Queen's reign, before Thomas Herbert, Knight, William Cecil, and Henry Herbert, Esquires, and John Waters, Clerk of the peace.

2. L.H. Margin: "xii Jur[atores] pro corpore Com[itatus]", '12 jurors from the body of the County.'

William Morgan, gentleman	John Rosser
John Gunter, gentleman	William Powell
Reginald William Gough	Henry David Powell
William Hughes, gentleman	Philip Howell Gwilym
Richard Gunter, gentleman	Morgan Parry

Edmund Richards
Howell Edwards
Roger Evans
John Rees Gwilym
Robert Gout[?]

3. L.H. Margin: 'Assault and Affray.'
"QUI DICUNT super sacramentum suum quod Williamus Thomas nuper de Trilleg ... yoman, duodecimo die Maij in nocte eiusdem diei anno regni Domine Elizabeth ... decimo octavo vi et armis etc. apud Trilleg predictam ... in quendam Morum Waters in pace Dei et predicte Domine Regine adtunc et ibidem existentem insultum fecit, Et predictus Williamus Thomas cum quodam falcastro vocato Abearyng byll quod ipse in ambabus manibus suis tunc et ibidem habuit et tenuit predictum Morum Waters in alta via ibidem equitantem et super Johannem Waters patrem eius tunc et ibidem attendentem violenter percussit ea intencione ad ipsum Morum Waters super caput eius percussendum, Et predictus Williamus Thomas cum falcastro predicto eundem Morum Waters super ulnam eius sinistram adtunc et ibidem graviter percussit verberavit et maletractavit ac ipsum Morum Waters et predictum Johannem Waters in pace Dei et predicte Domine Regine tunc et ibidem existentes in magnum timorem et periculum vitarum suarum adtunc et ibidem imposuit ad malum exemplum aliarum personarum et contra pacem predicte Domine Regine."

'WHO DECLARE on their oath that William Thomas lately of Trilleg ... , yeoman, did on the twelfth day of May in the night of the same day in the eighteenth year of the reign of the Sovereign Lady Elizabeth ... with force and arms etc. at Trilleg aforesaid ... make assault upon a certain Morris Waters being then and there in the peace of God and of the aforesaid Sovereign Lady the Queen, And the aforesaid William Thomas with a certain pike called a 'bearing bill', which he then and there had and held in both hands, violently struck the aforesaid Morris Waters there riding on the highway and also John Waters his father then and there accompanying him with the intention of striking the said Morris Waters on the head, And the aforesaid William Thomas with the aforesaid pike grievously struck, smote, and maltreated the same Morris Waters then and there on his left elbow and put the said Morris Waters and the aforesaid John Waters, being manifestly then and there in the peace of God and of the aforesaid Sovereign Lady the Queen, into great fear and danger of their lives to the bad example of other persons and against the peace of the aforesaid Sovereign Lady the Queen.'

4. L.H. Margin: 'assault and affray.'
Indictment that David Williams of Carlyon, yeoman, assaulted Christopher Welshe, Esquire, Sheriff of the County, and Philip Edwards his servant, at Carlyon on 4th October of the same year, putting them in great fear and danger of their lives, etc.

5. L.H. Margin: 'assault and affray.'
And that William Saunders of Llangoven, gentleman, Walter Johns of Bethowesnewyth, gentleman, and Thomas Reynolds of Treerdonock, yeoman, assaulted a certain John Edwards at Uske on 18th October of the same year, 'it being at that time the market-day of the same town'. Also that Saunders and Johns assaulted William John Williams, David John Thomas, John ap Harry and Edward ap Harry, a cleric, who were 'preserving and keeping the peace ... as much as lay in their power and defending the said John Edwards'. Also that the said Thomas Reynolds joined in the last-mentioned assault.

6. SESSION OF THE PEACE held at Uske on 27th October in the 18th year of the Queen's reign before William Morgan of Lanternam, William Herbert of Colbroke, William Lewis, Rees Morgan, Edmund Morgan, and Mathew Herbert, Esquires.

7. L.H. Margin. '12 jurors from the body of the County.'

Thomas Meredith, gentleman	James ap Richard
George Morgan, gentleman	Roger Morgan
John Meredith, junior	John Arney
Rees Williams, gentleman	Watkin Philips
Saunders Morgan	Thomas John David Powell
Roger Llyder	

William John Thomas
Howell Watkins
David Jenkins
David Thomas Philips
John Bettyng

8. L.H. Margin: 'assault and affray.'
Indictment that Walter Morgan of Uske, gentleman, Howell John Philips of Uske, yeoman, Andrew Edwards of Uske, corvisor, John Edwards of Uske, yeoman, and George Reynolds of Llanbadock, yeoman, assaulted William Saunders at Uske on 18th October, the market-day.

9. L.H. Margin: 'Riot and rout.'
"Et quod cum Christoferus Welshe vicecomes comitatus Monmoth virtute brevis Domine Regine nunc de replegiando extra Cancellarium ipsius Domine Regine apud Westmonasterium eidem vicecomiti directi per Philippum Edwards servientem eius et Walterum Jones ballivos et ministros predicti vicecomitis in hac parte sufficienter deputatos et auctoritatos primo die Augusti anno regni Domine Elizabeth ... decimo octavo apud Skenffrith in Comitatu predicto Replegiarium et Deliberarium fecissent cuidam Thome Morgan generoso quindecim vaccas multrices, unum vitulum, et unum taurum de bonis et catallis ipsius Thome Morgan captos et iniuste detentos et imporcatos per Carolum Cockes generosum et Hugonem Cockes apud Skenffrith predictam ... et quod Hugo Cockes nuper de Skenffrith predicta ... generosus, Thomas Tanner nuper de Skenffrith predicta ... tanner, Davyd James Hoby de Skenffrith, predicta ... laborer, Williamus Butler alias dictus Williamus serviens predicti Caroli Cockes nuper de Skenffrith predicta ... laborer, Madock ap Howell nuper de Skenffrith predicta alias dictus Madock Laborer ... , et Riceus Morgan de Saynt Moughan ... yoman, aggregati sibi quum pluribus aliis malefactoribus et pacis predicte Domine Regine perturbatoribus ignotis in numerum xij personarum vi et armis videlicet baculis cultellis pugionibus falcastris lanceis arcubus et sagittis ac aliis armis defensivis die et anno supradictis apud Skenffrith predictam...se illicite et riotose assemblaverunt et congregaverunt ac in predictos Philippum Edwards et Walterum Jones inexecucione dicti brevis et warranti predicti vicecomitis

sibi directi pro execucione eiusdem brevis adtunc et ibidem insultum fecerunt et quantum in se potuissent rescussum et resistenciam tunc et ibidem fecerunt ad malum exemplum aliarum personarum et contra formam diversorum statutorum in huiusmodi casu nuper editorum et provisorum ac contra pacem predicte Domine Regine."

'AND THAT whereas Christopher Welshe, Sheriff of the County of Monmoth, by virtue of a writ of Replegiare of the present Sovereign Lady the Queen from the Chancery of the same Sovereign Lady the Queen at Westminster directed to the same Sheriff, by Philip Edwards his sergeant and Walter Jones, bailiffs and officers of the aforesaid Sheriff duly deputed and authorised in this behalf on the first day of August in the eighteenth year of the reign of the Sovereign Lady Elizabeth ... at Skenffrith in the aforesaid County had made recovery and delivery to a certain Thomas Morgan, gentleman, of fifteen milking cows, one calf, and one bull, from the goods and chattels of the said Thomas Morgan seized and unlawfully detained and impounded by Charles Cockes, gentleman, and Hugh Cockes at Skenffrith aforesaid in the aforesaid County, Hugh Cockes late of Skenffrith ... gentleman, Thomas Tanner late of Skenffrith ... tanner, David James Hoby of Skenffrith aforesaid, labourer, William Butler otherwise called William the servant of the aforesaid Charles Cockes late of Skenffrith, labourer, Madock ap Howell late of Skenffrith otherwise called Madock Laborer ... labourer, and Rees Morgan of Saynt Moughan ... yeoman, having gathered themselves together with several other unknown malefactors and disturbers of the peace of the aforesaid Sovereign Lady the Queen to the number of 12 persons, by force and arms, namely staves, knives, daggers, swords, pikes, lances, bows and arrows, and other offensive weapons, on the day and in the year above stated at Skenffrith aforesaid ... unlawfully and riotously assembled themselves and gathered together and there and then made assault on the aforesaid Philip Edwards and Walter Jones in the execution of the said writ and of the warrant of the aforesaid Sheriff directed to them for the execution of the same writ, and then and there made opposition and resistance as much as in them lay, to the bad example of other persons and against the form of divers statutes recently published and provided in such a case and against the peace of the aforesaid Sovereign Lady the Queen.'

10. L.H. Margin: 'Forced entry'.
Indictment that George Williams of Saynt Wollo, yeoman, entered the messuage of Anna Philpott on 15th October the same year, forcibly ejected her and retained possession himself in disregard of a statute of 8 Henry VI.

11. L.H. Margin: 'Assault'.
Indictment that Philip Edwards of Llanwerne, yeoman, on 13th October of
the same year assaulted John Watkins at Carlyon.

Newport

1. SESSION OF THE PEACE held at Newport on the Tuesday next after the Epiphany in the 19th year of the Queen's reign, before Charles Somerset, Knight, Rowland Morgan, William Morgan of Lanternam, Thomas Morgan, William Lewis, William Evans, Bachelor of Laws, Mathew Herbert, and William John ap Roger, Esquires, and John Waters, Clerk of the Peace.

2. The Sheriff, Rees Morgan, Esquire, returns fully executed in all points his writ of "Venire facias" directed to him for the proclamation and constitution of the present court.

3. The Sheriff reports that acting on a writ of attachment he failed to find Katherine Jenkins, wife of Thomas William John of Pennalth, required to answer concerning a certain trespass. A new order is made for her appearance at the next Easter Session.

> Original writ; 22nd March 18 Eliz.
> L.H. Margin: 'To be summoned.'

Similar reports of the Sheriff from Nos 4–12 (incl.):

4. In the case of John Richards, and Reginald John ap Jenkin, both yeomen, of Aberustoyth, Charles Watkin and William John David ap John, both yeomen of Llandylowe Barthalowe, William Herbert, gentleman, and William John Philips yeoman, both of Llanvehangell Cylcornell, William Roberts, yeoman, of the same town, John Philip Thomas, yeoman, of Comeyoy, David Williams of Llanveyre Kylgedyn, tinker, John Mathew of Llanysson, in the county of Glamorgan, gentleman, Morgan Spriggin of Llanysson aforesaid, yeoman, and John Miller of Bethowesnewyth, miller, required to answer concerning certain trespasses and contempts. A new order for their appearance at the next Easter Session.

> Original writ; Epiphany 18 Eliz.
> L.H. Margin: 'To be summoned.'

5. In the case of Reginald Roberts of Comeyoy, labourer, Richard ap Jenkyn of Bergevenny, corvisor, Robert James of Llantellyo Cryssenny, glover, Richard David Sant and John George, both yeomen of Grussemont, John Harries, Richard Sadde and Watkin ap Howell, all yeomen of Saynt Moughan, Henry Wilcocks, yeoman of Llangewa, John Parke, yeoman of Dyngestowe, Richard ap Howell Williams and Watkin Howell Thomas, both

yeomen of Llantellyo Cryssenny, and Richard ap Jenkins of Bergevenny, corvisor, required to answer concerning certain trespasses and contempts. A new order for their appearance at the next Easter Session.

Original writ; Easter 18 Eliz.

6. In the case of Margaret ferch Hopkin, widow, of Aberustoyth, required to answer concerning a certain trespass and 'entry where entry is not allowed by law.' A new order for her appearance at the next Easter Session.

Original writ; Michaelmas 18 Eliz.

7. In the case of William Hughes of Monmoth, William Prosser of Pennalth, John Morris of Carlyon also called John Morris Hughes of Carlyon, all yeomen, John William Hughes, James William Hughes, William Morris Hughes, all yeomen of Uske, Thomas Roberts of Dyngestowe, gentleman, and Rees Jenkins of Newport, tanner, required to answer concerning certain trespasses and contempts. A new order for their appearance at the next Easter Session.

Original writ; Trinity 18 Eliz.

8. In the case of John Morris, yeoman, of Carlyon, otherwise called John Hughes, yeoman of Carlyon, William Hughes of the town of Uske, tailor, William Morris Hughes of Uske, tanner, and Rees Jenkins of Newport, tanner, required to answer concerning certain divers trespasses and contempts. A new order for their appearance at the next Easter Session.

Original writ; Trinity 18 Eliz.

9. In the case of Philip ap David, Llangom, weaver, Jenkin David of the town of Monmoth, labourer, and Rees Jenkins of the town of Newport, tanner, required to answer concerning certain trespasses and contempts. A new order for their appearance at the next Easter Session

Origainal writ: Michaelmas 18 Eliz.

10. Similar report of the Sheriff in the case of Owen Sayre, yeoman, Rees Owen Sayre, corvisor, James Owen Sayre, corvisor, all of Monmouth, and Rees Jenkins of Newport, tanner, required to answer concerning divers trespasses and contempts. A new order for their appearance at the next Easter Session.

Original writ; Michaelmas 18 Eliz.

11. In the case of John David Powell David of Bergevenny, tinker, Mathew Llewelyn of Newport, yeoman, John Glover of Mynsterworth in the County of Gloucester, labourer, and David John of Tylo in the County of Glamor-

gan, labourer, required to answer concerning certain felonies. A new order for their appearances at the next Easter Session.

Original writ; Michaelmas 18 Eliz.

12. In the case of David Williams of Carlyon, William Thomas of Trylleg, Walter Morgan, gentleman, Howell John Phillips, Andrew Edwards, corvisor, John Edwards, all of Uske, George Reynolds of Llanbadock, Hugh Cocks of Skenffrith, gentleman, Thomas Tanner, labourer, William Butler, otherwise William the servant of Charles Cocks, servingman, Thomas ap Thomas, labourer, Madock ap Howell otherwise Madock Labourer, all of Skenffrith, Rees Morgan otherwise Rees Agweyth, of Saynt Moughan, and Philip Edwards of Llanwerne, all yeomen except where otherwise stated, required to answer concerning divers trespasses, riots, assaults and contempts. A new order for their appearance at the next Easter Session.

Original writ; 27th October 18 Eliz.

13. L.H. Margin: "Notificacio relaxationis [securitatis] pacis."
David Williams of Rompney, bound over by Thomas Morgan, Esquire, to keep the peace with Joanna Thomas is released from his recognisances.

14. L.H. Margin: "Relaxatio [securitatis] pacis."
Henry Williams of Matharne, gentleman, and James Parker of Matharne, yeoman, bound over by William Lewis, Esquire, to keep the peace with Thomas Young, Roger Edwards, William Edmonds, William Thomas, Thomas Williams, Philip John, Lewis John, William Bowen, Edmund Perkins, Thomas Jones of Matharne, John Roberts, and Henry Kemys, are released from their recoznisances.

15. L.H. Margin: "Magna Inquisitio ad inquirendum pro Domina Regina."
'Grand Jury to enquire on behalf of the Sovereign Lady the Queen.'

John Williams, gentleman	James John Richards
Philip Morgan, gentleman	William John Watkins
John Morgan, gentleman	Nicholas ap Richard
Simon William John	Thomas Watkins
James Herbert	William Prichard
Morgan Parry	

Philip Bettyng
John William Phillips
Morgan David ap John
John Walters
Morgan Watkins

16. L.H. Margin: 'Felony and trespass.'
Indictment that Thomas John Williams and Philip John Williams of
Llanvehangell Pontmoyle, both labourers, broke and entered on 3rd October
of the preceding year the house of John Gwilym Bowen at Llanvehangell
aforesaid and stole from him a ewe, white, valued at eight shillings. Also
that John William ap Jenkin of Llanvehangell aforesaid, yeoman, who,
knowing the aforesaid pair to have committed the felony, 'feloniously
received, encouraged, helped and maintained them.'
> Note over Thomas John Williams's name: 'Puts himself on the
> country, not guilty, did not flee'.

17. L.H. Margin: 'Felony and burglary.'
And that James ap James of Roathe in the County of Glamorgan, gentleman,
and Thomas John ap Jenkin of Llanvreghva, yeoman, burglariously entered
the house of Lewis Howells at Rompney on 5th October the preceding year
'about the eleventh hour of the night' and assaulted Lewis and Jane Howells.

18. L.H. Margin: 'Felony.'
And that John Lewis, labourer, and George Baker, labourer, both of
Bergevenny, stole at Bergevenny a purse containing three pounds in
"pecuniis numeratis", (numbered, i.e. coined, money), the property of
Richard Turvill.
> Note over both names: "po[nit] se [super patriam] cul[pabilem]
> ca[talla] null[a] sus[pendatur] per coll[um]." 'Puts himself on the
> country; guilty; no chattels; let him be hanged by the neck.'

19. L.H. Margin: 'Felony.'
And that Philip John Williams of Llanvehangell Pontmoyle, labourer, stole
a white ewe valued at 5s., the property of John Gwilym Bowen of Llanvehangell aforesaid.

20. L.H. Margin: 'Felony.'
And that Jevan John of Paynescastle in the County of Radnor, labourer, stole
a bay gelding valued at four marks from Morgan Jenkins of Llandylowe
Barthalowe on 10th September of the preceding year.
> Note over his name: 'Puts himself on the country, guilty, no chattels,
> let him be hanged by the neck.'

21. L.H. Margin: 'Riot and rout.'
And that William David Mathew of Uske, Morgan Phillips of Llangeby,
John Harry Adam, Edward Harry Adam, a cleric, both of Uske, William
Reynolds of Llanbadock, Roger Harry of Llanvehangell Pontmoyle, Philip

Howell Gwilym of Wolfesnewton, Howell Reynolds of Llantrissen, William Reynolds of Llangevewe, Jevan Harry of Llangom, Philip Leonard of Llangeby, Thomas Edwards of Uske, all yeomen, and other persons unknown, unlawfully assembled at Uske on a market-day, 18th October of the preceding year, and assaulted William Saunders.

> *Memorandum inserted at the end, in another hand:* "Et postea Justiciarii pacis Comitatus predicti miserunt indictamentum predictum coram dicta Domina Regina in Bancum suum apud Westmonasterium termino Sancte Trinitatis anno regni sui xix virtute brevis ipsius Domine Regine de Certiorari prefatis Justiciariis directi."
>
> 'And afterwards the Justices of the peace of the aforesaid County sent the aforesaid indictment before the said Sovereign Lady the Queen to her bench at Westminster in the Trinity Term in the 19th year of her reign in virtue of a writ of Certiorari of the same Sovereign Lady the Queen directed to the aforementioned Justices.'

22. L.H. Margin: 'Assault and affray.'
And that Thomas Yorath of Llandenny assaulted Katherine Morris, wife of John David Lewis, at Llandenny on 27th December of the preceding Year.

23. L.H. Margin: 'Trespass.'
And that Thomas Prosser of Llansoer, gentleman, broke and entered at Llangattock juxta Carlyon on 3rd January of the present year the close of Watkin John Watkins and stole three white sheep valued at 10s. and kept them for the space of four days causing deterioration of their condition.

24. L.H. Margin: 'Assault and affray. '
And that Richard Lewis of Llanvaughes, yeoman, broke and entered the close of James Morgan and assaulted his person on 5th September of the preceding year.

25. L.H. Margin: 'Assault and affray.'
And that the same Richard Lewis assaulted the same James Morgan on 3rd January of the present year.

26. L.H. Margin: 'Trespass.'
And that David Richards of Monmoth, yeoman, John Yevans of Tredonock, labourer, and others unknown on 25th October of the preceding year and on 'divers days and occasions before and after' took from several reaches of the River Uske belonging to the most noble Earl of Worcester at Llangeby, Tredonock, and Llantrissen Nundecim salmones Anglice eleven salmons ... cum quibusdam retibus Anglice nettes," to the grave hurt of the said Earl.

27. L.H. Margin: "Grandis Inquisitio", 'Grand Jury.'

Philip Morgan, gentleman	John ap Jenkin Powell
John Thomas John Prosser	Philip William Llewelen
Howell Morgan	John Giles
Gwilym Philip Jenkins	Thomas Powell Wilcock
Lewis Morgan	William John Lewis
Lewis ap Jenkin	

John Harry
Richard John Thomas Hopkin
Jevan David
Richard Morgan
David Thomas
Roger Llyder

28. L.H. Margin: 'Trespass.'
Indictment that John Edmunds of Llangeby, yeoman, on 28th December of the preceding year broke hedges belonging to John Llewelen of Llangeby and took away the wood.

29. L.H. Margin: 'Assault and affray.'
And that William John David ap John and William John Phillips, both yeomen, of Grussemont, assaulted John Thomas Stephens at Grussemont on 31st May of the preceding year.

30. L.H. Margin: 'Assault and affray.'
And that Richard Jeyn Morris of Llangeby on 14th October of the preceding year at Llangeby assaulted Philip Harry, Jenkin Phillips, Reginald David, Philip Thomas Gwilym, and Jenkin Thomas David.

31. L.H. Margin: 'Extortion.'
And that Thomas Powell of Bergevenny, gentleman, and lately deputy-sheriff of the County, and Meredith Howell Jenkins of Llanwennarth, yeoman, servant of Thomas Powell, took by extortion on 13th November of the preceding year, under colour of official duty, "unum saccum Anglice a sack et tres modios hordei Anglice three busshels of barly maulte and oten maulte." valued at 10s. belonging to John ap John of Llanbadock and William John of Uske.

32. L.H. Margin: 'Assault and affray.'
And that David John Thomas of Porthvaynor, yeoman, assaulted William Thomas at Llangoven on 25th December of the preceding year.

33. L.H. Margin: 'Assault.'
And that George Williams of Newport, yeoman, assaulted at Newport, Morgan Prichard Harry on 9th January of the present year 'at the time of the general Session of the peace held there.'

34. L.H. Margin: 'Entry by force.'
And that Howell John George of Newchurche, husbandman, Meredith Watkins of Trylleg, tailor, Alice, his wife, Anna George of Trylleg, and Howell Jenkins of Trylleg, labourer, on 1st January of the present year in disregard of a statute of 8 Henry VI entered the messuage and garden of Morgan Williams occupied by John Lace, a cleric, tenant of Morgan Williams, and ejected owner and tenant, retaining possession themselves.

35. L.H. Margin: 'Entry by force.'
Identical in form with 34 above: Elizabeth Williams, widow, of Llangattock Clennyg, Howell ap Rees, labourer, and Lewis Williams, labourer, of the same place, ejected James John Richards of Llangattock aforesaid, on 3rd January.

36. L.H. Margin: "pro defectione [reparationis] vie regie."
'For failure to repair the Queen's highway.'

Et quod cum omnes ligei Domine Regine a tempore cuius contrarii memoria homini non existit usi fuerunt habere communiam viam et passagium tam pedestribus quam equestribus quam plaustratis equis et catallis per quandam viam sive venellam intra parochiam de Saynt Wollo in Comitatu Monmoth ducentem a villa de Newport in Comitatu predicto versus Bassaleg in eodem Comitatu quam quidem viam sive venellam intra predictam parochiam de Saynt Wollo in Comitatu predicto tenentes et inhabitantes eiusdem parochie a tempore supradicto reparare escurare et emendare debent solebant et usi fuerunt, eadem tamen via sive venella modo in tali decasu et ruina existit pro defectu reparationis quod predicti ligei predicte Domine Regine per viam sive venellam illam laborare transire seu itinerare non possunt absque magno periculo vitarum suarum et perdicione rerum et bonorum suorum ac in malum exemplum aliorum in tali casu delinquentium et contra pacem predicte Domine Regine, Necnon contra formam statuti in huiusmodi casu nuper editi et provisi.

'And that whereas all the subjects of our Sovereign Lady the Queen from the time the contrary of which is not within living memory have been used to have a common way and passage as well for foot-travellers as for horse-travellers and for draught horses and cattle along a certain way or path within the parish of Saynt Wollo in the County of Monmoth leading from the town of Newport in the aforesaid County towards Bassaleg in the same County and whereas this same way or path within the aforesaid parish of Saynt Wollo in the aforesaid County the land-holders and inhabitants of the same parish are bound, were wont, and have been used from the time above mentioned to repair, attend to, and mend, nevertheless this same way or path is now in such bad state and ruin for want of repair that the aforesaid subjects of the aforesaid Sovereign Lady the Queen cannot work on, cross over, or travel on that way or path without great danger of their lives and destruction of their property and goods and to the bad example of others offending in like manner and against the peace of the aforesaid Sovereign Lady the Queen, And furthermore against the form of the statute recently published and provided in a case of this kind.'

'Fines, charges and amercements at the foregoing Session'

37. Charge upon the freeholders and inhabitants of Llanhenock for non-appearance to show reason why they have not repaired the high-road in their parish leading from Carlyon towarde Uske.

R.H. Margin: 8*s.*

38. Similar charge on Tredonock in relation to the road leading from Carlyon to Uske.

R.H. Margin: 8*s.*

39. Also on Llantryssen in relation to the road leading from Llanllowell towards Pull Baugh.

R.H. Margin: 8*s.*

40. Also on Chrystchurche in relation to the road leading from Chryst-churche towards "Stonen Brydge" on the outskirts of Somerton.

R.H. Margin: 8*s.*

41. Also on Pantege in relation to the road leading from Bergevenny towards Newport.

42. Also on Lewis John Treharon of Chrystchurche, Thomas Williams of Westercoyde, and Lewis James of Chrystchurche, all yeomen, in relation to a road leading towards their lands within the parish of Chrystchurche, leading from that town towards Llanwerne. Fine: 2*s.* each.

R.H. Margin: 6*s.*

43. Also on Wonastow in relation to the road leading from Monmoth towards Uske.

R.H. Margin: 3*s*. 4*d*.

44. Also on Dyngestowe in relation to two roads, one leading from Monmoth to Raglan, the other from Monmoth to Treergayre.

R.H. Margin: 6*s*. 8*d*.

45. Record of fines, each 3*s*. 4*d*., on defaulting jurors from the Hundred of Newport; Howell John Jeyn Here and Thomas John Gayner of Bassaleg, Jenkin Jenkins of Michelstowe, William Taylor of Saynt Mellens, John Mathew, David Wylly, John Collins, Arthur Hughes, and John Baylis of Rompney, John Blethyn and Richard Durban of Peterston, Jenkin Thomas and Bernard Bruer of Saynt Bryede.

R.H. Margin: 43*s*. 4*d*.

46. Similar record relating to defaulting jurors from the Hundred of Trilleg; William John of Llantryssen, John Roberts of Llangoven, Thomas Edwards of Llansoy, John ap Howell of Cylgornick(?), William Hopkin of Llansoy, and Thomas ap John of Llannyssen.

R.H. Margin: 20*s*.

47. Similar record relating to defaulting jurors from the Hundred of Skenffrith; John ap Adam of Llangattock, John Charles of Grussemont, William Thomas Griffiths and Thomas Phillips of Dyngestowe.

(No marginal entry.)

48. Similar record relating to defaulting jurors from the Hundred of Uske; Thomas John ap Jenkin, Henry George, Thomas William John, all of Llandenny, Morgan Rosser and Henry ap Jenkin of Gwernesseny, Thomas William Cradock of Llangom, William Morgan Phillips of Tredonock, Morgan William Vregh and Morgan David Gwilym of Llanvreghva.

R.H. Margin: 30*s*.

49. Record of a payment of a fine for forcible entry imposed at the special Session at Uske on 27th October on George Williams of Newport; the fine paid 'into the hands of Charles Somerset, Knight.'

R.H. Margin: 2*s*.

50. Record of another fine paid by the same George Williams for assault, imposed at Uske on 27th October.

R.H. Margin: 2*s*.

51. Record of payment of a fine for trespass imposed at the present Session on John Edmonds of Llangeby; 'paid into the hands of John Waters, Clerk of the peace.'

R.H. Margin: 12*d*.

52. Philip Edwards, yeoman, Dionina his wife, and John Edwards, yeoman, all of Uske, 'admitted to their fines' imposed for resisting arrest at Bergevenny at the preceding Easter Session; 2*s*. each. The aforementioned Philip Edwards stands surety.

R.H. Margin: 6*s*.

53. William Morris Hughes of Uske, tanner, admitted to his fines; 'twice indicted of several assaults' at the preceding Trinity Session. Jacob (or James) Morris Hughes, tailor, of Uske, stands surety.

R.H. Margin: 4*s*.

54. The above mentioned Jacob Morris Hughes admitted to a fine at the preceding Trinity Session. William Morris Hughes stands surety.

R.H. Margin: 2*s*.

55. Stephen ap Rees of Llanvehangell Ystemllewren, James David Williams of Grussemont, and John ap Jenkin of Dyngestowe, all yeomen, admitted to their fines, 12*d*. each, imposed at the preceding Easter Session for selling ale without the licence of the Justices. John Cockes of Llantellyo Cryssenny, gentleman, stands surety for Stephen ap Rees, Rees Philip Williams, of Grussemont, gentleman, for James David Williams, and John Richards of Treergayre, yeoman, for John ap Jenkin.

R.H. Margin: 3*s*.

56. For the same offence William Gwilym *alias* Manyon of Llangattock, yeoman, and John Philip Weyth of Llantellyo Cryssenny, yeoman, admitted to their fines, 12*d*. each, imposed at the preceding Easter Session. For the former William Cockes of Rochefylde, gentleman, stands surety; for the latter John Morgan of Skenffrith, gentleman.

R.H. Margin: 2*s*.

57. For the same offence Thomas Stephens of Grussemont, yeoman, Philip Jenkin ap Howell Williams of Llangattock, yeoman, Elizabeth Badam of Llanvehangell, Watkin Williams *alias* Tavarnor, of Llantellyo Cryssenny, yeoman, and David ap David of Llantellyo aforesaid admitted to their fines, 12*d*. each, imposed at the preceding Easter Session. The fines paid into the hands of Rowland Morgan, Esquire.

R.H. Margin: 5*s*.

58. Walter Morgan, gentleman, Howell John Phillips, yeoman, John Edwards, yeoman, Andrew Edwards, corvisor, and George Reynolds, yeoman, all of Uske, despite a protest that 'they are in no wise guilty therof' admitted to fines, 2*s*. each, for assault, imposed at the special Session at Uske on 27th October. The fines paid into the hands of Thomas Herbert, Knight, and Henry Herbert, Esquire.

R.H. Margin: 10*s*.

59. William Saunders of Llangoven, gentleman, Walter Johns of Bethowes-newyth, gentleman, and Thomas Reynolds of Tredonock admitted to fines, 2*s*. each, for assault imposed at the special Session at Uske on 27th October; paid into the hands of William Morgan of Lanternam and Mathew Herbert, Esquires.

R.H. Margin: 6*s*.

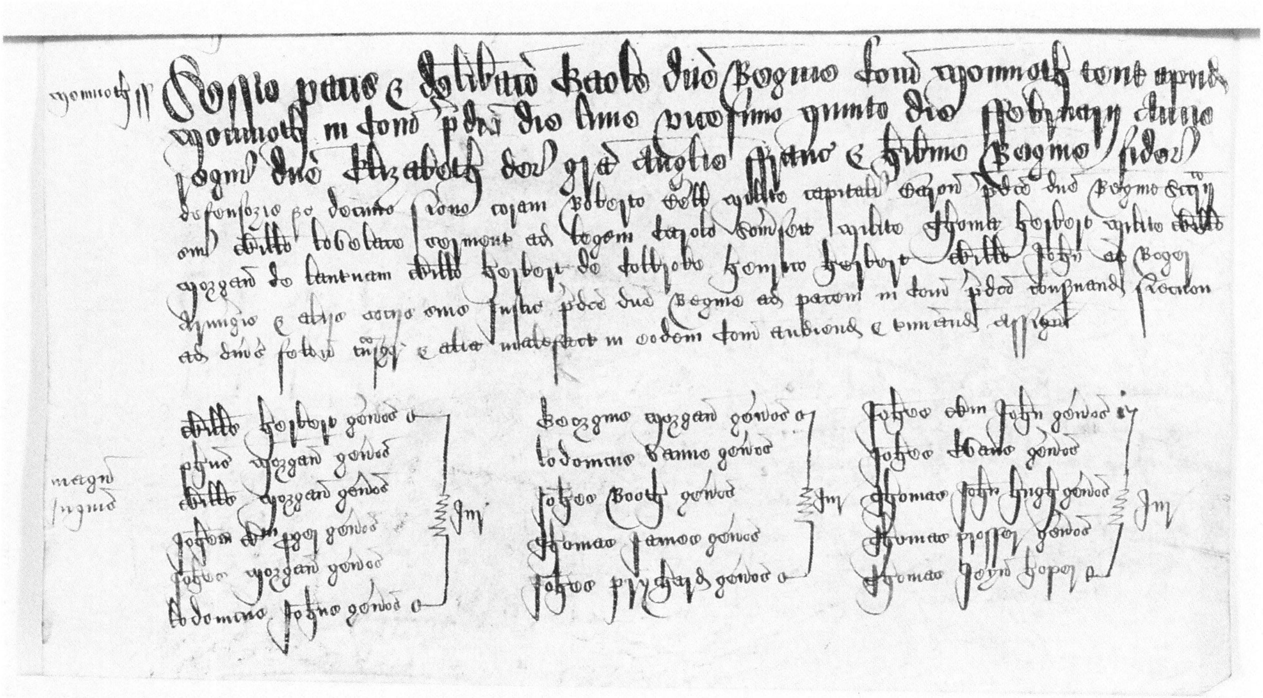

Plate 2. The first two entries of the first Monmouth Sessions of the Peace and Gaol Delivery, transcribed and translated opposite.

Monmouth I

1. "SESSIO PACIS et DELIBERACIO GAOLE Domine Regine Comitatus Monmoth tenta apud Monmoth in Comitatu predicto die Lune vicesimo quinto die ffebruarii anno regni Domine Elizabeth Dei gratia Anglie Ffrancie et Hibernia Regine Fidei Defensoris etc. decimo nono coram Roberto Bell, milite, Capitali Barone predicte Domine Regine Scacarrii sui, Williamo Lovelace serviente ad legem, Carolo Somersett, milite, Thoma Herbert, milite, Williamo Morgan de Lanternam, Williamo Herbert de Colebroke, Henrico Herbert, Williamo John ap Roger, armigeris, et aliis sociis suis justiciariis predicte Domine Regine ad pacem in Comitatu predicto conservandam, Necnon ad diversas felonias, transgressiones, et alia malefacta in eodem Comitatu audienda et terminanda assignatis."

'SESSION OF THE PEACE and GAOL DELIVERY of the Sovereign Lady the Queen, of the County of Monmoth, held at Monmoth in the County aforesaid on Monday 25th February in the nineteenth year of the reign of the Sovereign Lady Elizabeth, by the grace of God of England, France and Ireland Queen, Defender of the Faith etc. before Robert Bell, Knight, Chief Baron of the Exchequer of the aforesaid Sovereign Lady the Queen, William Lovelace, Serjeant-at-law, Charles Somerset, Knight, Thomas Herbert, Knight, William Morgan of Lanternam, William Herbert of Colebroke, Henry Herbert, William John ap Roger, Esquires, and other their colleagues, Justices of the aforesaid Sovereign Lady the Queen assigned to preserve the peace in the aforesaid County and also to hear and determine divers felonies, trespasses and other misdemeanours in the same County.'

2.	William Herbert	John William John
	Philip Morgan	John Evans
	William Morgan	Thomas John Hugh
	John William Proger	Thomas Prosser
	John Morgan	Thomas Jeyn Hoper
	Lewis Johns	George Morgan
	Lewis Vanne	
	John Booth	
	Thomas James	
	John Prichard	

In L.H. Margin: "magn[a] Inquis[itio]", 'Grand Jury';

N.B.: Each one of the jurors, except Hoper, is styled "gener[osus],"
'gentleman';

3. L.H. Margin: 'Felony and Treason'.
Indictment that Thomas ap John, *alias* Mason, of Brecon, on 15th December
of the preceding year 'at Monythusloyn ... falsely, feloniously and traitor-
ously made, fashioned and counterfeited ten pieces of false money of copper,
tin and other false metals admixed in the image and likeness of the money
and coin of the Sovereign Lady Elizabeth ... called half-shillings of sixpence
apiece, now current in this realm of England'.
    Over his name: "Po[nit] se[super patriam] cul[pabilem] nec re[traxit]";
'puts himself (on the country), guilty, did not flee'.[1]

4. L.H. Margin: 'Felony and Homicide'.
And that John Philip Thomas of Mamhylad, husbandman, assaulted Henry
Lewis at Mamhylad on 21st October of the preceding year, which assault
resulted in the death of the said Henry Lewis.

5. L.H. Margin: 'Felony'.
And that Jevan ap Rees of Llanbadock, labourer, and John ap Jenkin of
Glascoyed, labourer, on 11th November of the preceding year, stole two
heifers, one "pyed", the other red, each valued at 20*s*., from Thomas Harry
Lewis of Comeyoy.
    Over Jevan ap Rees's name: 'Puts himself on the country, guilty, no
chattels, let him be hanged by the neck.'

6. L.H. Margin: 'Felony'.
And that Richard ap Robert of the town of Bergevenny, corvisor, on 21st
October, preceding, stole a linen garment valued at 10*d*., the property of
William Lewis.
    Over his name: "Po[nit] se cul[pabilem] nec re[traxit]", 'Puts himself
(on the country), guilty, did not flee'.

7. L.H. Margin: 'Felony'.
And that Thomas Taylor of Monmoth, tailor, on 4th January of the present
year, stole a bay mare, the property of Lewis William Tucker.

[1] Cf. 2nd Monmouth Gaol Delivery, No 21. See also No 30 below.

8. L.H. Margin: 'Felony '.
And that the same Thomas Taylor stole on the same day a grey gelding
valued at seven pounds, the property of John Philpott, gentleman.

9. L.H. Margin: 'Felony'.
And that Philip Meele Phillips of Keynechurche in the County of Hereford,
labourer, on 5th June preceding, at Llanthonye stole six young steers of
divers colours, each valued at 20s., and four heifers of divers colours, each
valued at 20s., the property of William Cecil and Oliver Thomas.

10. And "quod cum Nichalaus ap Robert nuper de Cayrewent ... laborer ad
Generalem Deliberacionem Gaole Domine Regine castri sui Monmoth de
prisonibus in ea existentibus coram Edwardo Saunders Capitali Barone
Domine Regine Scacarrii sui et Williamo Lovelace serviente ad legem
Justiciariis ipsius Domine Regine ad Gaolam illam deliberandam assignatis
apud Monmoth ... die Veneris xxvij die Julii anno regni Domine Elizabeth
... decimo octavo secundum legem et consuetudinem regni Anglie convictus
et attinctus fuisset de quadam felonia per ipsum Nicholaum ap Robert adtunc
ante nuper facta et perpetrata ... videlicet pro uno spadone coloris browne
bay precii trium librarum de bonis et catallis cuiusdam Watkyn Williams
alias Howell per predictum Nicholaum felonice capto et abducto et super hoc
postea certis de causis et consideracionibus prefatos Justiciarios moventibus
idem Nicholaus ap Robert per eosdem Justiciarios apud Monmoth predictam
... adtunc commissus fuisset communi Gaole predicte Domine Regine ...
apud Carlyon in eodem Comitatu sub salva custodia Johannis Hughes de
Carlyon ... yoman, tunc custodis eiusdem Gaole ibidem moratur quousque
predicti Justiciarii ulterius inde advisari voluissent prout per Recordum inde
plene liquet et apparet, ET quod predictus Johannes Hughes tunc custos
Gaole predicte habeus onus et custodiam predicti Nicholai ap Robert modo
et forma prout predictum est in Gaola predicta existentis postea scilicet xxiiij
die Octobris anno regni predicte Domine Regine nunc xviij supradicto
prefatum Nicholaum ap Robert apud Carlyon predictam ... extra Gaolam
predictam a custodia ipsius Johannis Hughes felonice et voluntarie adtunc et
ibidem evadere escapiare et ad largum ire permisit contra pacem predicte
Domine Regine."

'that, whereas Nicholas ap Robert late of Cayrewent ... labourer, at the
General Gaol Delivery of the Sovereign Lady the Queen's castle of
Monmoth of the prisoners who were in it, before Edward Saunders, chief
Baron of the Exchequer of the aforesaid Sovereign Lady the Queen and
William Lovelace, Serjeant-at-law, the justices of the aforesaid Sovereign
Lady the Queen assigned for the delivery of that Gaol at Monmoth ... on

Friday, the 27th day of July in the eighteenth year of the reign of the Sovereign Lady Elizabeth had been convicted and attainted according to the law and custom of the realm of England of a certain felony then recently before committed and perpetrated by the same Nicholas ap Robert ... namely in the matter of a brown bay gelding of the value of three pounds of the goods and chattels of a certain Watkin Williams, alias Howells, feloniously taken and led away by the aforesaid Nicholas and (whereas) in addition later, for certain reasons and considerations which moved the said Justices, the same Nicholas ap Robert had been committed by the same Justices at Monmoth aforesaid ... to the common Gaol of the aforesaid Sovereign Lady the Queen ... at Carlyon in the same County in the safe custody of John Hughes of Carlyon ... yeoman, then the keeper of the same Gaol, he still abides there until the aforesaid Justices might wish to be further advised thereon as it is fully clear and evident by the Record thereof, AND that the aforesaid John Hughes, then the Keeper of the aforesaid Gaol, having the responsibility and custody of the aforesaid Nicholas ap Robert, being in the Gaol in the manner and fashion as has been aforesaid, afterwards, that is to say on the 24th day of October in the above-mentioned eighteenth year of the reign of the aforesaid Sovereign Lady the Queen that now is feloniously and of his own free will allowed the aforesaid Nicholas ap Robert at Carlyon aforesaid ... then and there to go out, escape and go at large out of the aforesaid Gaol out of the custody of the same John Hughes against the peace of the aforesaid Sovereign Lady the Queen.'

11. L.H. Margin: 'Felony'.
And that the abovementioned Nicholas ap Robert broke Gaol in the manner described.

12. L.H. Margin: 'Felony'.
And that Howell James late of Llantellyo Cryssenny ... yeoman, otherwise called Howell Herbert of Llantellyo Cryssenny, gentleman, was 'taken and arrested' at Grussemont by Simon John Yevor, constable of the peace, on 12th October preceding for having on that day assaulted a certain Joanna Llogarden at Grussemont and 'then and there committed rape and had carnal knowledge of her against the will of the same Joanna.' Having been brought by the constable before Rees Morgan and William ap Roger, Esquires, he was by these Justices committed to the Gaol at Carlyon in the custody of Christopher Welshe, Esquire, at that time Sheriff of the County. Indictment is now made that on 24th October he 'did by force at Carlyon feloniously and of his own free will break Gaol and withdraw himself then and there from the custody of the said Sheriff, escape, and flee, against the form of the statute in such a case ...'

13. "KALENDARIUM DELIBERACIONIS GAOLE Domine Regine Castri sui Monmoth de prisonibus in ea existentibus coram Roberto Bell, milite, Capitali Barone predicte Regine Scacarii sui et Williamo Lovelace, serviente ad legem, Justiciariis ipsius Domine Regine ad Gaolam illam deliberandam assignatis apud Monmoth in Comitatu Monmoth die Lune vicesimo quinto ffebruarii anno regni Domine Elizabeth ... decimo nono."

'KALENDAR of the GAOL DELIVERY of the Sovereign Lady the Queen's Castle of Monmoth of the prisoners being therein, before Robert Bell, Knight, Chief Baron of the Exchequer of the aforesaid Queen and William Lovelace, Serjeant-at-law, the Justices of the same Sovereign Lady the Queen assigned for the delivery of that Gaol at Monmoth in the County of Monmoth, on Monday the twenty-fifth day of February in the nineteenth year of the reign of the Sovereign Lady Elizabeth ...'

14. L.H. Margin: "r[emandatus] p[risoni]."
"Nicholas ap Robert nuper de Cayrewent in Comitatu Monmoth, laborer, attinctus prout prepositum in Kalendaris quadragesime anno regni Domine Regine nunc decimo octavo, Et tunc remandatus prisoni."

'Nicholas ap Robert late of Cayrewent in the County of Monmoth, labourer, attainted as set forth in the Lent Kalendar in the eighteenth year of the reign of the present Sovereign Lady the Queen, and then remanded to prison.'

15. L.H. Margin: 'remanded to prison'.
John William Baker of Bergevenny, labourer, indicted as the accessory of Thomas Baker in the matter of the death of Watkin Herbert and 'remanded to prison at the last (Session) because the principal (defendant) was not yet outlawed.'

16. Jevan Cadogan of Llangeby, Howell James of Llantellyo Cryssenny, yeoman, Walter Griffith of Llangom, David Morgan of Llangeby, William ap Jenkin ap Rees of Bydweltey, husbandman, Mathew Williams of Bydweltey, yeoman, Thomas John ap Jenkin of Llanvreghva, William John Thomas of Sherenewton, John James of Bergevenny, all labourers, except where otherwise stated.
   List bracketed on the right hand side with the marginal note: 're-manded to prison in the matter of good behaviour as set forth in the last Kalendar.'

17. William Thomas of Trilleg, yeoman, committed for failing to keep the peace towards John Waters and Morris Waters, his son, and others the

servants of the said John, being bound over to do so, as set forth in the last Kalendar.

18. L. H. Margin: 'remanded to prison.'
William Jenkins of Llanvapley, yeoman, committed for the rape of Jane ferch Howell "iuxta regiam viam" ('near the Queen's highway') at Llanthewy Brythergh on 1st March in the seventeenth year of the Queen's reign.

19. John Lewis of Bergevenny, labourer, and George Baker of the same place, labourer, committed for the theft on 13th November preceding of three pounds in "numbered money" contained in a purse, the property of Richard Turbill.
    Note over each name: 'Puts himself (on the country), guilty, no chattels, let him be hanged by the neck.'

20. Jevan Rees of Llanbadock, labourer, committed for the theft on 11th. November preceding, at Comeyoy, of two heifers, one "pyed", the other red, each valued at 20s., the property of Thomas Harry Lewis.
    Over his name: as No 19 above.

21. John ap John Tryley of Bergevenny, "bocher", arrested "pro suspecione felonie" and committed to prison by William Herbert of Colbroke, Rees Morgan, and Mathew Herbert, Esquires, in the matter of a heifer belonging to William Thomas.
    Note over his name: as No 19 above.

22. John David ap Howell David of Bergevenny, tinker, committed for the theft on the Feast of St Bartholomew preceding of a piece of cloth called "Welshe ffryse", black, valued at 46s. 8d., the property of Thomas Sadler.
    Over his name: 'Puts himself (on the country), not guilty did not flee'.

23. Roger Williams, *alias* Tinker, of Langston, tinker, arrested at Langston on suspicion of felony and committed by William Morgan of Lanternam, Esquire, in the matter of a mare (owner not mentioned).
    Over his name: as No 19 above.

24. Roger Long of [*Blank*] in the County of Glamorgan, 'arrested at Newport on suspicion of felony and committed by Thomas Morgan, Esquire.'

25. Lewis William Richards of Llaneserryng, labourer, arrested at Skenffryth and committed by William John ap Roger for petty larceny.

Over his name: 'Puts himself (on the country), guilty, no chattels.' (No note of penalty.)

26. Thomas Griffith of Newport, "bochor", arrested on suspicion of felony and committed by Thomas Morgan and now charged in the matter of a cow belonging to Samuel Johns.

Over his name: as No 19 above.

27. Anna Davies of Chepstowe, "spynster", arrested there on suspicion of felony, committed by William Lewis, Esquire, and now charged. (offence not specified).

Over her name: "Po[nit] se[super patriam] cul[pabilem] ad valenciam x*d.* Ca[talla] null[a]". 'Puts herself (on the country), guilty to the value of 10*d.*, no chattels'. (No note of penalty.)

28. John David of Llanworda in the County of Carmarthen, glover, arrested on suspicion of felony at Bergevenny, committed by William Herbert of Colbroke and William John ap Roger and now charged. (Offence not specified.)

Over his name: "Po[nit] se[super patriam] cul[pabilem] ad valenciam iij*s.* ij*d.* Ca[talla] null[a] legit ut clericus". 'Puts himself (on the country), guilty to the value of 3*s.* 2*d.*, no chattels, reads as a cleric'.

29. John Harry of Uske, labourer, arrested at Llandenny on suspicion of felony and committed by William John ap Roger.

30. Thomas ap John, *alias* Mason, of Brecon town, labourer, arrested at Bergevenny on suspicion of felony and committed by William Herbert of Colbroke and William John ap Roger.

31. William Rosser of Dyngestowe, labourer, arrested there on suspicion of felony, committed by William Evans, Bachelor of Laws, and now charged on two accounts. (Neither specified.)

Over his name: as No 19 above.

32. Richard Ffowkes of Monmoth, labourer, arrested there on suspicion of felony and committed by the bailiffs of the town of Monmoth.

33. Griffin John Hugh of Basseleg, John Smith, *alias* Gove, of Bassaleg, David ap Rees of Bassaleg, Howell Lewis of Bassaleg, John Hugh Bedowe of Maughan, Howell Owen of Bassaleg, Thomas Philip David of Coydkernewe, Howell Morgan of Newport, William Powell of Newport, Lewis John Llewelen of Tredegar, all yeomen; list bracketed on right hand side with the marginal note: "Missi a concilio Domine Regine in marchiis Wallie pro suspecione felonie"; 'Sent by the Council of the Sovereign Lady the Queen in the Marches of Wales on suspicion of felony'.

L.H. Margin, by each name, except the first: 'remanded to prison.'

34. L.H. Margin: 'remanded to prison.'
John ap John Grothor of Llantony, tailor, arrested there on suspicion of felony and committed by Rees Morgan.

35. William Prichard Morgan of Mamhylad, yeoman, arrested there on suspicion of felony, committed by William John ap Roger, and now charged in the matter of a sheep valued at 12*d*.

Over his name: 'Puts himself (on the country), not guilty, did not flee.'

36. William Griffith of Llanvehangell Tonne-y-groes, husbandman, arrested there on suspicion of felony and committed by Thomas Morgan and Thomas Watkins.

37. Philip Prosser of Carlyon, husbandman, sent by the Council of the Marches on suspicion of felony.

38. John Harry of Comeyoy, husbandman, sent by the same Council.

39. Thomas Parke of Comcarvan, husbandman, arrested there on suspicion of felony and now charged therewith.

Over his name: 'Puts himself (on the country), guilty, did not flee.'

40. "Jevanus Vrane nuper de Bergevenny ... laborer, modo indictatus super Statutem de Rogez pro secundo defectu, Et modo manucaptus ad serviendum Johanni Morgan et comparendum coram Justiciariis hic ad finem duorum annorum nunc proximum futurorum sub pena predicti Johannis Morgan x lib., etc."

'Jevan Vrane late of Bergevenny ... labourer, now indicted on the Statute of Rogues for a second default, And now bound over to serve John Morgan and to appear before the Justices here at the end of the two years next hereafter following, under a penalty of the aforesaid John Morgan of ten pounds, etc.'
   Over his name: 'Puts himself (on the country), guilty, no chattels.'

41. Rees Williams, *alias* Corvyser, of Newport, labourer, there arrested on suspicion of felony and now charged with the theft of a purse and 40s. in numbered money, the property of Jane ferch Rees.
   L.H. Margin: "r[emandatus] p[rison]i sine Ballio."
   'Remanded to prison without bail.'

42. Thomas ap Howell of Pennalth, yeoman, committed for failing to keep the peace.
   L.H. Margin: "remandatus prisoni pro pace," 'remanded to prison in the matter of keeping the peace'.

Crick

1. SESSION OF THE PEACE held at Cryck on 13th February in the nineteenth year of the Queen's reign, before William Lewis and Thomas Watkins, two of the Justices of the County, and John Waters, Clerk of the Peace.

2. L.H. Margin: '12 jurors for the body of the County.'

William Hughes, gentleman	Thomas Watkin Thomas
Howell Thomas ap David	Watkin ap Howell
Howell Kynvyn	Richard Howell
Philip Morgan Lawrence	John Charles
Thomas Lawrence	Richard John Jenkins

John William Tanner
Charles Howell Jenkins
John David
Howell William Thomas

3. L.H. Margin: 'Assault and common brawl.'
Indictment that William Bunting of Monmoth, yeoman, is guilty of a series of assaults and of common brawling. viz. 18th June, 17 Eliz., on John Howell; 7th November, 17 Eliz., on Thomas ap John, senior; 31st October, 17 Eliz., on William Hughes, one of the bailiffs of the town of Monmoth 'there and then doing and executing his duty in the court-house of the said town'; 20th February, 18 Eliz., on John Howell; 21st October, 18 Eliz., 'with a certain piece of iron called an iron pike' on Thomas Williams of Trylleg, gentleman, again in the court-house, adding 'many opprobrious, hateful and scandalous words'; 29th December, 18 Eliz. 'out of pure spite' towards John Morgan of Skenffryth, gentleman, addressed in a loud voice to one John Bannor, being a serjeant at the keys of the said town, the opprobious etc. words, "Arreste yonder knave", and to the said John Morgan, "Thou art a perjured knave. Thou art a brybyng thyffe. Thou art a beggarly knave by kynde." Also that together with Thomas ap Richard and the aforesaid John Bannor he assaulted John Morgan inflicting with a dagger a wound four inches deep in his leg, and that on 20th February of the preceding year and on divers days and times afterwards has been and is a common rioter, brawler, and disturber of the Queen's peace.

4. L.H. Margin: 'Riot and unlawful assembly.'
And that Arnold Welshe of Llanwerne, gentleman, Richard Thomas of
Llanwerne, *alias* Dick Swaysshe, Robert Miller of Carlyon, otherwise known
as a miller, Roger James of Llanwerne, Watkin Taylor of Llanvehangell in
Netherwent, tailor, John Howell of Chrystchurche, Morgan Thomas of
Tredonock, David ap Jenkin of Llanwerne, William Lawrence of Llanwerne,
Howell Nicholas of Denham, Thomas Nicholas of Denham, David Olway,
Llanwerne, John Parker of Denham, all labourers, except where otherwise
stated, and others unknown, to the number of twenty persons, did on the
25th January of the present year take and detain in a house at Denham a
certain Katherine Prichard, widow of William Prichard.

5. L.H. Margin: "[*Erasure*] and Assault."
And that the same men assaulted Walter Vaughan, one of the chief
constables of the Hundred of Caldycott, who acting on information received
went to Denham to arrest 'the aforesaid rioters and malefactors' and to bring
them before the Justices, Arnold Welshe urging on the assailants with the
words "Kyll hym, kyll hym; thruste hym throwe, meanynge the said Water
(*sic*) Vaughan."

6. L.H. Margin: 'Resistance' (to arrest).
And that Morgan Lewis Holder on 13th February resisted arrest at Shere-
newton and with the aid of others unknown assaulted James David, the
Sheriff's bailiff sent to arrest him.

Raglan

1. SESSION OF THE PEACE held at Raglan on 14th March in the 19th year of the Queen's reign, before Edward, Lord Herbert, William Herbert of Colbroke, William Cecil, William John ap Roger, Walter Jones, Esquires, and John Waters, Clerk of the peace.

2. The Sheriff, Rees Morgan, Esquire, returns fully executed in all points his writ of "Venire facias" directed to him for the proclamation and constitution of the present court.

3. L.H. Margin: '12 jurors for the body of the County'.

John Gunter, gentleman	Jenkin Richards
Philip Cocks, gentleman	Owen Lawrence
John Evans, gentleman	Philip Powell David
Philip Powell Gwilym	John Hopkin
Philip Ygove[1]	

John Lewis
Thomas Prichard
Thomas Watkin Thomas
John Charles
William John Badam
John Thomas Yoroth

4. L.H. Margin: 'Trespass.'
Indictment that William Atkins of Chepstowe on several occasions trespassed on the land of Lewis Herbert, gentleman, allowing pigs of his to tread down and consume growing barley.

5. Indenture recorded on 25th February, 19 Eliz., in the presence of William Morgan of Lanternam, William Herbert of Colebroke and John Waters, Clerk of the peace. A verbatim copy is given in Latin. The following is an abstract of the contents:

George West of Naysshe, yeoman, in consideration of the sum of a hundred pounds conveys to John Arney, his heirs and assigns,

---

[1] Presumably 'Y Gof'.

50

messuages and lands recently the property of John West, his father, in the parish of Naysshe, also messuages and lands of his own recently in the occupation of John Bettyng the elder, of Naysshe, now deceased, also the annual revenue of 18*d*. accruing from lands and tenements occupied by [*Blank*] Madocks and a similar revenue of 13*d*. from lands occupied by John Tappe.

6. Indenture recorded on 26th February, 19 Eliz., in the presence of William Morgan, of Lanternam, Esquire, and John Waters, Clerk of the Peace. A verbatim copy, dated 31st January, is given in English. The following is an abstract, with quotations, of its contents:

William Herbert of Saynt Julyan, "in consideracion as well of the summe of fowre hundryd pounds of lawful money of England ... as also of the yerely rent charge of fyve pounds" conveys to Jenkin David ap Jenkin "all that his mannor or lordshypp of Llanveyre Kylgeaden, alias Cullgeaden, with thappurtenance ... which he had purchasyd of William Herbert of Cardiff, Esquire, late decessyd and all and syngular messuages howses barnes buyldyngs curtylages gardens orchyds lands tenements meadowes leasses pastures feadynge woodde underwoodde rents possessyons servyces advowsons patronages Knyghte ffees courte wardes maryadges relysses prouffects warrens waters lybertyes ffranchezes advantages ryghts comodytyes and other heredytaments what so ever."

7. Indenture recorded on 28th March, 19 Eliz., in the presence of Thomas Herbert, Knight, and Henry Herbert, Esquire, and John Waters, Clerk of the peace. A verbatin copy, dated 26th March, is given in English. The following is an abstract, with quotations, of its contents:

Roger Williams of Llangeaby, Esquire, "in consyderacion of the summe of one hundryth and fortye pounds of lawful money of England" conveys to William Baker of Bergevenny, gentleman, his heirs and assigns, the messuage and lands commonly known as "Bydhey ferme" now in the occupation of the said William Baker and recently in the occupation of Roger ap John, deceased, in the parishes of Llangeaby and Llanbadock.

Abergavenny

1. SESSION OF THE PEACE held at Bergevenny on the Tuesday next after the Close of Easter in the nineteenth year of the Queen's reign, before William Herbert, of Colebroke, William Powell, Thomas Morgan, William John ap Roger, Mathew Herbert, Walter Jones, Esquires, and other their colleagues, and John Waters, Clerk of the peace.

2. The Sheriff, Rees Morgan, Esquire, returns fully executed in all points his writ of "Venire facias" directed to him for the proclamation and constitution of the present court.

3. The Sheriff reports that acting on a warrant he has summoned Thomas Baker of Bergevenny, labourer, and Nicholas Thomas of Comeyoy, husbandman, required to answer concerning divers felonies and murders, to his county court on five occasions, viz. at Monmoth on 6th December preceding, at Newport on 3rd January, at Monmoth on 31st January, at Newport on 28th February, and at Monmoth on 28th March, at none of which did they appear. "Ideo ipsi per indicium Williami Cockes, generosi, et Williami Jones, generosi, coronatorum predicte Domine Regine Comitatus predicti utlagati sunt et uterque eorum utlagatus est." 'Therefore by the declaration of William Cockes, gentleman, and William Jones, gentleman, coroners of the aforesaid Sovereign Lady the Queen of the aforesaid County, they are outlawed and each one of the two is outlawed.'
Original writ: 22 March. 18 Eliz.

4. The Sheriff reports that acting on a writ of attachment he failed to find Roger Roberts of Comeyoy, labourer, Richard ap Jenkin of Bergevenny, corvisor, Robert James of Llantellyo Cryssenny, glover, Richard David Evans and John George, of Grussemont, John Harry and Watkin ap Howell, of Saynt Moughan, Henry Wilcocks, of Llangewa, John Parke, of Dynge-stowe, Richard ap Howell Williams and Watkin Howell Thomas, all yeomen, of Llantellyo Cryssenny, and Richard ap Jenkin of Bergevenny, corvisor, required to answer concerning divers trespasses and contempts. A new order for their appearance at the next Michaelmas Session.
Original writ; Easter, 18 Eliz.
L.H. Margin: 'To be summoned.'

Similiar reports of Sheriff, from 5 to 17 (incl.):

5. In the case of John David Howell David of Monmoth, tinker, John Booke of Mynsterworth in the County of Gloucester, labourer, and David John of Tylo, in the County of Glamorgan, required to answer concerning divers trespasses and contempts. A new order for their appearance at the next Trinity Session.
    Original writ; Michaelmas, 18 Eliz.
    L.H. Margin: 'To be summoned.'

6. In the case of Margaret ferch Hopkin of Aberustoyth, widow, required to answer concerning certain trespasses and entry 'where entry is not allowed by law.' A new order for her appearance at the next Michaelmas Session.

7. In the case of William Hughes of Monmoth, William Prosser of Pennalth, John Morris, *alias* John Morris Hughes, of Carlyon, John William Hughes of Uske, James William Hughes of Uske, Thomas Roberts of Dyngestowe, all yeomen, and Rees Jenkins of the town of Newport, tanner, required to answer concerning divers trespasses and contempts. A new order for their appearance at the next Trinity Session.
    Original writ; Trinity, 18 Eliz.

8. In the case of John Morris, *alias* John Hughes, of Carlyon, yeoman, James William Hughes of Uske, labourer, and Rees Jenkins of the town of Newport, tanner, required to answer concerning divers trespasses and contempts. A new order for their appearance at the next Trinity Session.
    Original writ; Trinity, 18 Eliz.

9. In the case of Philip ap David of Llangom, weaver, Jenkin David of the town of Monmoth, labourer, and Rees Jenkins of the town of Newport, tanner, required to answer concerning certain trespasses and contempts. A new order for their appearance at the next Trinity Session.
    Original writ; Trinity, 18 Eliz.

10. In the case of Owen Sayre, yeoman, Rees Owen Sayre, corvisor, James Owen Sayre, corvisor, all of Monmoth, and Rees Jenkins of Newport, tanner, required to answer concerning divers trespasses and contempts. A new order for their appearance at the next Trinity Session.
    Original writ; Michaelmas, 18 Eliz.

11. In the case of David Williams of Carlyon, yeoman, and Philip Edwards of Llanwerne, yeoman, required to answer concerning divers trespasses and contempts. A new order for their appearance at the next Trinity Session.
Original writ; 27th October, 18 Eliz.

12. In the case of David Mathew of Uske, Morgan Phillips of Llangeby, John Harry Adam of Uske, all yeomen, Edward Harry Adam of Uske, a cleric, Philip Leonard of Llangeby, Thomas Edwards of Uske, Thomas Yoroth of Llandenny, all yeomen, Thomas Prosser of Llansoer, gentleman, Richard Lewis of Llanvaughes, William John David ap John of Grussemont, William John Phillips of Grussemont, Richard Lewis of Llanvaughes, and David John Thomas of Porthvaynor, all yeomen, required to answer concerning divers trespasses and contempts. A new order for their appearance at the next Trinity Session.
Original writ: Epiphany, 19 Eliz.

13. In the case of Philip John Williams of Llanvehangell Pontmoyle, labourer, James ap James of Roathe in the County of Glamorgan, gentleman, and Thomas John ap Roger of Llanvregva, yeoman, required to answer concerning certain felonies and burglaries. A new order for their appearance at the next Trinity Session.
Original writ; Epiphany, 19 Eliz.

14. In the case of Arnold Welshe of Llanwerne, gentleman, Richard Thomas, *alias* Dick Swaysshe, of Llanwerne, Robert Miller of Carlyon, otherwise known as a miller, Roger James of Llanwerne, Watkin Taylor of Llanvyhangell in Netherwent, tailor, John Howell Dee of Chrystchurche, Morgan Thomas of Tredonock, David ap Jenkin of Llanwerne, William Lawrence of Llanwerne, Howell Nicholas of Denham, David Olway of Llanwerne, all labourers, except where otherwise stated, John Parker of Denham, husbandman, and William Bunting of Monmoth, yeoman, required to answer concerning divers trespasses, riots, and contempts. A new order for their appearance at the next Trinity Session.
Original writ given at the special Session held on 13th February, 19 Eliz.

15. In the case of all the persons named in the immediately preceding with the addition of Morgan Lewis Holder of Sherenewton, labourer. A new order for their appearance at the next Trinity Session.
Original writ; the same special Session.

16. In the case of Thomas Taylor of Monmoth, tailor, Philip Meels of Keynechurche in the County of Hereford, labourer, Thomas ap John of Brewenock in the County of Brecon, mason, John Philip Thomas of Mamhylad, husbandman, John Hughes of Carlyon, yeoman, Nicholas ap Robert of Cayrewent, labourer, and Howell James of Llantellyo Cryssenny, yeoman, otherwise styled gentleman, required to answer concerning divers trespasses and contempts. A new order for their appearance at the next Trinity Session.
Original writ; 25th March, 19 Eliz.

17. In the case of Thomas Taylor of Monmoth, tailor, and John ap Jenkin of Glaskoyed, labourer, required to answer concerning divers felonies. A new order for their appearance at the next Trinity Session.
Original writ; 25th March, 19 Eliz.

18. L.H. Margin: "relax[atio securitatis] pacis." (Release from recognisances.)
William Rawlings, yeoman, and Anna Williams, his wife, of Penhowe, bound over to keep the peace towards John Mulgray and Wenllian his wife, are released from their recognisances.

19. L.H. Margin: "recogn[itio] ffin[is]."
John Harries alias Smith of Tynterne, smith, bound over in the sum of ten pounds to keep the peace towards Blanche Calys, and to appear at this Session, has failed to appear. His ten pounds and another ten pounds for which Thomas Williams, gentleman, of Trylleg, stood surety, declared forfeit to the Crown.

20. L.H. Margin: "Magna Inquisicio pro corpore Comitatus." 'Grand Jury for the body of the County.'

Richard Herbert, gentleman	Thomas Prees Llewelen Morgan
John Wrothe, gentleman	Thomas Prosser
David ap Richard, gentleman	Gwilym Phillips
John David Powell Gwilym	Richard Watkin Apye
Roger Williams, gentleman	Howell Richards
John William Prees Eghan	

William Morgan Phillips
Philip John ap Jenkin
John Rosser
Howell John ap Howell
John William Philip John

21. L.H. Margin: 'Felony.'
Indictment that Matilda ferch Wyllym, spinster, *alias* Matilda Parry of Uske,
on 8th April 'at about midnight of the same day' stole five yards of woollen
cloth called "fflanen" valued at ten pence and a cloak called a "parkelett"
valued at two shillings, the property of William Jenkins.

22. L.H. Margin: 'Felony.'
And that Morgan John Rees, yeoman, and John Corser, corvisor, both of
Merther in the County of Glamorgan, on 6th August at Bydwelty stole three
red cows valued at ten pounds, the property of Gwilym Phillips.

23. L.H. Margin: 'Felony.'
And that Morgan Philip Morgan of Llangeby, yeoman, on 13th August, at
Pengrege stole "one payre of lynnen hose" valued at 10*d*., the property of
George Morgan, gentleman.

24. L.H. Margin: 'Felony.'
And that John James Kynvyn of Bergevenny, yeoman, on 1st March broke
and entered the house of Howell John ap Jenkin and stole a grey horse
valued at £3 6*s*. 8*d*. the property of the said Howell.

25. L.H. Margin: 'Assault and affray.'
And that Edward Thomas of Cryckehoell in the County of Brecon, weaver,
on 26th May of the present year 'with force and arms, namely a staff and a
dagger' assaulted Walter ap Watkin, *alias* "Ygove", at Bergevenny and so
seriously wounded him that his life was despaired of.

26. L.H. Margin: 'Assault and common brawl.'
And that John ap John of Llanwenarth, labourer, on 20th May of the present
year assaulted Lewis ap John. Also that on that day and on several other
occasions before and after that day he has been a common brawler and
disturber of the Queen's peace.

27. L.H. Margin: 'Assault and affray.'
And that George West of Naysshe, yeoman, assaulted Rowland Jones at
Newport on 2nd April of the present year.

28. L.H. Margin: 'Trespass.'
And that Thomas William Lewis of Llandenny, yeoman, broke and entered
the house of Richard ap Rhydderch at Llandenny on 23rd March of the
present year.

29. L.H. Margin: 'Trespass.'
And that Howell Jeyn Davy, yeoman, John Watkins, labourer, and William Ogans, labourer, otherwise styled servant of the aforesaid Howell Jeyn Davy, all of Redwyck, on 2nd July of the preceding year trespassed in a meadow called "Broade Meade" belonging to William Herbert, of Colbroke, Esquire, and cut down and carried off hay therefrom.

30. L.H. Margin: 'Entry by force.'
And that John Williams of Llanvapley, labourer, on 2nd March, in disregard of a statute of 8 Henry VI, entered by force a messuage, a barn, an orchard, a garden, twelve acres of meadow, thirty acres of pasture, and thirty acres of woodland at Penrose, the property of Philip Thomas Williams in the occupation of his son David Philip, and having ejected both retained possession himself.

31. A declaration that, in disregard of a statute of the present Queen's Parliament held at Westminster from the 8th May to the last day of June in the 14th year of the Queen's reign, Lewis Gruffyth late of Hay in the County of Brecon, labourer, John Lewis late of Aberustoyth, labourer, Elizabeth ferch David of the same town, spinster, and Gwenllian ferch Thomas of the same town, spinster, 'heeding in no wise the aforesaid statute nor fearing in any way the penalty in the same statute', on 12th April were caught at Saynt Moughan 'begging, wandering, and straying and mis-behaving themselves against the tenor of the same Act in contempt of the same Sovereign Lady the Queen ...' Also that these four persons have been brought to the present court in the custody of Rees Morgan, Esquire, Sheriff of the County. 'And the aforesaid indictment having been read to them now in full court ... order is made to the Sheriff by the aforesaid Justices to carry out sentence against the aforesaid Lewis Gruffyth, John Lewis, Elizabeth ferch David, and Gwenllian ferch Thomas in the following form, namely to brand the aforesaid Lewis Gruffyth on his right ear and to whip him according to the form of the aforesaid statute, and because the aforesaid John Lewis, Elizabeth ferch David, and Gwenllian ferch Thomas are below the age of fourteen years, therefore order is made to the same Sheriff to whip the said John, Elizabeth and Gwenllian according to the form of the statute, etc.

32. L.H. Margin: 'secunda Inquisitio.'

William Taylor
Thomas Lewis
James John Richards
Richard Gunter
Morgan Rees
John Rees Philip Williams

Philpott Taylor
Morgan David Philip Jenkins
Thomas Llewelen of Llangattock
William John ap Adam
Morgan David ap John

Henry Morgan
William John
William John Llewelen
Richard John Thomas Hopkin
Henry Llewelen

33. L.H. Margin: 'Assault.'
Indictment that Philip Jones of Trilleg, gentleman, on 8th September preceding entered the house of Jane Batchelor and assaulted her and Jenett ferch Thomas.

34. L.H. Margin: 'Assault.'
And that Edward ap Harry of Uske, a cleric, on 29th March preceding assaulted Lewis Morris; also that the same Edward ap Harry and John ap Harry, yeoman, assaulted the said Lewis and Anna his wife on another occasion on the same day.

35. L.H. Margin: 'Trespass.'
And that Lewis Thomas of Llangeney in the County of Brecon, on 20th March preceding and on divers occasions before and after broke and entered the close of John Llewelen at Llandylowe Barthalowe, broke down the hedges and carried the material away.

36 L.H. Margin: 'Assault and affray.'
And that George West of Naysshe, yeoman, and William West of Newport, yeoman, on 2nd April preceding assaulted George Dawkes of Newport, tanner, 'one of the jurors impanelled, sworn, and charged according to the due form of the law and the custom of the town of Newport aforesaid to try a certain issue in the court of the town of Newport joined between the aforesaid William Weste and a certain Rowland James of Bergevenny ... glover.'

> An inserted note indicates that the case was later sent before the Queen's Bench at Westminster in the Trinity Term in virtue of a Certiorari directed to the Justices.

37. L.H. Margin: "Vend[itio] cervic[ie] absque licenc[ia]." 'The selling of ale without a licence.'
Presentment that Thomas Doberlowe of Broyngwyn, yeoman, sold bread, ale, and other victuals at his house on 14th April preceding and at divers other times without the licence of the Justices.

Similiar presentments follow, from No 38 to No 47 (incl.):

38. L.H. Margin: "pro consimili". 'for the like [offence]'.
Gwilla David, spinster, Thomas ap Richard, yeoman, John ap Jeyn Gruffyth, yeoman, and Agnes Wenne, spinster, all of Treegayre, committed the same offence on 12th April and at other times.

39. L.H. Margin: 'for the like offence.'
Richard Williams of Llaneserrynge, yeoman, committed the same offence on 10th April.

40. L.H. Margin: 'for the like offence.'
James Pargwyn of Llanthewy Skyrryd, yeoman, and Adam Richards of the same place, yeoman, committed the same offence on 9th April and at other times.

41. L.H. Margin: 'for the like offence.'
Joanna Gruffyth of Llanvapley, spinster, committed the same offence on 11th April and at other times.

42. L.H. Margin: 'for the like offence.'
Henry Phillips, yeoman, Margery ferch John, spinster, and Madock ap Rees, yeoman, all of Llangattock Clenyg, committed the same offence on 6th April.

43. L.H. Margin: 'for the like offence.'
John Roberts, yeoman, Hugh Llyvor, yeoman, and John Crose, yeoman, all of Goytre, committed the same offence on 4th April.

44. L.H. Margin: 'for the like offence.'
Henry Gough of Saynt Mougham, yeoman, and William Gwilym of Llangattock Vybon Avell, yeoman, committed the same offence on 8th April.

45. L.H. Margin: 'for the like offence.'
William John Weyth of Chrystchurche, labourer, committed the same offence on 9th April.

46. L.H. Margin: 'for the like offence.'
William Rhydderch of Portskewett, labourer, committed the same offence on 8th April.

47. L.H. Margin: 'for the like offence.'
John William ap Jenkin, yeoman, and John George Howell, yeoman, both of Raglan, committed the same offence on 12th April.

48. Record of an indictment at the preceding Epiphany Session at Newport that Elizabeth Williams, widow, Howell ap Rees, labourer, and Lewis Williams, labourer, all of Llangattock Clennyg, on 3rd January of the present year entered and took possession of an enclosure of land belonging to James John Richards, keeping out the owner in disregard of a statute of 8 Henry VI; the defendants appeared and 'they say that they are in no way guilty thereof and that no one of them is guilty thereof in the form as by the aforesaid indictment ... And concerning this matter they put themselves severally on the country ... Accordingly order is made to the Sheriff of the County that he should cause to come before the Justices at the next general Session of the peace ... to be held at Bergevenny ... on the Tuesday next after the Close of Easter next occurring, 12 etc. ... The same day is appointed for the aforementioned Elizabeth, Howell, and Lewis, etc.'
     On the appointed day (that of the present Session) the Sheriff, Rees Morgan, Esquire, returns his 'writ in order' fully executed in all points with a panel of 24 names attached to the same writ or order. Twelve of these are sworn: Henry Howell of Llangattock, Roger James, Nicholas ap Richard, James Prichard, William Lawrence, Morgan Philip Jenkins, David Morgan, Thomas Prosser, James Howell ap Howell, William Thomas ap John, William ap Jenkin Rosser, and John Thomas ap Jenkin David. These 'say on their oath that the aforesaid Elizabeth Williams, Howell ap Rees, and Lewis Williams are not guilty of the aforesaid trespass, riot, unlawful assembly and entry by main force ... Therefore it is granted by the Court that the aforesaid Elizabeth Williams, Howell ap Rees and Lewis Williams ... should be acquitted "sine die" and that each one of them ... should go acquitted and "sine die".'

49. Another record, identical in form with that immediately preceding, of the indictment and trial at the same two Sessions respectively of Thomas ap Howell of Bergevenny, gentleman and lately Deputy Sheriff of the County, Meredith Howell Jenkins, yeoman, and John ap John, yeoman, and servant of Thomas ap Howell, both of Llanwennarth, for taking by extortion under colour of their duty a sack and three bushels of "barly-malte" valued at 10s., the property of John ap John of Llanbadock and William John of Uske. They

are acquitted by a jury of 12: Thomas David ap John, gentleman, John Evans gentleman, Robert John Williams, Morgan Thomas, Philip Jenkin ap Jenkin. Howell ap Howell Howell (*sic*), Philip Prosser, John William Lewis, William John ap Howell Hawkins, Henry Howell of Llangattock, John William James, and William David ap Jenkin.

50. Similar record of the indictment at the General Session and Gaol Delivery held at Monmoth on 25th February preceding that Richard ap Robert of the town of Bergevenny, corvisor, stole a linen garment valued at 10*d.*, the property of William Lewis. The accused appears at the present Session in the custody of the Sheriff, pleads not guilty, puts himself 'on the country', and is acquitted by a jury of 12: Howell Thomas Williams, Morgan Philip Jenkin Eghan, Jevan Llewelen, Roger James, Richard James, Roger Evans, John David Penry, Thomas Jeyn Apoyrkin, Philip Parry, Jevan Williams of Llannover, Watkin David ap Jenkin, and David Morgan of Penrose.

L.H. Margin: "Non culp[abilis] nec re[traxit]. Ideo ex[oneratur]". 'Not guilty, did not flee. Therefore he is acquitted.'

51. Similar record of the indictment at the preceding Epiphany Session at Newport that William David Mathew of Uske, yeoman, Morgan Phillips of Llangeby, yeoman, John Harry Adam of Uske, yeoman, Edward Harry Adam of Uske, a cleric, William Reynolds and Richard Watkins, yeomen, of Llanbadock, Roger Harry of Llanvehangell Pontmoyle, yeoman, Philip Howell Gwilym of Wolfesnewton, yeoman, Howell Reynolds of Llantryssen, yeoman, William Reynolds of Llangevewe, yeoman, Jevan Harry and Philip Leonard, yeomen, of Llangom, Thomas Edwards of Uske, yeoman, and others unknown, engaged in rioting and unlawful assembly at Uske on a market-day, 18th October preceding, and at that time assaulted one William Saunders. Seven of them, William Reynolds, Richard Watkins, Roger Harry, Philip Howell Gwilym, Howell Reynolds, William Reynolds of Llangevewe, and Jevan Harry appeared, put themselves 'on the country', having put themselves not guilty.

At the present Session these seven are acquitted by a jury of 12: John David ap Howell of Llangoven, Lewis Thomas of Llansoy, James Williams of Trillege Graynge, John William Llewelen of Llanthewy, Henry David ap Howell of Llangenock, Henry Richards of Penhowe, Thomas John Hopkins of Llanllowell, Lewis John ap Rosser of Mamhylad, Thomas ap Rosser of Llantryssen, John Thomas John Phillips of Trilleg, John Morris ap Howell of Llanvehangell, and John ap John David of Llanvetherynge. An order is made for the appearance of the others at the next Corpus Christi Session, to be held at Uske.

'Fines, charges and amercements at the foregoing Session'

52. Record of fines imposed on defaulting jurors from the Hundred of
Newport: William Watkin of Peterston, Thomas Morse of Marshefield,
William Portree of Peterston, and David Wylly of Rompney; each 3s. 4d.

R.H. Margin: 13s. 4d.

53. Similar record of fines on defaulting jurors from the Hundred of
Caldycott: John Mulray of Portskewett, Jenkin ap Howell of Wylcryck,
Thomas Bole of Wytston, William Watkins of Sherenewton and Walter ap
Howell of Magor.

R.H. Margin: 16s.8d.

54. Similar record fines on defaulting jurors from the Hundred of Raglan:
Thomas John ap Watkin, and John Adam Howell.

R.H. Margin: 6s. 8d.

55. Similar record of fines on defaulting jurors from the Hundred of Uske:
Thomas ap Robert of Gohelog, gentleman, Philip Jenkins of Llancayo,
Howell Edwards of Uske, Siprius Phillips, Thomas John ap Jenkin, Thomas
James of Pantege, Watkin John Wyllym of Llangattock, and Lewis Meredith
of Llandegveth.

R.H. Margin: 26s. 8d.

56. Charge upon the freeholders and inhabitants of Llanhenock for
non-appearance to show reason why they have not repaired the high road in
their parish leading from Carlyon to Uske ... 6s. 8d.

57. Similar charge on Tredonock in relation to the road leading from Carlyon
towards Uske. 6s. 8d.

58. Also on Chrystchurche in relation to the road leading from there towards
"Stonen Brydge" on the outskirts of Somerton ... 6s. 8d.

59. Also on Llantryssen in relation to the road leading from Llanllowell to
Pull Baugh ... 6s. 8d.

60. Also on Pantege in relation to the road leading from Bergevenny towards
Newport ... 6s. 8d.

61. Also on Lewis John Treharon of Chrystchurche, yeoman, Thomas
Williams of Westercoyde, yeoman, and Lewis James of Chrystchurche,

yeoman, in relation to a road leading towards their lands within the parish of Chrystchurche, leading from that place towards Llanwerne. Fine: 2*s.* each ... 6*s.*

62. Thomas ap Richard of Treergayre, yeoman, admitted to his fine, 2*s.* for selling ale without the licence of the Justices. Robert Lace of Dyngestowe, stands surety.

R.H. Margin: 2*s.*

63. Lewis Thomas of Llangeney in the County of Brecon, labourer, indicted at the present Session for trespass, admitted to his fine of 2*s.* The fine paid into the hands of William Herbert of Colbroke.

R.H. Margin: 2*s.*

64. James Williams of Redwyck, yeoman, and John Goseling of Magor, yeoman, each admitted to a fine of 2*s.* for selling ale without the licence of the Justices, Richard Thomas of Redwyck and Watkin Tanner of Magor stand surety.

R.H. Margin: 4*s.*

65. For the same offence Richard Lace, yeoman, John Bedyck, *alias* Smith, yeoman, and John Powell, yeoman, all of Caldycott, admitted to a similar fine.

R.H. Margin: 6*s.*

66. For the same offence Henry Yoroth of Redwyck, labourer, and William John Badam of Sherenewton, yeoman, admitted to similar fines, 2*s.* each, fines paid into the hands of William Herbert of Colbroke.

R.H. Margin: 2*s.* (not 4*s.*)

67. For the same offence Jenkin ap John of Llangattock Vybon Avell, yeoman, admitted to a fine of 12*d.* paid into the hands of John Waters, Clerk of the peace.

Usk II

1. SESSION OF THE PEACE held at Uske on the Tuesday next after the Feast of Corpus Christi, the 11th June in the 19th year of the Queen's reign, before Edward, Lord Herbert, William Morgan of Llanternam, William Herbert of Colbroke, Thomas Morgan, William Lewis, Edmund Morgan, Mathew Herbert, William John ap Roger, Walter Jones, and John Waters, Clerk of the peace.

2. The Sheriff, Rees Morgan, Esquire, returns fully executed in all points the writ of "Venire facias" directed to him for the proclamation and constitution of the present court.

3. The Sheriff reports that, acting on a writ of attachment, he has failed to find John Richards of Aberustoyth, Roger John ap Jenkin of the same town, Charles Watkins of Llandylowe Barthalowe, William John David ap John of the same town, William John Phillips of Llanvehangell Cylcornell, William Probert of the same town, all yeomen, David Williams of Llanveyre Cylgedyn, tinker, John Mathew of Llannyssen, yeoman, Morgan Spryggen, yeoman, and John Miller, miller, of Bethowesnewyth, required to answer concerning certain trespasses and contempts. A new order for their appearance at the next Epiphany Session.
    Original writ; Epiphany, 18 Eliz.
    L.H. Margin: "utlagat[us] de transgr[essione]". 'Outlawed for trespass.'

Similar reports of the Sheriff, from Nos 4 to 17 (incl.):

4. In the case of Philip John Williams of Llanvehangell Pontmoyle, labourer, James ap James of Roathe in the County of Glamorgan, gentleman, and Thomas John ap Jenkin of Llanvrighva, yeoman, required to answer concerning certain felonies. A new order for their appearance at the next Epiphany Session.
    Original writ; Epiphany, 18 Eliz.
    L.H. Margin: "ex[igi]", 'to be summoned.'

5. In the case of Thomas Taylor of Monmouth, tailor, Philip Mele of Keynchurche in the County of Hereford, labourer, Thomas ap John of Brewenock in the County of Brecon, mason, John Philip Thomas of Mamhylad, husbandman, John Hughes of Carlyon, yeoman, Nicholas ap Robert of Cayrewent, labourer, and Howell James of Llantellyo Crysenny,

yeoman, *alias* Howell Herbert of Llantellyo aforesaid, gentleman, required to answer concerning divers felonies. A new order for their appearance at the next Epiphany Session.
Original writ; 25th February, 19 Eliz.
L.H. Margin: 'to be summoned.'

6. In the case of Thomas Taylor of Monmoth, tailor, and John ap Jenkin of Glascoyed, labourer, required to answer concerning certain felonies. A new order for their appearance at the next Epiphany Session.
Original writ; 25th February, 19 Eliz.
L.H. Margin: 'to be summoned.'

7. In the case of Rees Jenkins of the town of Newport, tanner, John Morris, *alias* John Morris Hughes of Carlyon, yeoman, James William Hughes of Uske, labourer, and William Prosser of Pennalth, yeoman, required to answer concerning certain trespasses, assaults, and contempts. A new order for their appearance at the next Epiphany Session.
Original writ; Trinity, 18 Eliz.
L.H. Margin: 'To be summoned.'

8. In the case of Rees Jenkins of the town of Newport, tanner, and William Hughes of Monmoth, yeoman, required to answer concerning certain trespasses and contempts. A new order for their appearance at the next Epiphany Session.
Original writ; Trinity, 18 Eliz.
L.H. Margin: 'To be summoned.'

9. In the case of John Morgan, *alias* John Hughes, of Carlyon, yeoman, James William Hughes of Uske, labourer, Thomas Roberts of Dyngestowe, gentleman, Philip ap David of Llangom, weaver, Jenkin David of Monmoth, labourer, and Rees Jenkins of Newport, tanner, required to answer concerning certain trespasses, assaults and contempts. A new order for their appearance at the next Epiphany Session.
Original writ; Trinity, 18 Eliz.
L.H. Margin: 'To be summoned.'

10. In the case of Margaret ferch Hopkin of Aberustoyth, widow, required to answer concerning a certain trespass and 'entry where entry is not allowed by law.' A new order for her appearance at the next Epiphany Session.
Original writ; 27th July, 18 Eliz.

11. In the case of Owen Sayre, yeoman, Rees Owen Sayre, corvisor, James Owen Sayre, corvisor, all of Monmoth, and Rees Jenkins of Newport, tanner, required to answer concerning divers trespasses and contempts. A new order for their appearance at the next Michaelmas Session.
Original writ; Michaelmas, 18 Eliz.

12. In the case of David Williams of Carlyon, yeoman, and Philip Edwards of Llanwerne, yeoman, required to answer concerning certain trespasses and contempts. A new order for their appearance at the next Michaelmas Session.
Original writ; given at the Special Session held on 27th October, 18 Eliz. (i.e. at Usk).

13. In the case of Matilda ferch Watkin of Uske, *alias* Matilda Parry, spinster, Morgan John Rees, yeoman, and John Corvyser, corvisor, both of Merther in the County of Glamorgan, and John James Kynvyn of Bergevenny, yeoman, required to answer concerning divers felonies. A new order for their appearance at the next Michaelmas Session.
Original writ; Easter, 19 Eliz.

14. In the case of Arnold Welshe, gentleman, Richard Thomas, *alias* Dick Swaysshe, both of Llanwerne, Robert Miller of Carlyon, labourer, otherwise known as a miller, Roger James of Llanwerne, yeoman, Watkin Taylor of Llanvehangell in Netherwent, tailor, John Howell Dee of Chrystchurche, Morgan Thomas of Tredonock, husbandman, David ap Jenkin, William Lawrence, both of Llanwerne, Howell Nicholas of Denham, Thomas Nicholas of Denham, David Olway of Llanwerne, all labourers except where otherwise stated, and John Parker of Denham, husbandman, required to answer concerning certain trespasses, riots, and assaults. A new order for their appearance at the next Michaelas Session.
Original writ; 13th February, 19 Eliz.

15. In the case of all those mentioned in No 14 with the addition of Morgan Lewis Holder of Sherenewton, labourer, required to answer concerning certain trespasses, riots, and resistance to arrest. A new order for their appearance at the next Michaelmas Session.
Original writ; 13th February, 18 Eliz.

16. In the case of Thomas Prosser of Llansoer, gentleman, Richard Lewis of Llanvaughes, Thomas Yoroth of Llandenny, William John David ap John of Grussemont, William John Phillips of the same town, Richard Lewis of

Llanvaughes,[1] and David John Thomas of Porthvaynor, all yeomen, required
to answer concerning certain trespasses, assaults and contempts. A new order
for their appearance at the next Michaelmas Session.
   Original writ; Epiphany, 19 Eliz.

17. In the case of John Williams of Llanvapley, labourer, Edward Thomas
of Crickhowell in the County of Brecon, weaver, John ap John of Llanwenarth, labourer, George West of Naysshe, Thomas William Lewis of
Llandenny, Howell Jenkin David, John Walter, labourer, William Ogans,
labourer, *alias* William Lewis servant of the aforesaid Howell Jenkin David,
all of Redwyck, Edward ap Harry, a cleric, and John ap Harry, both of Uske,
Thomas Doberlowe, Sibyl David, spinster, John ap Jenkin Gruffyth, Agnes
Wenne, spinster, all of Bryngwyn, Richard Williams of Llanesserynge, James
Parkgwyn, and Adam Richards, both of Llanthewy Skyrryd, Joanna Gruffyth
of Llanvapley, spinster, Henry Phillips of Llangattock Clennyg, Margaret
ferch John, spinster, and Madoc ap Rees, both also of Llangattock Clennyg,
Henry Gough of Saynt Moughan, William Gwilym of Llangattock Vybon
Avell, William John Weyth of Chrystchurche, Thomas Robert of Langston,
John Robert, Hugh Llyvor, John Croft, all of Goytre, William Rhydderch of
Portskewett, John William ap Jenkin, and George Thomas Howell, both of
Raglan, all yeomen except where otherwise stated, required to answer
concerning divers trespasses and contempts. A new order for their appear-
ance at the next Michaelmas Session.
   Original writ; Easter 19 Eliz.

18. L.H. Margin: "M[emorandum] pro [securitate] pacis r[emandatus] ad
prox[imam]". 'Memorandum in the matter of surety for keeping the peace;
remanded to the next [Session.]'
Lewis Phillips of Llanvreghva, a cleric, is bound over to keep the peace
towards Morgan Harry of Pantege and to appear at the next Michaelmas
Session. John Thomas of Micheltroy, yeoman, and Maurice Thomas of
Trilleg, yeoman, stand surety each in the sum of a hundred shillings; Lewis
Phillips himself in the sum of ten pounds.

19. L.H. Margin: identical with No 18.
The abovementioned Morgan Harry is bound over to keep the peace towards
the said Lewis Phillips and to appear at the next Michaelmas Session. Robert
Waters of Llanbadock, gentleman, and Philip John Howell of the same town,

---

[1] This name is here entered a second time on the list.

yeoman, stand surety, each in the sum of a hundred shillings; Morgan Harry himself in the sum of ten pounds.

20. L.H. Margin: 'Memorandum in the matter of surety for keeping the peace; remanded to the next Trinity Session.'
Thomas Jones of Uske, gentleman, is bound over to keep the peace with Reginald Hugh and to appear at the next Trinity Session. John Herbert of Llangevewe, gentleman, and Morgan Howell of Uske, yeoman, stand surety, each in the sum of a hundred shillings; Thomas Jones himself in the sum of ten pounds.

21. L.H. Margin: identical with No 20.
The abovementioned Morgan Howell is bound over to keep the peace towards the same Reginald Hugh and to appear at the next Trinity Session. Thomas Jones, gentleman, and John Adam, yeoman, both of Uske, stand surety, each in the sum of a hundred shillings; Morgan Howell himself in the sum of ten pounds.

22. L.H. Margin: "pro felon[ia]; R[emandatus] ad proximam Gaole Deliberac[ionem]". 'In the matter of a felony, remanded to the next Gaol Delivery.'
John Thomas David of Uske, yeoman, remanded on bail to the next Gaol Delivery, wheresoever held in the County, to answer concerning a certain felony. William Thomas ap Morgan of Pantege, gentleman, and William Thomas Gruffyth of Llanbadock, yeoman, stand surety, each in the sum of twenty pounds, and John Thomas David himself in the sum of forty pounds.

23. L.H. Margin: identical with No 22.
Robert Waters of Llanbadock, gentleman, remanded on bail to the next Gaol Delivery, to answer concerning 'all and singular charges which shall then and there be made against him.' William David ap John of Llannarth, gentleman, and Nicholas William Gruffyth of Uske, yeoman, stand surety, each in the sum of ten pounds and Robert Waters himself in the sum of twenty pounds.

24. L.H. Margin: identical with No 22.
John ap John Gwynne and William John Gough both yeomen of Uske, bound over each in the sum of ten pounds, to appear at the next general Gaol Delivery and give evidence against John Thomas David 'and others' who are to be charged with a certain felony.

25. L.H. Margin; "Magna Inquisicio pro corpore Comitatus." 'Grand Jury for the body of the County.'

Andrew Jones, gentleman
William Herbert, gentleman
William Morgan, gentleman
John Thomas John Prosser
Morgan David ap John

Henry David Powell
William John Powell Hawkins
Thomas Eghan
William Powell
Edward Williams

John William Phillips
William John Thomas
George Williams
Reginald William Thomas
Thomas Jeyne Apoyrkin

26. L.H. Margin: 'Felony and murder.'
Indictment that John Williams the elder of Stavorney, yeoman, on 31st January preceding, at about 'the eighth hour of the night, murdered John Williams the younger by stabbing him with a dagger valued at 2s.'

> *Over his name:* 'Puts himself (on the country), guilty, no chattels, let him be hanged by the neck.'

27. L.H. Margin: 'Felony.'
And that Thomas William Jenkin Wyllym, labourer, John William Jenkin Wyllym, labourer, and William Rees, weaver, all of Llanygon in the County of Brecon, on 13th October preceding at Comeyoy stole two calves, each valued at 34*s*. 4*d*. and a heifer valued at 34*s*. 4*d*., the property of Simon ap Richard.

28. L.H. Margin: 'Felony.'
And that Gladys ferch Thomas, spinster, and Katherine ferch John, spinster, both of Goytre, on 25th May at Goytre stole a lamb valued at 10*d*., the property of John Williams.

> *Over both names:* 'Puts himself (on the country), not guilty, did not flee.'

29. L.H. Margin: 'Trespass.'
And that John Richard ap Jenkin, labourer, Roger Richard ap Jenkin, labourer, William Richard ap Jenkin, labourer, Gwenllian Rees, spinster, and Amabel Richards, spinster, all of Trethvyn, on 13th February entered by force 'into a messuage or tenement, two acres of land and three acres of meadow and molested the owner, John David Powell Eghan.'

30. L.H. Margin: 'Trespass.'
And that Morgan David Morgan, yeoman, and Roger James, yeoman, both of Llanwerne, trespassed at Wytford on 28th May preceding. 'They broke and entered a close belonging to a certain Giles Powell within the liberty of Henry, Earl of Pembroke and then and there unlawfully distrained upon the said Giles Powell for a heifer of red colour, of the goods and chattels of the aforesaid Giles Powell.'

31. L.H. Margin: 'Assault and affray.'
And that Edmund Coole of Monmoth, yeoman, on 8th June preceding assaulted Morris Waters at Monmoth.

32. L.H. Margin: 'Trespass.'
And that Joanna ferch Thomas, wife of Thomas Jeyn, deceased, of Trillegge Graynge, widow, on 7th June preceding entered the close of William Bedowe at Pennalth, breaking the hedge and driving off three cows, the property of the said William Bedowe.

33. 'Trespass.'
And that the same Joanna ferch Thomas together with Matilda ferch Thomas, spinster, on 24th May preceding at Pennalth entered a close and a house belonging to Walter Jones, Esquire, unlawfully retaining possession against the said Walter Jones.

34. L.H. Margin: 'Trespass.'
And that Jevan Lewis of Llanwerne, labourer, on 9th June preceding allowed a mare of his to tread down and consume growing oats and barley belonging to Morgan Harry at Llanwerne.

35. L.H. Margin: 'Assault and affray.'
And that William David of Llannelly in the County of Brecon, yeoman, and Griffin Miller of Llangreyney in the County of Brecon, miller, assaulted David Thomas Phillips at Bergevenny on 3rd May.

36. L.H. Margin: 'Assault and affray.'
And that Richard Herbert of Goytre, gentleman, on 9th June preceding and 'on divers occasions before and after' assaulted Philip Richard at Goytre.

37. L.H. Margin: 'Trespass.'
And that William Morgan Rosser of Carlyon, yeoman, on 19th May preceding trespassed in a close belonging to William Thomas Lewis at Llanthewy and broke fences recently erected around the said close.

38. And 'that whereas by divers statutes of the laws of England hitherto made, it stands ordered and enacted that all villages within this realm of England are bound to have, to repair, and to maintain within the same village posts called "stockes" at the charges and expenses of that village, and this under a fixed penalty contained and determined in the same statutes, nevertheless, those statutes notwithstanding, the village of Skenffryth has for a long time not had and still has not stocks in the village of Skenffryth aforesaid in the aforesaid County to the pernicious and evident example to other villages in the aforesaid County and to the great and ready encouragement, incitement, and emboldening of all felons, malefactors, trespassers, and other suspect persons there lingering near or passing by, and also against the form of the aforesaid statutes and against the peace of the aforesaid Sovereign Lady the Queen.'

39. L.H. Margin: 'For the sale of ale without the licence of the Justices.'
Presentment that Richard Powell Jenkins, and William Grono, tailor, both of Skenffryth, Richard Taylor, and Philpott John, both of Grussemont, David Philip Jenkins, and Howell ap Rees Gough, both of Skenffryth, Rosser Thomas of Llangom, Hugh Reynolds of Rochefyld, tailor, George James of Caldycott, Elizabeth Webb, spinster, and Anna Warner, spinster, both of Caldycott, William Gwilym of Llangattock Vybon Avell, John Philip Weyth of Llanveyre, and Milo ap Harry of Buckeholte, all yeoman, except where otherwise stated, on divers occasions sold "victualia" without the licence of the Justices.

40. L.H. Margin: "Pro defectu alte vie." 'For failure to repair the high road.'
Presentment that the land-holders and inhabitants of Llanbadock failed to repair and maintain the road within their parish leading from Uske to Llandegveth.

Similar presentments from No 41 to No 54 (incl.):

41. L.H. Margin: 'Failure to repair high road.'
Relating to Llantryssen in respect of a road leading from Castell Trogie towards the house recently occupied by Walter ap Howell of Llantryssen and now occupied by Henry, Earl of Pembrock.

42. L.H. Margin: 'Failure to repair high road.'
Relating to Llandegveth in respect of a road leading from Uske via Llanbadock towards Llandegveth and thence to Lanternam.

43. L.H. Margin; 'Failure to repair high road.'
Relating to Llanvreghva in respect of a road leading from Uske via
Llanbadock towards Llanvreghva and thence to Lanternam.

44. L.H. Margin: 'Failure to repair high road.'
Relating to Uske in respect of a road leading from Uske to Pontmoyle.

45. L.H. Margin: 'For the like offence. '
Relating to Llanbadock in respect of a road leading from Uske to Pontmoyle.

46. L.H. Margin: 'For the like offence.'
Relating to Llanvyhangell Pontmoyle in respect of a road leading from Uske
to Pontmoyle.

47. L.H. Margin: 'For the like offence.'
Relating to Llangattock-iuxta-Uske in respect of a road leading from
Tryssawen towards Bergevenny.

48. L.H. Margin: 'For the like offence.'
Relating to Grussemont in respect of a road leading from the dwelling-house
of Morris Williams towards Gryge Vaugh.

49. L.H. Margin: 'For the like offence.'
Relating to Llantellyo Cryssenny in respect of a road leading from the same
dwelling-house towards the same Gryge Vaugh.

50. L.H. Margin: 'For the like offence.'
Relating to Skenffryth in respect of a road leading from Bergevenny through
Tyre Marsshy to Trynante and thence to the town of Rosse.

51. L.H. Margin: 'For the like offence.'
Relating to Rochefyld in respect of a road leading from Monmoth towards
Bergevenny between Crosse Lloyde and Mouse Well in the aforesaid parish
of Rochefyld.

52. L.H. Margin: "pro non veniendo ad adiuvandum emendare altas vias."
'For not coming to help repair highways.'
Presentment 'that George Morris of Llangevewe ... yeoman, John Williams
of Llangevewe aforesaid ... labourer, Thomas ap Gwilym of the same town
... labourer, William Thomas alias Meyrick, of the same town ... labourer,
and Jane John Wyllym of the same town ... widow, did not come on the
days appointed for them by the overseers of the parish of Llangevewe to

help to mend and repair the highways within the same parish according to the form of the statute recently set forth and provided in such a case, but made default on six several days in coming to work in the form aforesaid, having sufficient notice and warning given them previously in this behalf by the aforesaid overseers, against the form of the aforesaid statute and against the peace of the aforesaid Sovereign Lady the Queen. Therefore they have forfeited and lost the penalty contained in the statute, that is to say each of them for each day thus making default through them 12*d*.'

Similar presentments from No 53 to No 57 (incl.):

53. L.H. Margin: 'For the like offence.'
James David, labourer, Howell Wyllym, labourer, Gwenllian Howell, widow, and John Morgan, labourer all of Llangevewe, made default on 'four several days', the same penalty.

54. L.H. Margin: 'For the like offence.'
Morgan Williams, labourer, Thomas Williams, labourer, James John Watkins, labourer, Thomas John Williams, labourer, and Roger John Watkins, labourer, all of Llangevewe, made default on 'three several days'; the same penalty.

55. L.H. Margin: 'For the like offence.'
Howell Hopkins, labourer, and Robert William Glace, labourer, both of Llangevewe, made default on 'two several days'; the same penalty.

56. L.H. Margin: 'For the like offence.'
John ap John, labourer, William Reynolds, yeoman, and Jenkin Thomas Cecil, labourer, all of Llangevewe, made default 'on one day'; the same penalty.

57. L.H. Margin: 'For the like offence.'
David Johns of Llangevewe made default on 'five days'; the same penalty.

58. 'Grand Jury for the body of the County.'

John Robnett, gentleman	William Roberts
David Thomas Phillips	Roger Jenkins
Morgan Watkins	John Lewis
Philip John ap Jenkin	John Howell Turner
Thomas Harry	John Adam Howell
William John Lewis	

Thomas Williams
John Philip John Williams
David Meyrick David
Philip Gwilym Lawrence
Philip Powell

59. L.H. Margin: 'Felony.'
Indictment that John Thomas David, yeoman, and Rhydderch John Morgan, yeoman, both of Uske, on 4th September preceding entered the close of John ap John at Uske and stole therefrom a black heifer valued at forty shillings.
Over his name: 'Puts himself (on the country), guilty, did not flee.'

60. L.H. Margin: 'Trespass.'
And that William Laborer, labourer, and Matilda Edwards, spinster, both of Llanbadock, on 2nd March preceding, entered 'where entry is not allowed by law' at Llanbadock and ploughed up with oxen belonging to Wenllian ferch John a close belonging to Henry John.

61. L.H. Margin: 'Assault and resistance to arrest.'
And that John James, yeoman, Henry Johns, labourer, Edward Johns, labourer, William Thomas Sennon, labourer, Gwenllian ferch John, spinster, and Alsona ferch John, spinster, all of Llanwerne, on 12th June preceding, assaulted Elizabeth Williams, wife of Morgan Harry, as she was driving away for impounding, a cow which she found 'trespassing in a close called Tyre Erowe' belonging to her husband and for forcibly recovering the cow from her.

62. L.H. Margin: 'Assault and affray.'
And that Henry Thomas of Rompney, yeoman, on 10th June preceding assaulted John Crede at Peterston by striking him with his fist 'on the mouth and the teeth ... violently drawing the blood.'

63. L.H. Margin: 'Assault and affray.'
And that Philip John Bona of Aberustoyth, labourer, assaulted William Meyrick David with a staff at Aberustoyth on 21st April.

64. L.H. Margin: 'Trespass.'
And that Rees ap Jenkin, yeoman, and Hugh David, yeoman, both of Kemys, on 28th May preceding entered by force the messuage at Kemys of John Rawlings and his wife Jane, 'which the same John and Jane held by an indenture of lease from Thomas John ap Gwilym, Marcialia his wife, and Thomas their son, for a term of years still current', and unlawfully ejected the said John and Jane.

65. L.H. Margin: 'Assault and affray'
And that William ap Jenkin of Llanwenarth, mason, assaulted Philip John Jenkin at Bergevenny on 3rd May.

66. L.H. Margin: "Uske."
Record of an indictment at the General Session at Bergevenny held on the Tuesday after the Close of Easter preceding that Morgan Philip Morgan of Llangeby, yeoman, on 13th August preceding at Pencrege stole "unum par calligarum videlicet one payre of lynnen hose" valued at ten pence, the property of George Morgan, gentleman. He appears at this Session in the custody of the Sheriff, Rees Morgan, Esquire, pleads not guilty, puts himself 'on the country', and is acquitted by a jury of 12: William Powell of Uske, gentleman, Lewis Morgan of Llangeby, William John Lloyde, John David Lewis, Thomas John Williams, Jenkin Thomas ap John, John Robert Thomas, William James, Watkin Philip Gwilym, Robert Watkins, Richard Williams, and William John Thomas.
        L.H. Margin: "Non cul[pabilem] nec re[traxit] I[de]o ex[oneratur]".
        'Not guilty, did not flee. Therefore he is acquitted.'

67. Similar record of the indictment at the present Session that Gladys ferch Thomas, spinster, and Katherine ferch John, spinster, both of Goytre, on 24th May preceding entered the close of John Williams at Goytre and stole therefrom a lamb, colour [*Blank*], valued at 10*d*. They appear, plead not guilty, put themselves 'on the country' and are acquitted by a jury of 12: James Thomas Reynolds, gentleman, Ciprius Phillips, David John Howell, John Lewis, Howell ap Jenkin, William Meyricke David, Roger John ap Rosser, Roger David ap Jenkin, Roger Thomas ap John, Thomas Jenkin ap John, Henry Jenkin Eghan, and Richard John.
        L.H. Margin: identical with No 66.

'Fines charges and amercements at the aforesaid Session'

68. Record of fines, each 3*s.* 4*d.*, imposed on defaulting jurors from the Hundred of Trilleg; William John of Llanyssen, Edmund Saunders of Llangoven, Philip Williams, and David Bennett.

R.H. Margin: 13*s.* 4*d.*

69. Similar record relating to defaulting jurors from the Hundred of Skenffryth; Charles Hughes, gentleman, Edward Mason of Bychenor, John Leighton of Englysshenewton, and Thomas William Jenkin.

R.H. Margin: 13*s.* 4*d.*

70. Similar record relating to defaulting jurors from the Hundred of Newport; Walter Hopkins, William Roberts of Tregwyllym, John Thomas of Mychelston, David Wylly of Rompney, John Morgan of the same place, Howell David of Malpas. Howell Thomas ap Jenkin of Monythusloyn, William John Treharon of Saynt Wollo, and Maurice Williams of Bassaleg.

R.H. Margin: 30*s.*

71. Similar record relating to defaulting jurors from the Hundred of Caldycott. Walter John, David Gwilym, John Harry Prichard of Naysshe, Laurence John Lewis of Redwyck, John Williams of the same place, and Lambroth Robnett of Saynt Bryede.

R.H. Margin: 16*s.* 8*d.*

72. Charge upon the land-holders and inhabitants of Saynt Wollo for non-appearance to show reason why they have not repaired the highway within their parish leading from Newport to Bassaleg.

R.H. Margin: 3*s.* 4*d.*

73. Similar charge on Pantege in relation to the road leading from Bergevenny towards Newport.

R.H. Margin: 3*s.* 4*d.*

74. Also on Dyngestowe in relation to the road leading from Monmoth to Bergevenny.

R.H. Margin: [*Erasure*]

75. Also on Llanhenock in relation to the road leading from Carlyon towards Uske.

R.H. Margin: 3*s.* 4*d.*

76. Also on Chrystchurche in relation to the road leading from there towards the bridge called "Stonen Brydge" on the outskirts of Somerton.

R.H. Margin: 3*s.* 4*d.*

77. Also on Tredonock in relation to the road leading from Carlyon towards Uske.

R.H. Margin: 3*s.* 4*d.*

78. Also on Lewis John Treharon of Chrystchurche, yeoman, Thomas Williams of Westercoyed, yeoman, and Lewis James of Chrystchurche, yeoman, in relation to a road leading towards their lands within the parish of Chrystchurche, leading from that place towards Llanwerne ... 2*s.* each.

R.H. Margin: 6*s.*

79. Record of payment of a fine for assault imposed at the special Session at Uske on 27th October preceding on William Thomas of Trylleg, yeoman. Paid 'into the hands of' Thomas Morgan, Esquire.

R.H. Margin: 3*s.* 4*d.*

80. Record of payment of fines for assault imposed at the preceding Michaelmas Session on Thomas James, gentleman, and Walter Williams, yeoman, both of Uske. 2*s.* each. Paid into the hands of Mathew Herbert, Esquire.

R.H. Margin: 4*s.*

81. Hugh Cocks, gentleman, Thomas Tanner, tanner, David James Holby, the younger, labourer, William Butler *alias* William the servant of Charles Cocks, Thomas ap Thomas, labourer, Madock ap Howell, labourer, all of Skenffryth, and Rees Morgan *alias* Rees Agweyth of Saynt Moughan, yeoman, indicted for riot and unlawful assembly at the Special Session of 27th October are 'admitted to their fines', each 2*s.* Charles Cockes of Skenffryth, gentleman, stands surety for them all.

R.H. Margin: 14*s.*

82. Record of payment of a fine for assault imposed at the preceding Michaelmas Session on Philip Meyrick of Naysshe, yeoman, and Agnes Phillips his wife. Paid into the hands of Mathew Herbert, Esquire.

R.H. Margin: 3*s.* 4*d.*

83. Record of payment of a fine for assault imposed at the preceding Epiphany Session on Thomas Yoroth of Llandenny, yeoman. Paid into the hands of Rowland Morgan, Esquire.

R.H. Margin: 2s.

84. John Jevans of Tredonock, labourer, indicted (offence not stated) at the preceding Epiphany Session is admitted to his fine. [Blank] stands surety.

R.H. Margin: 3s. 4d.

85. Richard Jenkin Morris of Llangeby, yeoman, indicted for assault at the preceding Epiphany Session is admitted to his fine ... David John Morris of Tredonock stands surety.

R.H. Margin: 3s. 4d.

86. John William Hughes of Uske, tanner, indicted 'with others' for assault and riot at the general Session at Trinity of the preceding year is admitted to his fine. Reginald Williams of Llanbadock, gentleman, stands surety.

R.H. Margin: 3s. 4d.

87. "MEMORANDUM quod decimo die Junii anno regni Domine Elizabeth ... decimo nono, coram Thomas Watkyns armigero uno justiciarorum pacis predicte Domine Regine ad pacem in Comitatu predicto .... Et Johanne Waters Clerico pacis Comitatus predicti venerunt Roulandus Morgan armiger et Thomas Morgan de medio templo in London armiger in propriis personis suis et cognoverunt quandam indenturam inter eos ex una parte et Thomam Morgan de Grayesynne generosum ex altera parte factam sigillatam et deliberatam fore factum ipsorum Roulandi Morgan et Thome Morgan de medio templo et predicti Thomas Morgan de Grayesynne et Philippus Madocke petierunt habere indenturam predictam irrotulari secundum formam statuti in huismodi casu editi et provisi Et at peticionem et requisicionem ipsorum Thome Morgan de Grayesynne et Philippi Madocke indentura predicta irrotulatur in hec verba."

('MEMORANDUM that on the tenth day of June in the nineteenth year of the reign of the Sovereign Lady Elizabeth ... before Thomas Watkins, Esquire, one of the justices of the peace of the aforesaid Sovereign Lady the Queen ... and John Waters, Clerk of the peace of the aforesaid County, came Rowland Morgan, Esquire, and Thomas Morgan of the Middle Temple in London, Esquire, in their own proper persons and acknowledged a certain indenture made, sealed and delivered between them of the one part and Thomas Morgan of Gray's Inn, gentleman, of the other part, to be the deed of the same Rowland Morgan and Thomas Morgan of the Middle Temple; and the aforesaid Thomas Morgan of Gray's Inn and Philip Madock sought to have the aforesaid indenture enrolled according to the form of the statute in such cases published and provided; and on the petition and request of the same Thomas Morgan of Gray's Inn and Philip Madock the aforesaid indenture is enrolled in these words'.)

"THIS INDENTURE made the seventh day of June in the nyneteenth yere of the raygne of o[u]r soveraygne Lady Elizabeth ... between Rowland Morgan of Maughen in the county of Monmoth, Esquyer, and Thomas Morgan of the Middle Temple in London, Esquyer, of thone partye, and Thomas Morgan of Grayesynne in the County of Myddlesex, gentleman, and Philip Madock of Saynt Wollo in the seid County of Monmoth of thother partye WYTNESSETH that the seid Rowland Morgan and Thomas Morgan of the Middle Temple for and in consyderacion of a certen summe of money to theym by the seid Thomas Morgan of Grayesynne and Philip Madock well and truly at thensealynge herof contentyd and payed whereof the same Rowland Morgan and Thomas Morgan of the Middle Temple knowledge and confesse theym sylffe truly answeryd and satysfyed and therof do dyscharge and acquyt the seid Thomas Morgan of Grayesynne and Philip Madock theyr executors and admynystrators by these presents have grauntyd and bargayned and sould and by these presents do graunt bargayn and sylle unto the seid Thomas Morgan of Grayesynne and Philip Madock theyr heyres and assygnes to the only use and behuffe of the same Thomas Morgan of Grayesynne and Philip Madock theyr heyres and assygnes for ever all that mannor and capytall messuage and chyffe mansyon howse of Tredeger with thappurtenences sett lyenge and beynge within the parysshe of Bassaleg within the seid county of Monmoth togeather with all and every the demeasnes landes tenements and heredytaments thereunto belongyng and with the same now used and occupyed and all and syngler those messuages lands tenements and heredytaments with thappurtenances sett lyeng and beyng in the severall parysshes townes ffyldes or hamletts of Newport, Saynt Wollo, Bettus, Malpas, Coydkernewe, Bassaleg, Marshefyld, Saynt Bryedes, Saynt Mellones, and Tredonock in the seid County of Monmoth and in all and every or any of theym wich be mencioned and specified in a payre of indentures bearyng date of the tenth day of Apryll in the seid nyneteenth yere of the raygne of our Soveraygne Lady the Quenes maiestie that is now made betwen Myles Morgan of Tredeger in the County of Monmoth, Esquyer, of thon party and Rowland Morgan of Maughen in the County of Monmoth, Esquyer, and Thomas Morgan of the Middle Temple in London Esquyer and Edmond Morgan of Bydweltye in the seid county of Monmoth Esquyer of the other partye and all and syngler suche and those messuages lands tenements and heredytaments within the seid countie of Monmoth late the lands of the seid Myles Morgan wich be and are comprysed and conteyned in a ffyne levyed in th courte of the Quenes maiesty that now is of the comen pleas at Westminster byffore Her Highnes Justyces there this present Trynytys tearme or in Ester terme now last past between the seid Rowland Morgan and Thomas Morgan of the Middle Temple and Edmond Morgan Esquyer complaynant and the seid Myles Morgan deforcyant TO HAVE AND TO HOULD the seid capytall mesuage and chyffe mansyon howse of Tredeger with thappurtenances togeather with all and every the seid demeasne lands tenements thereunto belongyng and all other the premysses with all and syngler theyr appurtenances unto the seid Thomas Morgan of Grayesynne and Phylyp Madock theyr heyres and assygnes to the only use and behuffe of the same Thomas Morgan of Grayesynne and Phylyp Madock theyr heyres and assygnes for ever IN WYTNES wherof the partyes afforeseyd to these presents entchayngeably have put theyr seales.

Geven the day and yere above wrytten."

Monmouth II

1. SESSION OF THE PEACE AND GAOL DELIVERY held at Monmoth on Thursday the eleventh of July in the nineteenth year of the Queen's reign before Robert Bell, Knight, Chief Baron of the Queen's Exchequer, Nicholas Barham, Serjeant-at-law, Thomas Herbert, Knight, William Morgan of Lanternam, William Herbert of Colbroke, Christopher Welshe, William Lewis, Thomas Morgan, William Cecil, Edmund Morgan, Henry Herbert, William John ap Roger, Esquires, and other their colleagues.

2. L.H. Margin: 'Grand Jury.'

John Cocks, gentleman	John James Williams
Thomas ap Rosser, gentleman	David Prichard, gentleman
Hugh Philip Saunders, gentleman	Simon William John
John ap Jenkin Morris	Morgan ap Harry
William Powell of Dyfferyn	Thomas ap Rees

Lewis Vanne, gentleman
Walter Hopkins, gentleman
John Arney of Newrey
Richard Morgan, gentleman
Philip Powell Wyllym

3. L.H. Margin: 'Felony and murder.'
Indictment that Watkin John Rosser of Pantege, labourer, on 18th April preceding at Llanvyhangell Pontmoyle, 'not having, in his cups, any fear of God, but seduced by instigation of the devil', assaulted Laurence John Williams with a "pykyd staffe" valued at 6*d.*, inflicting on the back of his head 'a mortal blow two inches in depth and half an inch wide' from which blow Laurence John Williams died on 8th May. The assailant also delivered with the same staff another mortal blow on the victim's left elbow and another on his back, from each of which, it is affirmed, he would have died if he had not died from the head wound.

L.H. Margin: 'accessory.' Also that Roger Harry of Pantege, yeoman, and Henry John Richards of Pantege, yeoman, aided and abetted the said Watkin John Rosser in the assault. Also that the said Roger Harry 'received, harboured, comforted and maintained' the said Watkin John Rosser at Pantege, knowing him to have committed felony and murder.

4. L.H. Margin: 'Felony.'
And that Geoffrey Thomas of Aberustoyth, yeoman, on 20th January
preceding at Newport stole a grey mare valued at 43s. 4d., the property of
George Williams.

5. L.H. Margin: 'Felony.'
And that Edward Nicholas of Bergevenny, *alias* Edward Burt, labourer, on
20th March preceding at Bergevenny, stole a grey horse valued at 40s., the
property of John Bentall.

6. L.H. Margin: 'Felony.'
And that Philip ap Rees Howell of Talgarth in the County of Brecon aided,
abetted, comforted and maintained at Newport on 11th of July preceding one
Thomas Philip Rees Howell of Talgarth, gentleman, knowing him to have
been charged previously, jointly with John Rees Howell of Gellygaer in the
County of Glamorgan, yeoman, with the theft at Uske of a bay horse valued
at four pounds, the property of William Berowe.

7. L.H. Margin: 'Trespass.'
And that James ap Jenkin of Stavarney, gentleman, and John Thomas of
Newport, *alias* John Thomas Veyn, labourer, on 26th June preceding entered
a close and a wood at Trethvyn belonging to William Morgan of Lanternam
and stole therefrom three "sparohawkes" in a nest.

8. L.H. Margin: 'Assault.'
And that William ap William, *alias* William Grussemont, of Monmoth,
cutler, and John Watkins of Llansoy, tailor, on 23rd May preceding at
Monmoth, at 'about twelve o'clock in the night', 'after taking drink'
assaulted William Morris and William Hugh Wever, two sworn watchmen
of the Sovereign Lady the Queen.

9. L.H. Margin: 'Trespass and assault.'
And that Richard Herbert of Llanvaughes, gentleman, and William Webb of
Caldycott, yeoman, on 9th July preceding entered the house or tenement and
36 acres of land belonging to Joanna Smith, *alias* Bettyng, of Naysshe,
assaulting and forcibly ejecting her, retaining possession themselves.

10. L.H. Margin: 'Assault and affray '
And that William ap Jenkin of Llanwenarth, mason, made three separate
assaults on Philip John Jenkins, at Llanvyhangell Ystem Llewerne on 20th
April of the preceding year, at Monmoth on 10th June of the preceding year,
and at Bergevenny on 3rd May of the present year.

11. KALENDAR OF THE GAOL DELIVERY of the Sovereign Lady the Queen of her castle of Monmoth of the prisoners in it, before Robert Bell, Knight, Chief Baron of the Exchequer of the aforesaid Sovereign Lady the Queen, and Nicholas Barham, Serjeant-at-law, the Justices of the same Sovereign Lady the Queen assigned for Gaol Delivery at Monmoth on Thursday the eleventh of July, 19 Elizabeth.

12. John David Powell David of Bergevenny, tinker, John ap John Grothor of Llanthony, tailor, William John Ssela of Llanvyhangell Cylcornell, labourer.

> Bracketed in the R.H. Margin: 'Remanded to prison, in the matter of good behaviour as set forth in the last Kalendar "tempore xlesie". ('in the time of Lent').

13. Thomas ap Howell of Penalth, yeoman.

> R.H. Margin: 'Remanded to prison in the matter of keeping the peace as set forth in the aforesaid last Kalendar'.

14. John Smith, *alias* Gove, of Bassaleg, David ap Rees of Bergevenny, Howell Lewis of Bergevenny, John Hugh Bedowe of Maughen, Howell Owen of Bassaleg, Thomas Philip David of Coydkernewe, Howell Morgan of Newport, William Powell of Newport, Lewis John Llewelen of Tredeger, all yeomen.

> R.H. Margin: 'remanded to prison as set forth in the aforesaid last Kalendar.'

15. William James of Llanarth, yeoman, indicted as set forth in the Kalendar of the time of Lent, 18 Elizabeth, having been summoned but not yet tried.

[6. William Jenkins of Llanvapley, yeoman, indicted as set forth in the last Kalendar and then remanded to prison.

> *Over his name:* 'Puts himself (on the country), guilty, did not flee.'

17. John William ap Jenkin of Llanvyhangell Pontmoyle, yeoman, indicted as an accessory and remanded to prison at the last Session 'because the principal defendant has not yet been outlawed.'

18. 'Rees Williams, *alias* Corvysor, late of Newport ... , indicted and acquitted at the last (Session) and then committed to prison without bail until he should pay 40s. to Jane ferch Rees; he is now delivered.'

19. John Williams the elder of Stavarney, yeoman, indicted for the murder at Stavarney on 31st January preceding of John Williams the younger by striking him, of malice aforethought, with a dagger valued at 2*s*.

20. John Thomas David of Uske, yeoman, indicted on the charge that he, with others, entered the close of John ap John at Uske on 4th September of the preceding year and stole a heifer valued at 40*s*.
    Over his name: 'Puts himself (on the country), not guilty, did not flee.'

21. Thomas ap John Mason, mason, of Brecon, indicted on the charge that, on 15th September, 19 Elizabeth, at Monythusloyn, he counterfeited 'ten pieces of false money ... after the likeness ... of the ... coinage called half shillings and six pence apiece, now current in this realm of England.'
    Over his name: "Po[nit] se[super patriam] cul[pabilem] nec re[traxit]"; 'puts himself (on the country), guilty, did not flee.'[1]

22. Thomas Philip Prees Howell of Talgarth in the County of Brecon, gentleman, taken at Uske on suspicion of felony and committed by William Cecil, Esquire, in the matter of a horse belonging to William Berowe.
    Over his name: 'Puts himself (on the country), guilty, no chattels.'

23. John Rees Howells of Gellygaer in the County of Glamorgan, yeoman, taken at Uske on suspicion of felony and committed by William Cecil, Esquire, on the same charge as the immediately preceding.
    Over his name: as No 22 above.

24. Griffin David of Westbury in the County of Wiltes, labourer, taken at Chepstowe on suspicion of felony and committed by Thomas Morgan, Esquire, and now charged. (The offence is not specified.)
    Over his name: "Po' se ...", the formula being left thus incomplete.

25. Morgan Howell of Maughen, labourer, taken there on suspicion of felony and committed by Rowland Morgan, Esquire, and now charged.

26. Richard Jenkin of Bergevenny, taken there on suspicion of felony and committed by Edmund Morgan, Esquire.

27. Gwenllian ferch Lawrence, of Bergevenny, spinster, taken there on suspicion of felony and committed by William Herbert of Colbroke, Esquire.

---

[1] Cf. 1st Monmouth Gaol Delivery, No 3.

28. John Howell Dee of Chrystchurche, labourer, taken there on suspicion of felony and committed by William Morgan of Lanternam, Esquire.

   Over his name: "Po[nit] se[super patriam] cul[pabilem] de parvo latrocinio ad valenc[iam] vj*d*." 'Puts himself (on the country), guilty of petty larceny to the value of 6*d*.'

29. George Treavor of Wylton in the County of Wiltes, taken at Devawden, within the parish of Newchurch, on suspicion of felony and committed by Edward, Lord Herbert, and now charged with felony and burglary.

   Over his name: 'Puts himself (on the country), guilty, no chattels.'

30. Matilda ferch Morgan, servant of George Thomas Howell of Raglan, spinster, taken at Raglan on suspicion of felony and committed by William Powell, Esquire.

31. George Thomas Powell of Raglan, taken there on suspicion of felony and committed by the aforesaid William Powell.

32. William Brown of Raglan, labourer, there taken on suspicion of felony and committed by the aforesaid William Powell.

33. John Griffith of Bassaleg, labourer, taken at Chrystchurche on suspicion of felony and committed by Thomas Watkins, Esquire, and now charged.

   Over his name: identical with No 29 above.

34. Howell Thomas ap Howell of Llantryssen, labourer, there taken on suspicion of felony and committed by William Lewis, Esquire.

   Over his name: "Po[nit] se[super patriam] cul[pabilem] ca[talla] null[a], legit ut clericus. I[de]o ardetur in manu sua sinistra." 'Puts himself (on the country), guilty, no chattels, reads as a cleric. Therefore he is branded on his left hand.'

35. Matilda ferch William of Stavarney, spinster, there taken on suspicion of felony and murder 'that is to say the death of John Williams the younger,' and committed by William, Earl of Worcester, one of the Justices of the peace of the County.

36. David ap David Wyllym of Clytha, labourer, there taken on suspicion of felony and committed by the aforementioned William Lewis and now charged.

   Over his name: 'Puts himself (on the country), not guilty. '

37. John Thomas of Cardyff in the County of Glamorgan, labourer, taken at Llanwerne on suspicion of felony and committed by Christopher Welshe, Esquire, and now charged with petty larceny.

> *Over his name:* 'Puts himself (on the country), guilty, no chattels.

38. Robert Simons of Crockehorne in the County of Somerset, butcher, taken at Chrystchurche on suspicion of felony and committed by William Morgan of Lanternam.

39. Roger Harry of Pontmoyle, yeoman, there taken on suspicion of felony and murder, namely the death of Laurence John Williams, and committed by the aforementioned William Herbert of Colbroke.

40. Harry John Richards of Pantege, yeoman, there taken 'for the same reason' and committed by Thomas Herbert, Knight.

41. David Rees of Carmarthen in the County of Carmarthen, labourer, taken at Bergevenny on suspicion of felony and committed by William John ap Roger.

42. Jenett ferch David of Ostrood Gonles in the County of Brecon, spinster, taken at Bergevenny on suspicion of felony, committed by Mathew Herbert, Esquire, and now charged in the matter; 'the shearing of sheep to the value of 12*d*.'

> *Over her name:* "Po[nit] se[super patriam] cul[pabilem] de parvo latrocinio." 'Puts herself (on the country), guilty of petty larceny.'

43. Rachel Edmondes of Llanvaughes, spinster, taken at Saynt Bryedes on suspicion of felony and committed by the aforementioned Edmund Morgan.

44. William Beere of Raglan, yeoman, there taken on suspicion of felony and committed by Charles Somerset, Knight, Thomas Herbert, Knight, William Morgan of Lanternam, William Herbert of Colbroke, William John ap Roger, Thomas Watkins, Henry Herbert, William Powell, and Walter Jones, all Esquires.

45. John Thomas of Trilleg, yeoman, taken at Raglan on suspicion of felony and committed by the aforesaid Charles Somerset, Knight, Thomas Herbert, Knight, and 'the other Justices aforesaid.'

> L.H. Margin: "p'i pro b'n' ger' (prisoni pro bene gerendo)." 'To prison in the matter of good behaviour.'

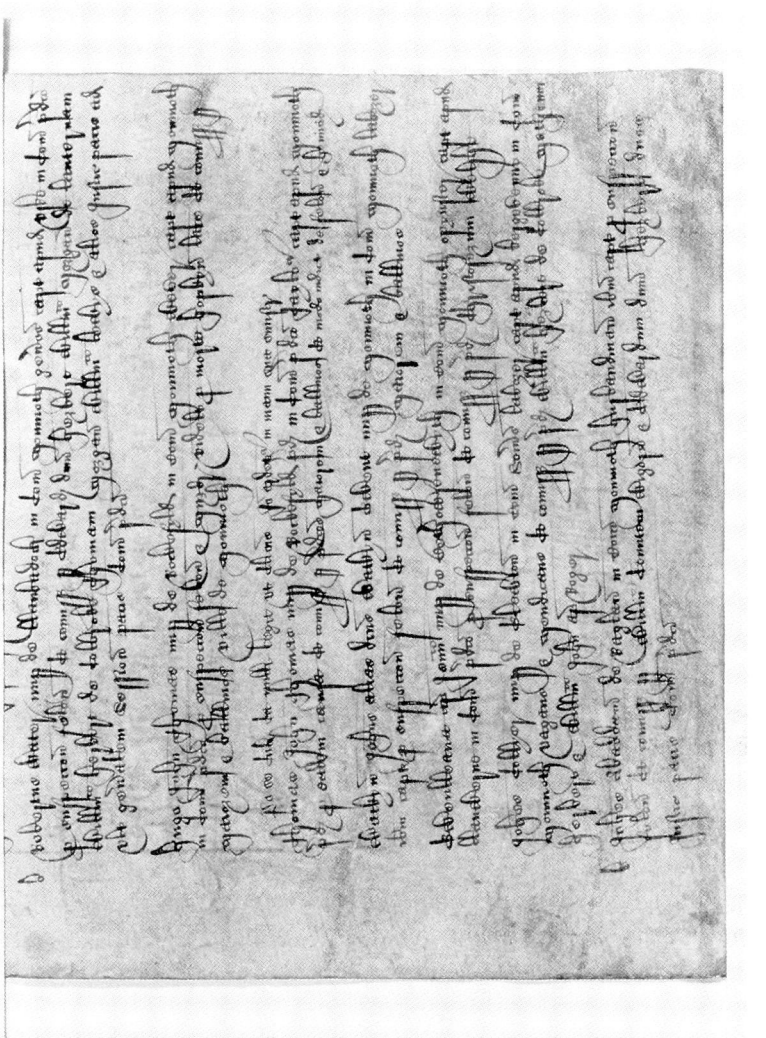

Plate 3. Entries from the second Monmouth Sessions of the Peace and Gaol Delivery (Nos 46–52 in the calendar overleaf). Note the entry concerning Thomas John Thomas (No 48), an example of claiming 'benefit of clergy'.

46. Robert Waters of Llanbadock, gentleman, taken at Uske on suspicion of felony and committed by Edward, Lord Herbert, William Morgan of Lanternam, William Herbert of Colebroke, Thomas Morgan, William Lewis and other Justices at the last general Session of the County.

47. Hugh John Thomas of Rochefyld, weaver, taken at Monmoth on suspicion of felony and of the murder of Hopkin Lace and committed by the mayor and bailiffs of the town of Monmoth.

48. Thomas John Thomas of Rochefyld, tailor, taken at Monmoth on the same charge as that immediately preceding and committed by the mayor and bailiffs of the town of Monmoth and now charged with felony and homicide.
　　Over his name: "Po[nit] se[super patriam] cul[pabilem] ca[talla] null[a] legit ut clericus I[de]o ardetur in manu sua sinistra"; 'Puts himself (on the country), guilty, no chattels, reads as a cleric. Therefore he is branded on his left hand.'

49. Watkin Johns, *alias* Watkin Gwent, of Monmoth, labourer, taken at Monmoth on suspicion of felony and committed by the aforesaid mayor and bailiffs.

50. Gwenllian ap (*sic*) Jenkin of Bethowesnewyth, spinster, taken at Llanwerne on suspicion of felony and committed by the aforementioned Christopher Welshe.

51. John Collyer of Glewton in the County of Somerset, labourer, taken at Bergevenny 'wandering and begging' and committed by William Herbert of Colbroke, Mathew Herbert and William John ap Roger.

52. John Abaddam (ap Adam) of Raglan, husbandman, there taken on suspicion of felony and committed by William Earl of Worcester and Edward Lord Herbert.

53. James (*no other name*) of Goytre, husbandman, there taken on suspicion of felony and committed by William Herbert of Colbroke and William John ap Roger.

54. Margaret ferch David of Henllys, spinster, there taken on suspicion of felony and committed by the aforesaid Thomas Morgan and Edmund Morgan.

55. William Morgan of Marshefyld, yeoman, there taken on suspicion of felony and committed by the aforesaid Thomas Morgan and Edmund Morgan.

L.H. Margin: "r[emandatus] p[rison]i ad gen[er]al[em]." 'remanded to prison until the general (Session).'

56. Lewis Phillips of Saynt Bryedes, yeoman, there taken on suspicion of felony and committed by the aforesaid Thomas Morgan and Edmund Morgan.

L.H. Margin: identical with No 55.

57. David Williams of Rompney, yeoman, there taken on suspicion of felony and committed by the aforesaid Thomas Morgan and Edmund Morgan.

58. David Phillips of Trethvyn, yeoman, there taken on suspicion of felony and committed by the aforesaid Thomas Morgan and Edmund Morgan.

59. Thomas David Willym of Porteskewett, husbandman, there taken on suspicion of felony and committed by William Lewis, Esquire and now charged.

Over his name: identical with No 48.

60. Alsona ferch Philip Gwilym of Llantellyo Cryssenny, widow, there taken on suspicion of felony and committed by William Herbert of Colbroke and William John ap Roger.

L.H. Margin: "r[emandatus] p[rison]i ad Brecon." 'Remanded to prison until the Brecon (Sessions).'

61. William Grussemont of Monmoth, labourer, there taken on suspicion of felony and committed by the mayor and bailiffs of the town of Monmoth.

62. John Hughes, formerly gaoler of the common gaol at Carlyon, charged at the General Session and Gaol Delivery held at Monmoth on 25th February preceding with having allowed Nicholas ap Robert to escape from the gaol, now remanded to prison on a charge of having stolen a brown bay gelding valued at three pounds, the property of Watkin Williams, *alias* Howell.

Over his name: 'Puts himself (on the country), not guilty, did not flee.'

63. John Watkins of Talgarth in the County of Brecon, yeoman, 'returned by the Chief Justice of the Great Sessions of the same place.'

64. Roger Watkins of Talgarth also returned by the same Chief Justice.

65. William George of Wondy, labourer, charged with the murder of Watkin Howell on 3rd November in the sixteenth year of the Queen's reign, by striking him on the head with a stone, inflicting a wound from which he died on 18th November of that year.

66. David ap Jenkin of Ouldecastell, labourer, there taken. [*No further particulars given*].

Index of Persons

There is no wholly satisfactory method of indexing Welsh personal names of the sixteenth century, when some families had adopted hereditary surnames whereas others continued to use patronymics, with or without the element 'ap'. In this index, an arbitrary but consistent decision has been made to invert all names, treating the final element as a surname, and to omit 'ap', even when it appears in the text.

Index of Places

Places in Monmouthshire are arranged under the parishes used in Sir Joseph Bradney's *History*. County suffixes are given only for places elsewhere.